THE COOK'S ALMANAC

THE COOK'S ALMANAC

Jacqueline Hériteau

A Stonesong Press Book

World Almanac Publications
New York, New York

Interior design: Cris Graña
Cover illustration: Nancy Stahl
Illustrations: Ivy Sky Rutsky, pp. 34, 58, 109, 155, 219, 229, 232, 238
Jeanette Eng, pp. 1, 37, 69, 127, 181, 225, 247

The "Dried Fruit Soup" recipe is reprinted from *A Feast of Soups*
© 1981, 1982, by Jacqueline Hériteau, published by The Dial Press,
One Dag Hammarskjold Plaza, New York, NY 10017

A Stonesong Press Book

First published in 1983

Distributed in the United States by Ballantine Books, a division of Random
House, Inc., and in Canada by Random House of Canada, Ltd.

Library of Congress catalog card number: 82-061796
Newspaper Enterprise Association ISBN 0-911818-40-5
Ballantine ISBN 0-345-31035-7

Printed in the United States of America

Newspaper Enterprise Association, Inc.
World Almanac Publications
200 Park Avenue
New York, NY 10166

To Maggie, my daughter-in-love,
and Krishna Littledale.

Other Books by Jacqueline Hériteau

A Feast of Soups
Oriental Cooking the Fast Wok Way
The How to Grow and Cook It Book
The How to Grow and Can It Book
Take It Along Cookbook
Potpourris and Other Fragrant Delights
The Office Gardener
Small Batch Pickling and Preserving
Small Fruits and Vegetable Gardens
Small Flower Gardens
50 Easy Garden Projects
The Best of Electric Crockery Cooking

ACKNOWLEDGMENTS

To publish in one go everything there is to know about cooking would require volumes from here to Peking. This volume includes only some of what its author finds fascinating about cooking, along with some handy tables and charts. And a very few basic recipes that are favorites. To pull together even this modest compilation I had lots of help. My very sincere thanks to Karen Scott, three-star chef, for work on the glossary and meat charts among other items; to Kate Alfriend, communications officer with the United States Department of Agriculture (and to the department itself and the government and people who support it); to Ann Tilsen, author and researcher and food enthusiast; and to Jean Taylor, good friend and sometime assistant.

A very special thank you to Patricia Fisher, the editor, who contributed so many good ideas and put in so much solid work.

CONTENTS

1

A COOK'S EYE VIEW OF HISTORY

PEOPLE AND COOKING

Food has been all things to man. An invitation to intimacy (remember the hilarious sequence in the movie *Tom Jones*); an investigative tool in the hands of scientists (the USSR's Pavlov who used dogs' feeding habits to study conditioned reflexes in man); a weapon (the purpose of a siege was to starve the citadel into submission).

At various times, one food or another has been proposed as the answer to man's search for vitality, health, wealth, good looks, longevity, or love. Beans, rosewater, prunes, wine, basil, sugar, coffee, cod liver oil, and, more recently, yogurt, have been seen as panaceas. Pepper, oysters, tomatoes, cocoa, and vanilla, to name a very few, have been considered aphrodisiacs. While it may not be true that fish feeds the brain, as Mark Twain proposed, in many respects it is true that you are what you eat, and that how you eat tells a lot about what you are. The raw materials of meals—until recently a function of season and geography—are the essentials of survival. So, at its most basic, food is the life support system of man on earth.

Through the aeons of prehistory, the search for food and water dictated the movements of peoples across the face of the continents. There is no record of cooking before 360,000 B.C. Early men and women ate their catch raw and sometimes frozen. About 10,000 to 12,000 years ago, man became a herdsman, learned to roast and bake, turned grains into flour and made flat breads, brewed drinks, notably mead, of honey and fruit, and by 8000 B.C., was planting and on his way to becoming a farmer.

We catch a glimpse of our hunting/fishing selves in *The Explorers Cookbook*. Published in 1971, the book is a compendium of eating experiences among pre-technology societies. It is a natural sequel to the Explorers Club banquet which annually offers delicacies such as yak patties, rounds of lion's tail, and witchety grub soup (a New Zealand delicacy) to be-medalled men and be-jewelled women at a black-tie gala in Manhattan.

> In the United States there are 17,000,000 registered hunters, and 60,000,000 fishermen.

The Explorers Club and its annual banquet were founded by a handful of men who lived through three terrible winters in the frozen Arctic wastes early in the 1880s. As yet undiscovered, the North Pole and the uncharted lands around it held the imagination of the explorers of the period, including General Adolphus Washington Greely. Greely was looking for the Pole in 1882. The supply ship due to rendezvous with him in that year failed to appear. No relief came when

the Arctic waters opened in 1883, and a naval vessel did not reach him until June 1884. Of the twenty-three men who began that final winter, only Greely, his aide Colonel David L. Brainard, and five others survived. After that, Greely and Brainard made it a custom to meet for a sumptuous dinner on the anniversary of their rescue. The dinner grew into a club. Seventy-five years later, Explorers Club members are walking memory banks of what life was like aeons ago when man first started to explore the planet. Judging by present-day explorers, the good old days were pretty bad. Sir Ernest Shackleton, for instance, survived an 800-mile Antarctic journey in a twenty-two-foot open rowboat by going without sleep for sixteen days. To get through one trip to the North, Peter Freuchen had to cut off his own infected foot. Sven Hedin survived his Taklan Makan desert expedition to China by burying himself in the sand every day during the sunlit hours.

Our early ancestors' food supply system probably resembled an Arctic expedition gone wrong. Kenneth H. Armstrong, northern bush pilot, writes of exploring the Mulchatna River in Alaska with two companions: "We hunted eighteen straight days before getting a moose, hunting on short rations of one small hot cake per day, and one prune. Three prunes would not have looked so bad if we had had a smaller pot to cook them in. The day prior to getting the moose, we were out of flour, and each of us upon our return to camp could feel a definite drop in energy."

WHEN FAT WAS GOOD

Among Eskimo and other peoples where food has been in short supply, fat is considered a mark of status. Traditionally, the upper classes of the Western world, and others who do not have shortages of food in their backgrounds, are slimmer. The belle of the turn of the century in America would be put on a Weight Watchers diet at once if she applied to the Ziegfeld Follies for a job today.

Armstrong got the moose, but then began to fear because eating quantities of the lean meat left the men "unsatisfied," with less energy than one hot cake would have offered.

Later, on the trek back toward civilization, Armstrong and his group were invited to dine with an Eskimo family, who "sent the kids out with a basket to gather willow buds." These their Eskimo hostess cooked in two skillets greased with a quarter inch of bear fat. First, she browned the buds with salt and cooked them through, then she added cubed beaver tail and cooked all together for another fifteen minutes.

Armstrong describes the meat as somewhat sweet, "similar to wild sheep," and says the willow buds were delicately flavored.

FLOWERY FOODS

The twelfth-century Crusades reintroduced to Europe the elegance of the fabled Oriental courts and many Eastern uses of fragrant herbs (or sweet herbs) and flowers. Rose water, as well as orange water, are distillations that were used as flavorings. Rose petals were used in jams in the last century, and candied violets are still sold to place on desserts and decorate confections. Today, rose petals and accacia buds are made into fritters and Germany has a rose petal wine cup.

Primroses and nasturtiums are used as garnishes for soups and salads. Nasturtium leaves may be used for *dolmas* in place of vine leaves and are shredded to add peppery accents to salads. Mignonnette and lime blossoms are used in wine cups and the Japanese and Chinese use dried chrysanthemums as herbs. The buds of cottage pinks and the blooms of mock oranges may also be used to decorate cakes.

There was a time when we didn't have pots to cook in. A description by Justice William O. Douglas of a snakebake is informative. The recipe applies to pythons, which may be twenty feet long, and to watersnakes as well.

First, you build a fire the length of the snake, then two people hold the dead snake, one at either end, turning it often, until its nervous system stops twitching. Then it is set on the ground and incisions are made along both sides of the backbone to sever the sinews. It then is rolled into a ball, tied with strings, and baked for thirty minutes on either side under hot embers. The entrails are removed. It is cut into steaks and served.

Snakes have a reputation for good flavor, particularly diamondbacks. The cave paintings found near Aurignac in southern France, dating back 40,000 years, show people who caught salmonlike fish and gathered berries and wild grains.

No doubt greens and insects were part of the larder. They cooked on hearth fires and steamed food in wet leaves.

Theodore P. Bank, II, Executive Director of the American Institute of Exploration, Professor of Social Science at Western Michigan University, and a Fullbright scholar, describes some of the unusual stews he came across in his years in the North with the Aleut-Eskimo and the Ainu. The Aleuts are a nearly extinct people living on the fringes of the USSR in the Aleutian Islands. The Ainu are Australoid-Japanese aborigines now almost absorbed into the mainstream culture of Japan.

Tundra berries, sour little fruits of a heath, *Empetrum nigrum*, are part of an Aleut delicacy made with salmon livers, cooked white, then mashed into a doughy paste. For the Aleut, the dish is flavored with hair-seal oil; for outsiders, there was a sauce of fish or vegetable oil, vinegar, and salt. Wild parsnip goes into a far North *bouillabaisse*, that includes rock tripe (*Fucus*), sea lettuce (*Ulva*), the roots of the white orchid (*Platanthera*), Indian rice (*Fritillaria*), and starchy tubers, cooked with fish such as octopus, halibut, salmon or cod, clams, and shrimp. Bank recommended the marrow of cow parsnip (*Heracletum lanatum*) for its licoricelike flavor, but warned against the juice of the skin which causes mouth sores unless peeled away.

The men and women who colonized America recorded eating nettles, milkweed, pokeweed shoots, marsh marigolds, and Jerusalem artichoke roots, to name a few, so none of the Aleut diet is too hard to understand. Professor Bank describes Aleut tea made with the dried leaves of wild Aleutian geranium (*Geranium erianthum*), and with dried raspberries and brambleberries (*Rubus spectabilis*), which are related to blackberries. However, insects as an item of diet is a little more difficult for most of us to accept. We can buy canned crisped grasshoppers from North Africa, but so far they have not diminished the potato chip market.

Richard Sterling Finnie, a Canadian explorer and filmmaker, speaks of a banquet including a caribou head with staring eyes. He says he "popped them into my mouth like oysters, in conformity with Eskimo custom." (Sheeps' eyes are similarly consumed by Arab nomads, and fish eyes by Frenchmen.) Mr. Finnie continues: "Squeamishness would mar enjoyment of two other delicacies." One, the partly digested contents of a caribou's stomach, "a sort of pureed salad." The other, the larvae of warble flies incubating in the hides of grazing caribou. "Esquimo squeeze out these maggots..."

Let's not continue, but let's remember that aborigines in New Zealand today eat witchety grubs, which have been described as looking like eggs; Africans eat the inner part of termites' nests and yellowjacket soup; fried Katanga termites are served in the Congo; and gourmets everywhere consider frogs' legs and snails as delicacies.

Explorers of this century have turned up a large assortment of other foods that are not to be found on supermarket shelves, but certainly were useful to early man: roasted fruit bats (hamlike); armadillo (multiplying now in the southern

United States), said to be good for sausages and good fried or grilled (on the pink side, please); murres, little auks, puffins, white fox, white whale (overly rich, but okay if you like the taste of cod liver oil), seal (pungent), caribou, reindeer (cooked raw, or frozen), Arctic hare, ptarmigan, ducks, geese, fish (frozen, dried, or raw), also quite edible.

And edible, for a very brief time to a very small number of people, was the marrow of the 50,000-year-old bones of a fossil horse. It had been found, according to Coleman S. Williams, on an American Museum dig in the frozen muck of a glacier in Alaska. The bones, in perfect condition, were brought back to New York for analysis, and the marrow was found to be fresh.

To devotees of *ossobuco*, and *sushi* and *sashimi* (those jewellike preparations of raw fish and rice that are a Japanese invention), the fare discussed above will come as no surprise. Under certain conditions, anything edible has appeal.

A feature of Charlie Chaplin's famous movie *The Gold Rush* was the sequence in which the little man, out of food, cooks and eats his shoes. This could be real life, according to explorer Richard Finnie. He tells the story of Bishop Stringer, a Canadian missionary to the Yukon territories who ate his moccasins when he was out of food (and dined out on the story for the rest of his days). After all, leather is animal hide, or jerky. A recipe in *The Explorers Cookbook* for making jerky out of pork hide instructs the reader to use the strips as laces, or to eat them fried, as the occasion warrants. Whale meat jerky is made of strips of eight by two-and-one-half-inch skin, sun dried—tough but nourishing. Just break off a piece, chew a while, then try to swallow. In South Africa a contemporary butcher shop offering is *biltong*, strips of dried elephant meat from animals culled from overcrowded herds multiplying in South Africa's Kruger National Park.

These stories give us insights into what cooking and food were like in the days when people and food were scarce. Under the circumstances, you might think people would be pretty stingy about sharing it. But they weren't. The following is a story told by Alonzo W. Pond, who served as archaeologist for Roy Chapman Andrews (Andrews discovered fossil dinosaur's eggs) in the Gobi dessert.

The time: *circa* 1925; the place: Biskra, Algeria, en route to Touggourt following a narrow-gauge railway through the desert. Lost and hungry, the party of eleven asked an elderly woman for food.

"A few minutes later, we heard the squawk of a rooster. We knew it would soon be boiling in the *couscousier* beneath a colander full of whole wheat pellets. The aromatic chicken broth would steam up through the colander and cook the pellets to the softness of steamed rice and make it most flavorful.

"While the *couscous* was steaming, our unexpected hosts discovered some olives. We had pleasant hors d'oeuvres while waiting for our meal. With all the meat cooked off the chicken bones, each of us had a taste of chicken. The broth, spiced good and hot with red peppers, was poured over the steamed wheat pellets. Still too civilized to make balls of the food with our fingers and plop them into our mouths as desert people do, we got out our spoons and ate a hearty meal. When the *couscous* was finished, our hosts brought a big basket of fresh dates and coffee.

"We decided that life on the desert might be pretty rough when you are not prepared, but none of us has ever forgotten the hospitality of that woman who killed her last rooster to feed strangers."

The willingness to share food seems to be common to many who live on the edge of starvation. The Hellenic Greeks traditionally fed any stranger who knocked on the door, and the Swedes still talk of the hospitality pot tradition of the barren lands. The pot was a big kettle hung over the embers of the hearth and filled with a thick soup. Any who came were entitled to a bowlful. Anything left was scraped back into the soup kettle so that nothing was lost, and this became the basis of the next day's hospitality pot.

No other creature on the planet, so far as we know, invites weakened peers in to dine, especially when provisions are scanty.

Food has been all things to man, but first and foremost, it is man's primary life support system, and the symbol of a nurturing love.

MYSTERY AND MAGIC

If food were merely fuel for biological machines, we need never have gone further than that primitive diet of raw meat and fish, starches, and greens. Through aeons of prehistory, man had been gathering and chewing wild barley, millet, and wheat. He knew (however he articulated it) that cooking makes the cellulose walls of plants more digestible and produces chemical changes in starches that remove the bitterness. Time would teach that a field of grain and a garden of dates were more reliable than a flight of grasshoppers. The history of cooking could have ended with *pita* bread and mutton stew since there was no physiological reason to go further. But we went much further.

To those educated in the West, geography tends to end on the eastern shores of the Mediterranean. But cooking's early history is seen much farther east, in lands already ancient when Egypt became a trading nation—about 2500 B.C.

By 6000 B.C., new stone-age farming people were settling in Iraq (Mesopotamia). By 3300 B.C., they had invented writing and developed the Sumerian culture of independent city states. Between 3300 B.C. and 524 B.C., the land was absorbed by a succession of peoples whose names we associate with the Bible, hanging gardens, and sybaritic pleasures—the Babylonians, the Assyrians, and the Chaldeans. Later Persians (Iranians) conquered the region, ousted by the Greeks under Alexander the Great (356 to 323 B.C.), whose followers held the land together in a league of Hellenic states that stretched from Egypt to India. Cleopatra was Greek and Macedonian by birth.

While the Sumerians were working out their Garden of Eden in Mesopotamia (Iraq), to the east beyond Persia at least one other Garden of Eden evolved in a valley centered on the Indus River bordering India, in a land we now call Western Pakistan. Since the 1920s, archaeologists have been uncovering Mohenjo-Dara and Harappa, towns dating from 4000 B.C., where well-organized societies flourished from about 2500 to 1750 B.C. Already some 100 ancient towns and villages have been identified, some with fortified citadels.

SOME PLANTS CULTIVATED 4,000 YEARS AGO IN THE MIDDLE EAST

Almonds	Cucumbers	Mulberries	Sorghum
Apples	Dates	Olives	Soybeans
Apricots	Eggplants	Onions	Tea
Bananas	Figs	Peaches	Turnips
Barley	Grapes	Pears	Watermelon
Beans	Mangoes	Quinces	Wheat
Cabbage	Millet	Rice	

Compiled from James Traeger's *The Food Book.*

In the Mesopotamian valley are records of what may be the first dates planted. Chicken was domesticated and stuffed—mutton, too—and roasted and stewed, types of yogurt and cheese were made, and ice cream and sherbets chilled by snows brought from the mountains were served. From the Indus valley, orange and lemon seeds and, perhaps, rice traveled east to India, Burma, and China. There, mortar and pestle were used to powder fragrant spices and herbs, and early curries were made from mustard seeds, turmeric, fennel, cumin, and tamarind rind, deliciously disguising the defects of meats soured by heat and time. Saffron, then as now, was gathered from fields of purple crocus which gave their orange stamens to the cause of culinary delight.

To the hunting societies and desert nomads who sought them out or came upon them, these twin cradles of civilized eating must have seemed like paradise. Drawn to the rich valleys as conquerors, beggars, or friends, tribes brought their own seeds, knowledge, and discoveries: how to bake flat cakes (variations on *pita* bread, those flat chewy cakes characteristic of Arab cooking as far west as Morocco); or how to build an oven by digging a hole in the ground and lining it with clay (in *The Food Book* [Avon, 1972], James Traeger goes into the details). Visitors to the Middle East today can find vestiges of the village life of the ancients. Despite the inroads of oil riches and international politics, town and village bazaars in Iraq and the Arab peninsula are still rich with the aroma of spice-scented roasted mutton and stewed lamb. Food is still cooked over small charcoal fires as it was in the days when civilization was the new way of life for shepherds. Now, as then, food is cooked in sheep fat and drippings, curries abound, and meats are made sweet with nuts and honey, just as in the *Arabian Nights*.

There's *tadjin ahmar*, a mutton stew made with prunes and onions, and *chervah*, mutton soup of tomatoes and onions. *Mechoui* is a young lamb roasted on a spit in a manner ancient when India was young. The lamb is cleaned and emptied except for the kidneys, partially stuffed with onions, and seasoned. Then, it is skewered on a spit. A big fire is built to one side, embers are placed under the lamb, which is turned on the spit and basted often as it roasts. *Kebash-el artarine*, thick parts of cooked mutton stuffed with crushed almonds and honey, is brushed with honey, covered with pounded pistachio nuts, and served on a layer of apricot jam. *Kebash-sakkar*, is boiled mutton coated with gooseberry jelly. Chicken may be pricked all over with a knife, rubbed with honey mixed with melted butter, and flavored with benzoin gum (a balsamlike resin) and attar (essence) of roses mixed with more honey. It is then cooked, halved, spread with chopped pistachio nuts, sprinkled with sugar, and garnished with cherries in syrup, preserved ginger, and more honey.

How did man get from barley porridge and baked snake to *kebash-el artarine*? Nervously. Optimistically. Courageously. Eve wasn't hungry when she took the apple. She was curious. The story of Eve and the apple tells us what it was like to introduce a new food to Eden. First reaction: It looks tempting! Second reaction: Delicious! The devil must have made it. Then phase three takes over: The food becomes inaccessible, taboo, possibly poisonous, and appears to have properties that are both medicinal and erotic. Phase four: The establishment bans it, making it totally irresistible. Phase five: Some hero brings it into the fold.

Take coffee, for instance. Coffee appeared in the Middle East in the thirteenth century A.D., along with a number of stories about its origins. A favorite tale locates its origins in Abyssinia (Ethiopia) and Yemen, which is just across the Red Sea from Abyssinia. There was a shepherd, whose name may have been Kaldi, who dozed while his sheep grazed. One day his sheep ate some bright red berries, and he awakened to find them dancing with joy and bleating prettily. The source of this behavior seemed to be bright red berries on some shrubs with glossy leaves and jasmine-scented flowers. Kaldi tried the berries, and hopped, skipped, and jumped all the way home to show his wife this new pleasure-giving stimulant. The wife became nervous, sniffing a snake in her little garden of Eden, and sent him off to the monastery to have his "heaven sent" gift checked out by the monks. Sure enough, the monks were alarmed at this obvious work of the devil and threw the berries into the fire.

TURKISH COFFEE

This is made in a special utensil called an *Ibrik*. Usually fashioned of copper or brass with a long handle and no spout, it has no cover, is tall, and tapers toward the top. To prepare the coffee, measure 1 *demitasse* cup of cold water into the coffeemaker for each cup desired. Heat until lukewarm. Add to the water 1 heaping teaspoon of pulverized dark-roast coffee and 1 teaspoon of sugar (more or less to taste) for each cup. Stir. Bring to a boil over medium heat. Pour off half the coffee into *demitasse* cups. Boil the remaining coffee again. Remove from the heat and spoon some of the creamy coffee foam into each cup. Fill the cups, but do not stir the coffee once it has been poured. In Arabic, the foam is called "the face of the coffee" and you lose face if you serve coffee without it!

Information from the Pan-American Coffee Bureau.

(If you find here some resemblance to the story of the apple and Eve, remember that thirteenth century Yemen was in the hands of the Ottomon Turks, followers of Muhammed, whose religion, Islam, was rooted in the Old Testament.)

Norman Kalpas, in a charming little book called *The Coffee Lover's Companion* (Quick Fox, 1977), writes: "At once, a most heavenly aroma came forth from the fire," drawing monks from all over the monastery to the room where Kaldi and his heavenly/hellish berries waited. One of these was the chief monk who knew that the way to translate an aroma into a flavor was to brew its source. So coffee was brewed and born. The monks liked it a lot.

In another story, coffee was first known in Mocha in Yemen, where it miraculously appeared with a traveling monk in search of peace and saved the townspeople from a mysterious illness.

In reality, the brew moved northward from Yemen, carried by dervishes to Mecca. The dervishes are wandering monks of Islam who incorporate strenuous howling and whirling into their religious rites. By the fifteenth century, there were coffee houses all over Mecca and in Cairo as well. Men and women drank the bitter brew in tiny cups inches deep in sediment while they listened to poets, scholars, and musicians.

HOW TO STORE COFFEE

In Bean Form:
Room Temperature	4 to 5 weeks
Freezing	5 to 6 months (grind amount needed only)
Refrigerator	Avoid

Ground Coffee:
Room Temperature	7 to 10 days
Freezer	5 to 6 weeks
Refrigerator	up to 3 weeks

Information from Simpson & Vail.

Coffee's journey toward acceptance was not easy. Muhammed's teachings expressly forbade stimulating and/or intoxicating beverages. Coffee was surrounded with strong circumstantial evidence against it on this count. Not only had the devout dervishes whirled under its influence, but at some point, the bean pulp had been fermented to make liquor. Perhaps because of this, coffee had been named kahwah, which is a word also used to describe wines. The big brew was in big trouble. In 1511, it influenced a trial that was knee deep in local politics. Mecca then was ruled by governor Kair Beg, servant of the Holy Ottoman Empire. Backed by local doctors who condemned coffee as damaging to the health, he banned those wicked meeting places where men were being corrupted by such nonreligious pleasures. Eventually, poor Kair Beg lost both his head and his ban to the Sultan in Cairo, who was a coffee drinker. The Sultan came down hard on Mecca, investigated certain allegations against Kair Beg, and found him to be an embezzler.

Moving westward, coffee immediately ran into trouble at the Vatican. It was described to Pope Clement VIII (1592-1605) as an unholy brew, the elixir of the Terrible Turks, who held the Near and Middle East and preyed on Eastern Europe and the Balkans continuously. Clement was a mild, thoughtful man. He tasted the accused brew, pronounced it good, and is said to have suggested that the drink be baptised and made into a Christian drink.

The great coffee vogue-and-scandal was repeated as a cycle in England and in France, the beverage being seen as a ruiner of men, sometimes an elixir, sometimes a medicine, sometimes an aphrodisiac.

With perhaps more justification, wines and various alcohols have shared the "new food" fate. Some stories claim wine as the discovery of the Hebrews, recording that Noah planted vineyards after his descent from Mount Ararat, the legendary location of the Ark. Ararat is in eastern Turkey on the border of Iran, once called Persia. The Iranians claim its discovery for a Persian prince. In any case, wine moved westward from Ararat. Solomon, who ruled in Jerusalem from about 972 to 932 B.C., is said to have drunk the wine of Cyprus, and Jesus of Nazareth served it at the last supper.

LOVE POTION

1 gill of good red wine

Add 1 teaspoon each of rosemary, anise seed, cloves, clear honey, orange rind. Add a pinch of cumin, 3 green leaves from rose geranium.

Mix in a sauce pan over fire. Bring to a boil gently and stir while slowly counting to one hundred. Remove pan to a cool place until the contents stop steaming.

Strain ingredients through a fine sieve and return pan to heat again on the fire. When sweet vapors rise, pour potion into a cup and deliver to the one whose love you would sweeten and want.

It shall not fail unless performed by one whose heart and household keep slatternly habits.

Spell of Love from *The Complete Book of Spells, Ceremonies and Magic* by Migene Gonzolas-Whipple (Crown, 1977).

Muhammed repudiated wine, and his followers, under the Ottoman Empire, all but eliminated vineyards from the Middle East. It flourished in Europe, however. The Greeks combined wine and fertility in the person of the same God, Dionysius. The Dionysian rites were festivals where drunkeness accompanied the orgiastic eating of the raw flesh of animals and possibly more sinister substances.

SOME FOODS CALLED APHRODISIACS

Absynthe	Fennel	Pheasant
Anise	Fish	Pimientoes
Artichokes	Fish soups	Pistachio nuts
Asparagus in seasoned	Garlic	Potatoes
butter sauce	Honey	Prunes
Avocados	Hot sauces	Radishes
Basil	Leeks	Raw beef
Beans and fava beans	Licorice	Rose water
Capon	Liver	Saffron
Carrots	Mandrake root	Shallots
Caviar	Marrow	Shark's fin soup
Celery	Mushrooms,	Shellfish
Cheeses	particularly morels	Snails
Chocolates	Mutton	Thyme
Chutneys	Nutmeg	Tomatoes
Cloves	Nuts	Truffled sweetbreads
Coca-cola	Olives	Truffles
Cocoa	Onions	Vanilla
Coffee	Oysters	Venison
Dill	Peas	White beets
Eels	Peppermints	Wine
Eggs	Peppers	

In all these cases, the evil, of course, was not in the wine, the coffee, or even in Eve's apple, but rather in the hearts of men. The pleasure in food is to be found in the hearts of men as well. Nowhere is this more clearly seen than in the myths surrounding aphrodisiacs. The connection between pleasure in food and pleasure in sensuality has encouraged dreamers to believe in the aphrodisiac properties of foods century after century. Candidates for the role of aphrodisiac have been fish, vegetables, especially those resembling genitalia (associative magic) such as mandrake root and ginseng, fruit, spices, drinks, and herbs. (The root word for vanilla is also the root word for vagina.) The human tendency to attribute to the unknown any quality we want it to have has conferred magical properties on an extraordinary number of foods.

Even though wine is classified today as a drug, there is nothing in it that can enhance sexual prowess or directly stimulate sexual desire, according to all authorities of note. Neither coffee nor wine, neither oysters nor vanilla, nor any other so-called aphrodisiac or love potion contains any chemical agents recognized by modern science as having the ability to stimulate a direct physiological reaction upon the genitourinary tract.

On the other hand, no one denies the subtle relationship between the sensual appreciation of food and the sensual appreciation of sex. A German nutritionist, H. Balzli, wrote authoritatively of a well-prepared meal of subtly seasoned foods as stimulating various sensuous reactions—visual, olfactory, and tactile—conducive to a state of general euphoria that could invite sexual expression. The French *cabinets particuliers*, small private dining rooms featured by certain Paris restaurants in recent centuries, linked food and sex, as have other ceremonial situations throughout history.

A relatively modern drink that was rich in sexual connotations was absinthe, a green liqueur that was poured over ice and mixed with water. It was invented by Dr. Ordinaire, a Frenchman who lived in Switzerland. Made of 70-80 percent alcohol, flavored with star anise (a licorice flavoring), and distilled from angelica root, sweet flag, and dittany with wormwood, it was the sipping drink of the café intellectuals in the early decades of the century and was credited with encouraging everything from the poetic muse to sexual desire. It was banned in Switzerland in 1908, in the United States in 1912, and in France in 1915, because it was believed to have a harmful effect on the nerves. Permitted, however, is Pernod, an approximation of absinthe and a close relative of the home brew distilled in basements all around the Mediterranean, *raki*, which is North African. In the region of Cannes where the jet set plays, the people call it *pastise*, and it is considered a good stomach remedy, a cure for tapeworms (though alcoholic drenchings did not cure Louis XIV's tapeworm), an appetite stimulant for invalids, and, sometimes, a flavoring for *bouillabaisse*, a fish stew. Too much of it, like too much of any alcoholic beverage, appears to make men and women impotent, a common symptom of intoxication.

It is theorized that alcohol and some drugs that seem to depress the inhibitions (such as marijuana), may open the way to sexual excitation. In addition, substances known as cantharides (Spanish fly, a skin irritant and diuretic), and yohimbine may have the capacity to affect sexuality. Yohimbine is described as a crystaline alkaloid found in Central Africa where it has been used for centuries to increase sexuality. However, the title of aphrodisiac is applied with reservations. Most investigators feel that any clinical changes in sexuality after its use are due to suggestion, since it actually requires lethal doses of the substance to have a stimulatory effect.

Another food that man has approached with fear and hopeful trembling is the tomato. All varieties of tomato are derived from a wild species that began in what is today Peru, Ecuador, and Bolivia. In Mexico, long before Columbus,

natives were cultivating types of tomatoes, and it is generally believed that the tomato moved from there to Europe. It was known in Italy in 1554 as *pomodoro* (golden apple), so it must have been a yellow variety. From Italy, the tomato spread to Spanish and English gardens in both yellow and scarlet forms, but it was seen as a horticultural curiosity and was called "love apple" because of its supposed aphrodisiac properties.

SUPREME COURT DECISION

Is the tomato a fruit or a vegetable? As horticulture classes things, it is a fruit. However, for the purposes of trade in the United States, it was classified as a vegetable by the United States Supreme Court in 1893. The reason the court ruled it a vegetable is that it is used most often in the main part of meals, when vegetables usually appear.

By the mid-1700s, the Europeans were eating tomatoes, but there is no record of the tomato's use in the United States until Jefferson grew them in 1781. The tomato was not used in the northeastern states until about 1835, but as late as 1900, many people still considered it poisonous. The genus name, *Lycopersicoon*, means "wolf peach" and probably alludes to its supposed poisonous characteristics, but the magic and the mystery of this food are long gone.

If the lowly tomato, the most common vegetable (by legal definition) in American gardens, can have been perceived in so many guises, it has to be because man seeks and finds in food much more than biological fuel. He attributes to food the powers of a god: the power to harm and the power to heal.

RITUALS

Psychologists say the infant perceives a world that is hazy and mysterious, in which feeding seems to be the unexplained, magical result of his powerful cry for food. To an infant civilization exploring a planet, it would seem wise to propitiate and to worship the invisible forces governing its food supplies. Early man sacrificed food and initiated food-related ceremonies. Abram of the Chaldees sacrificed a lamb at one of the watershed moments of the Old Testament, the time when human sacrifice came to an end. Catholic followers of Rome still strengthen self-discipline and prepare for Easter and the immortality of man by giving up favorite foods, including meat, for Lent. The Hindus and the Taoists had given up meat years before Jesus of Nazareth was born.

In its earliest period, India celebrated with banquets of young buffalo basted in clarified butter, birds baked in leaves, cheeses, sweets of milk and sugar, mango sauces, pepper, sesame oil, cardamom, cloves, and dozens more flavorings on fowl, rice, and breads. Honey was served on the great holidays (holy days) and at state banquets. These feasts would have appealed to the Aryans, the lean and wild warriors who conquered the Middle East and India itself in 1500 B.C. From the cold central steppes of Asia (USSR), these Turks brought with them the will to conquer and the art of roasting chunks of meat, *kebabs*, on swords over the campfire. The Hindus, who dominate India today, are the descendants of these Turkestani conquerors, and followers of a religion that is a synthesis of the thought of the Aryans and of the native peoples they overcame.

TYPES OF HONEY

Honey varies in color and flavor, depending upon the plant sources from which the bees gathered the nectar. It is generally classified and sold as liquid, comb, solid, or chunk.

Liquid has been forced from the comb and is free of crystals.

Comb Honey is sold in the comb as stored by the bees.

Solid Honey, partially or wholly solidified or granulated, is referred to as candied, creamed, or churned.

Chunk Honey is a combination of liquid and comb honey.

A thousand years later (when the people who were to found the Roman Empire were barely emerging among the Etruscans), food was being etherialized in India. In the fifth century B.C., references to food in early religious writings of India were put together. Food was classified for nutrition, flavor, and for aesthetic appeal. The *Bhagavad Gita* (Celestial Song), a Sanskrit poem whose lessons in spiritual discipline (yoga, for attaining enlightened consciousness) are the basis for both Hindu and Buddhist thought, says food that is savory possesses the quality of truth and is considered conducive to health and longevity. Bitter, acid food is seen as stimulating the passions, and therefore injurious. Spoiled food is gloom. Banquets of buffalo became few and far between in this century which saw the enlightenment of a young Indian nobleman later called the Buddha. Buddha's sorrow at seeing a family of insects destroyed by a farmer's plough is credited with inspiring the vegetarianism adopted by Buddhist groups.

Buddha eventually became more important in China than in India. A further impetus to vegetarianism came from the Chinese philosopher, Lao-Tze. Lao-Tze inspired the Taoist movement which promoted a spiritual approach to life, with nonstriving as an essential theme. Taoism pronounced barely cooked vegetables nutritionally superior, which was just as well since China early ran out of wood for cooking. The Taoists also evolved a ritualistic tea-drinking ceremony that may be the basis for the complex and beautiful tea-drinking ceremony that developed in Japan and is still taught today.

TO MAKE A PERFECT CUP OF TEA

Outstanding tea is clear and pale, with a delicate bouquet, and without a trace of bitterness. A second brewing of the leaves will produce very good tea, but discard the leaves after that. Dilute tea that seems too strong with boiling hot water.

Experts recommend the use of china or glazed clay tea pots: Metals flavor the tea unpleasantly. You will probably like best tea made in these proportions: for large quantities, use 2 tablespoons for each 4 cups of water. For smaller portions, use ½ to 1 teaspoon for each cup. Measurements should be slightly mounded spoonfuls.

Tea which is brewed correctly usually has two-thirds of the leaves floating in the beginning; incorrectly brewed tea will have about half its leaves floating.

Always buy the best quality tea you can afford; always draw fresh, cold water (not water from the hot faucet). Never heat water beyond the very first moment of boiling, or it will be flat because excessive boiling expels the oxygen in the water. Always have the tea pot hot by scalding it or by setting it on a warm stove top. Always pour the boiling water into the pot all at once to keep it as hot as possible. Steep the tea for 5 minutes before pouring.

The Japanese tea ceremony is said to be rooted in the Zen Buddhist principle that promotes the adoration of the beautiful in the daily routines of life, from the cleaning of a house to the preparation of a meal. The Japanese word for the ceremony is *cha-no-yu*, literally meaning "hot water tea." Zen is from a Sanskrit word, *dhyana*, meaning meditation or contemplation.

The tea ceremony is an upper-class way of entertaining guests. Everything follows established aesthetic rules of etiquette. The ceremony takes place in a tea room (*chaseki*), about nine feet square, built especially for the ceremony and designed to suggest refined poverty (so as not to be ostentatious, which is aggressive). In the room are a few ornaments and a small sunken fireplace where the kettle is heated in winter. A brazier and charcoal fire are used in summer. Guests approach the ceremony humbly by crawling through a three-foot door. Large mats are arranged in a predetermined way, with a smaller one for a servant. The tea—green tea as in China—is placed in a small bowl, boiling water is poured over it, and the tea master beats it with a bamboo brush, a *chasen*. When the tea is ready, each guest is offered a sip and after each sip, the edge of the bowl is wiped with a small paper napkin. All is solemn and silent.

The founders of the ceremony emphasized harmony between guests and utensils, respect for the people and the instruments, cleanliness (guests rinse their mouths and wash their hands before entering), and finally, the tranquility associated with the indefinable quality of mellowness which an article acquires by long and loving use.

STORING TEA

Tea should be kept in a tight-lidded can in a cool, dry place, as the leaves have a definite tendency to absorb moisture and odors. Unlike some wines, good tea does not improve with age but a tight container will preserve its fragrance and flavor longer.

The ritualistic approach to food still permeates Japan's cooking. In the home, beautiful, brightly lacquered wooden or porcelain bowls are set on trays as pretty as the bowls. Shapes and colors are carefully arranged with great artistry. Proportion and harmony in color, and extraordinary refinement go into the food itself. Whether or not you like raw fish, *sushi* and *sashimi*, now becoming popular in the West, these morsels are designed as exquisitely as a painting. A sprig of green seaweed, the coral of salmon flesh, the perfect precision of cut vegetables, are unmatched for delicacy even in the greatest cuisines of the West. Small portions and a dozen dishes elegantly combine variety with moderation. At banquets, though dozens of dishes are served, many of these are meant as gifts for departing guests and can be expected to remain untouched during the meal.

On the farthest eastern shore of the lands we call the Far East, food, as life, is presented in the most exquisite way and is treated in the most ritualistic fashion to be seen among contemporary societies. In western lands, rituals became celebrations, rather more robust in connotation, and perhaps more open to change.

CELEBRATIONS

The earliest celebrations were based on a successful hunt. Later celebrations involved the conquest of other people's stores of supplies. The *kebab*-roasters from Turkestan rode to plunder the riches of the Indus Valley, stayed to celebrate, and became Hindus. Near relatives of theirs conquered the Myceneans and Greeks, became the Hellenes, and under Alexander marched East, overwhelming the *kebab*-eaters, the curry-eaters of Pakistan and India, and spiceland itself. The Arabs, who took over as the Hellenistic states crumbled, lived on the spice trade for the next thousand years and more.

For a time, Persia (Iran) ruled the supplies of the Middle East and Egypt, spreading spices, sweetmeats, and the story of Aladdin's magic lamp. Then, Roman legions won the known world and exacted as tribute everything from pepper and Swiss cheese to Egyptian wheat. Rome, in its turn, collapsed.

Under the banner of Islam, a new wave of Turks carried their campfires and *kebabs* all the way to Morocco, conquered the Berbers, crossed to Spain, and taught the people to put a pinch of cinnamon and a dab of saffron in their food. There known as Moors, they almost took France in the eighth century and ruled Spain for the next 700 years.

In 1683, the Turks, under their flag of the crescent moon, besieged Vienna. Viennese bakers, who had learned the art of flaky pastry from the Middle East, began to make their breakfast rolls in the shape of crescents, inspired, perhaps, by the Turkish defeat by the King of Poland. Or maybe they made them that way one morning simply because they expected to be feeding them to the Turks. The siege was the last real effort by the Turks to conquer Europe's supplies, but the flaky *croissant* stayed to conquer Vienna. A hundred years later, Marie Antoinette, the Viennese bride of Louis XVI, brought *croissants* with her to Paris. Poor Marie lost her head to the people of France, who rebelled because the court had so much to eat when they had so little.

If you take the long view of history, it appears that the conquerors did the most to spread the wealth of cooking lore. And it certainly was from the palaces that the poor took lessons on how to live well.

In Old Testament stories, common people had their share in a number of fatted calves. In one big affair staged by King Solomon, the people consumed 22,000 oxen and uncountable fowl.

Slaves and commoners crowned the heads of Egypt's imperial guests with the sacred blue lotus, lit the spices that perfumed the banquet halls, baked the raised bread Egypt evolved after isolating yeast from the desert nomads' sourdough, roasted wild beasts and game birds, and pressed olives, another Egyptian first. These culinary skills so impressed the Romans, they turned Egypt into Rome's breadbasket.

GARLIC

Garlic has attracted more attention, perhaps, than any other herb. Throughout history a garlic diet has been promoted as the solution to everything from hardened arteries to wounds. Here's a partial list: aging skin, asthma, bladder disease, boils, bronchitis, cancer, cholera, colds, colitis, constipation, cramps, croup, diabetes, diarrhea, diphtheria, dysentery, ear inflammation, encephalitis, eye inflammation, flatulence, fluid retention, gallstones, high blood pressure, indigestion, insect bites, intestinal worms, kidney dysfunction, kidney stones, laryngitis, malaria, nervous tension, neuralgia, nicotine poisoning, paralysis, pimples, pleurisy, pneumonia, poison antidote, rheumatism, snake bite, tonsilitis, toothache, tuberculosis, tumors, ulcers, whooping cough, worms, wounds.

Garlic was considered an energy food by Pliny and Herodotus, and the slaves who built the pyramids are said to have lived on it and onions. Athletes ate garlic to stay fit. Muhammed, we are told, had high regard for it as an antidote for snake bites.

Greece, a poor and rocky land, taught the people more about attitudes than about cooking. The Stoics knew how to tighten their belts, and Epicurus perfected the art of discrimination. But the citizens of Greece who were enslaved by the Roman Empire ate very well. Delicacies were brought from every corner of the known world for the crowned heads of Rome to feast on and the poor to think over. Rose petals and wheat by the boatload crossed the Mediterranean from Egypt, and shiploads of spice came from Tyre to what is now Lebanon, brought overland from Yemen (Sheba) by Arab traders. The Romans learned to flavor spoiling meat and pep up tough grains and porridges by adding ginger, nutmeg, cinnamon, pepper, and other glories of the curry-eaters to the cooking pot.

Voracious for things good, they served suckling pig often enough to threaten the pork population, necessitating the declaration of piglet as taboo except for holidays. It was the Romans who taught farmers to geld roosters so they would grow into feast-sized capons. Theirs were the first pastas in Europe, doughy strips shaped according to the region they evolved in. Slaves brought to the banquet halls of the Emperors things of the sea and things of the forest.

In *The Food Book*, James Traeger tells us Roman appetizers included jellyfish and eggs, a pig's udder stuffed with sea urchins, brains cooked with oil, tree fungus with a peppery fish-fat sauce, peacock brains, and flamingo tongues. Main courses included roast deer flavored with arugula (the rue Ophelia spoke of), olive oil, and honey; ostrich; parrot and turtle dove; ham boiled with figs and bay and rolled in pastry; and flamingo boiled with dates. Desserts included roses fried with pastry and stuffed dates, peaches, plums, and pears. There were vats of wine. None of this was very refined, but Europe was learning from the civilized world, the Middle East.

The partygoers lolled, Oriental fashion, on couches at the banquet tables, belching in compliment to their hosts (another Arab custom, shared by the

THE MAGIC OF GOLD

The Middle Ages were preoccupied with the alchemists' determination to turn other substances into gold. This obsession spilled over even into food. A number of recipes evolved with gold as the most fashionable ingredient, and it was said to have healing capacities. Patients who could afford it had gold dust sprinkled on their food, and it also apparently was mixed into the corn fed to chickens being fattened for court households. Gold-flecked liqueurs still are to be found in Europe, among them *Danziger Goldwasser* and *Elizir d'Anvers*. In India, wafer-thin 14-carat gold leaf is used to garnish some sweets and desserts, and, recently, pralines (candy-coated almonds) with a tissue-thin coating of silver were sold in San Francisco.

Eskimo), dabbed wine-reddened lips with napkins (just invented), and invited slaves to tickle their throats in the *vomitorium* to get them through the eight-hour banquets.

The common people munched porridges of lentils and legumes, ate salt fish, and, occasionally, a little goat meat, and were given free bread and games when they got restless. Some of the glory that was Rome traveled to the provinces of France, Spain, and Britain, where the barbarians marveled, and they, too, learned. The Visigoths demanded 30,000 pounds of pepper as part of the tribute exacted from Rome in 408 A.D. as the price of peace.

As the Roman tidal wave receded, leaving North Africa and the Middle East in the hands of the Ottoman Empire, refined dining in Europe retreated to the monasteries along with Bibles, herbals, and recipes for making wine and cheese. The common people scoured forests and fields for wild sweet herbs—like thyme and oregano—and free meats. Spices were a magical memory from the good old, bad old days.

BUBBLING SYLLABUB

Eggnog and syllabub, which is made with wine, are related. Syllabub is a name derived from Sillery in the Champagne region of France, and the word "bub" is slang from Elizabethan times, meaning a bubbling drink. Traditionally, syllabub was made by placing a bowl of wine under a cow, and then milking the cow until the bowl had a froth on the top.

In the eighth century A.D., Charlemagne used Christianity to forge Europe into a semblance of the past and called it the Holy Roman Empire. In the thirteenth century, the Crusades and Marco Polo's journals of his stay in China reintroduced to the European table some of the splendors of the East. Marco Polo noted that great quantities of pepper were used in China and cultivated in the Orient, leading to the search for a sea route to the Far East that uncovered America in 1492. Europe could not forget the fact that spices could make poor-quality food more palatable, and the Arabs were blocking the ancient supply routes.

The Father of the Elizabethan age was Henry VIII of England, and his message was gluttony. As irresistibly scandalous as his capacity for wives was his capacity to consume food. He could eat for seven hours at a stretch and became so fat machinery had to be invented to get him up and down stairs. In the temperate climate where civilization began, the river valleys had yielded three crops a year. England's North Sea weather yielded one. Food was meat-focused. The herds were killed in fall when fodder became scarce, and the meat was sour by Christmas and dangerous by Lent—a good time to give it up. Whereas a single calf would have sufficed for a desert tribe, Henry could eat a whole chicken, several meat courses, and many loaves of bread in one go. There was nothing fancy about his food. Bay laurel, which appeared in Indian *pilafs* and had been used to crown the victor in Rome, was used less for cooking than for strewing on floors of homes fouled by odors in a land where doors and windows had to be closed much of the year.

Like Henry, the people ate white bread, drank beer, carried their own knives and spoons to help themselves from a common pot, put meat on a slab of bread, and ate with their fingers.

CAVIAR

Exuberance over caviar, one of the most expensive delicacies, is shared worldwide. Although it first became popular in France in 1741, it has been known in Western Europe since the sixteenth century: To quote from Hamlet, "His play...pleased not the million, 'twas caviare to the general."

Probably no other food has commanded such interest as to the proper way in which it should be served. The Russian czars are most noted for their obsession with its presentation.

Traditionally, caviar is eaten with a silver spoon and served in an elegant glass dish on a piller of ice. Condiments, such as crushed eggs, often accompany the dish for two reasons: restauranteurs feel its high price calls for additional pains in presentation; a more valid reason is that condiments make for a more balanced taste.

Technically, caviar is the roe or eggs of fish, such as sturgeon, salmon, whitefish, and lumpfish, which have been treated with salt. Beluga, Sevruga, and Osetra, imported from the Soviet Union and Iran, are the most pleasing to the gourmet palate and command the highest prices. Beluga is from a rare, large sturgeon that produces the most prized eggs, large and succulent. It is the most expensive caviar.

Osetra is a medium-sized egg and brown in color. Sevruga is smaller.

Roe from the American sturgeon is black or gray, softer than imported sturgeon, and more reasonably priced. American salmon caviar is reddish-orange. Caviar from lake whitefish, called American Gold, is champagne in color and the egg-size is medium.

Fresh caviar has the purest taste. Pasteurized caviar has a longer shelf life, but pasteurization causes some loss of flavor. The pasteurized less expensive varieties make good sauces and dips and lend elegance to any party.

Caviar must be served chilled. Store fresh caviar in the coldest part of the refrigerator and keep it no longer than two or three weeks. Pasteurized varieties sold in the jar should be chilled and turned every day so that the oils and caviar remain thoroughly mixed. When caviar is to be incorporated into a sauce to be cooked, add it at the last minute and never boil it. Excessive heat will dissolve the eggs.

The French countryside and climate offered a more diverse fare than the British, and added a touch of class to the gluttony of an age. Louis XIV (1643—1715) had such a prodigious appetite that people would travel miles to see him eat four kinds of soup, a whole pheasant and a whole partridge, a ham, mutton in casserole, salads, and sweets, followed by fruit and hard-boiled eggs.

Through the sumptuous halls of Versailles, past the one thousand silver-tubbed orange trees positioned to disguise the odors of the not-very-fastidious courtiers, trooped the servants, bearing eight times eight prepared dishes, eight courses of eight dishes each. From these, Louis chose twenty, ending always with hard-boiled eggs.

So intent were the nobles of the court on feeding their king that they took as truth the story of what has to have been the most frivolous suicide of all time. In a letter, Madame de Sevigne speaks of François Vatel, chef to the Prince de Condé, who committed suicide on a Friday when the king was coming to dinner and the fish failed to arrive on time.

The pursuit of sophistication in excess was introduced to a ready, willing, and able French food circle by an Italian who came to France as bride to the Duc d'Orléans in 1533. Catherine de Médici, the daughter of spice traders, had her Italian chefs and confectioners instill both artistry and confidence in the French court cooks. It was in Louis XIV's reign that the *Cordon Bleu* school of cookery with its rich sauces was set up in Paris for orphaned daughters of French noblemen in the military. But the complex cookery that evolved was the joint legacy of gluttony and the guillotine that ended it. Rendered jobless by the French Revolution, the court-trained chefs of France emigrated to other lands, including the Americas, opened restaurants, and spread the French court cooking traditions wherever they went.

Marie Antoinette's head came off in 1793, just 100 years after the Turks' last bid for Vienna. Exactly 200 years later, the great French chef, Georges Auguste Escoffier, created *pêches Melba* and served it to Dame Nellie Melba, the great Australian soprano at the newly opened Savoy Hotel in London. In that 200-year period, the people made clear their understanding that to control fool supplies, people must control the government. The centuries following the French Revolution bequeathed to Escoffier a legacy of simplified court cooking. He taught the world to orchestrate that repertoire as carefully as Mozart orchestrated a minuet.

Gourmet cooking has improved steadily since the Revolution, becoming simpler as it has been adapted to the needs of a developing middle class. The best food in France has always come from the provinces. Here, thrifty and discriminating *ménagères*, their palates educated by the availability of the best and freshest ingredients, have cultivated the art of making the most of everything from cockles to *foie gras*. They use only a handful of flavorings: herbs, cream, mushrooms, a little wine, lemon. There's no need to disguise perfection under peppery sauces.

PÊCHES MELBA

Poach the peaches in vanilla-flavored syrup. Put them in a timbale upon a layer of vanilla ice cream, and coat them with a raspberry puree.

From *The Escoffier Cookbook* (New York: Crown, 1941). This edition is an Americanization of the famous chef's *Le Guide Culinaire* with Phileas Gilbert and Emile Petu (1903). Other best-known books by the master chef are *Le Carnet d'Epicure*, (1911), *Le Livre de Menus* (1912), and *Ma Cuisine* (1934).

Today, food from the growers reaches every corner of the western world in relatively good condition. The industrialization of the West saw continent-spanning railroads begin the transportation of perishables from warm southern gardens to cold northern markets. Tin won the West as surely as the cowboys who packed canned beans in their saddlebags starting in the mid-1800s. Frozen food may not be as good as fresh, but it has made obsolete the root vegetable and starch-based cuisine of the North since the technique of freezing was perfected by Clarence Birdseye, a Brooklyn-born scientist in the 1930s. The jets that zoom fresh tulips daily from Holland, in and out of season, also bring just-baked French *croissants* to select New York establishments, which are now rivalled by *croissants* from local bakeries.

The crumbs that fell from the tables of the emperors may not have filled the bellies of the multitudes, but the information gained from such exploration of abundance fed the commoners' dreams. It was Napoleon's intuition that an army travels on its stomach. It is history's message that once the people want something, they get it. Persian princes sent fast horses to bring ice for sherbets from the distant mountains of Iraq. The humblest contemporary family has only to go to the corner supermarket for its frozen dessert. The supermarket of today routinely stocks what would have been ransom for a kingdom in hoysin sauce, mandarin oranges, canned snails, oil, vinegar, pepper, saffron, basil, and other spices and herbs.

FLAVORINGS

Herbs and spices today are that special touch of something, that color, that multiplies a food's flavor by as many shades as the cook knows how to use. In the past, they were used as remedies for ailments of every kind and were particularly useful in making spoiled food palatable. There was a time when all spices, and particularly pepper, were very expensive. Even today, we pay almost as much per pound for saffron as a drug dealer pays for opium.

Spices are seeds, bark, and dried flowers from tropical trees and plants, most of them from the Far East. Herbs grow there too, but are found in the Mediterranean area and also grow, at least as annuals, in most temperate regions. The Egyptians, Greeks, and Romans used spices and herbs, and, as in Biblical times, held spices to be among their most precious possessions. With the fall of the Roman Empire, Europe was cut off from the spice routes to the Far East and substituted the use of herbs. The lore of herbal uses was preserved in the monasteries of Europe and passed on to the people. In the Middle Ages, the mistress of the household was doctor and perfumer, as well as mistress to the cook. The heart of the home was the "stillroom," a special place where the still for distilling liquors and various medicinal preparations was kept, where potpourris were made to ward off bad odors, and where herbs were dried and

SPICES AND HERBS TO KEEP ON HAND

Among the most important herbs and spices to have handy for most modern and international cooking are: cinnamon, nutmeg, allspice, thyme, bay, parsley, cloves (whole and ground), marjoram, tarragon, celery seed, onion, garlic, oregano, basil, saffron, sage, cardamom, curry, turmeric, coriander, cumin, ground ginger, fresh ginger (which will keep for about a year in the refrigerator if peeled and covered with dry sherry in a jar with a tight-fitting lid; freezing the ginger will only make it mushy), soy sauce, paprika (imported from Hungary), cayenne, black peppercorns, sea or kosher salt.

stored. The "stillroom books," the diaries of homemakers and cooks, were the first cookbooks. In 1682, Mary Doggett wrote in *Mary Doggett: Her Book of Recipes*: "Take half a pound of Cypress Roots, a pound of Orris, ¾ lb. Rhodium (rosewood), a lb. of Coriander seed, ¾ lb. of Calamus, 3 oranges stuck with cloves..." This was a "receipt" for a "sweet bagg," to scent linens and make musty rooms smell good.

The earliest complete herbal, a record of the uses of herbs, was written in the first century after Christ by a Greek, Dioscorides. One compiled in the sixth

century was signed Pseudo-Apuleius. It was translated into Anglo-Saxon in the eleventh century, and many manuscripts and printed editions were available. In the years just after Elizabeth I came to the throne, two English herbals appeared, *The Grete Herbal* (1526) and *Banckes' Herbal* (1525). Browsing through recipes from these books, one catches a glimpse of the world those cooks dealt with, where the spoilage of food was fought with the same weapons as such modern ills as insomnia, depression, falling hair, and one we don't deal with much anymore, the plague. Not all recipes were refined.

VIN AIGRE

The most popular disinfectants in England and in Colonial America were herbal vinegars. Scented with many different garden herbs, they were used to ward off plague germs, to perfume sickrooms, and to improve poor ventilation. In the seventeenth century, vinegars were used to soak sponges which were to be sniffed if you felt faint. The heads of walking canes had compartments to hold vinegar-soaked sponges. During epidemics men and women washed their hands and faces in vinegar and sprinkled vinegar over linens and bedclothes.

In time, these aromatic vinegars went into *vinaigrettes* which Victorian ladies wore on chains around their necks. Those were the days when ladies, laced to their chins, fainted easily, and vinegar was used as a resuscitant. Herb vinegars were also used to scent the bath. Here is an example from *The Toilet of Flora*, written in the eighteenth century:

Handful of rosemary, wormwood, lavender, and mint to be put into a jar with a gallon of strong vinegar, keep near a fire for four days, strain, an oz. of powder camphor added, and then bottled for pleasure.

Vin aigre is French for sour wine.

In *The Food Book*, James Traeger quotes from a cookbook compiled about 1390 for Richard II's kitchen: "Take rabbits and smite them to pieces; seethe them in grease...Take chickens and ram them together, serve them broken..." The first printed cookbook, according to Traeger, was published in 1475. *The Cook's*

Oracle, by Dr. William Kitchiner, may have been the first to show weights and measurements. Mrs. Isabella Beeton's *The Book of Household Management*, published in 1861 in England, was the first of the modern cookbooks. The first book of English cookery, according to André L. Simon and Robin Howe, authors of *Dictionary of Gastronomy* (Overlook Press, 1978), was *The Forme of Cury*, written in 1147. Fannie Farmer's *Boston Cooking School Cookbook* was published in 1896. In *American Cookery*, published in Hartford in 1796, Amelia Simmons is credited with being the first to introduce to the printed page recipes for such native American foods as Indian pudding. Fannie Farmer's book and the 1930 edition of *The Better Homes and Gardens Cookbook* are still ranked as among the better general cookbooks available to American cooks. *Escoffier's Cookbook* is probably the preferred reference work of professional cooks, while Julia Child's series of books on French foods are certainly the best teaching books for anyone who wishes he or she could get to the *Cordon Bleu* school in Paris. Her work is patient, painstaking and, generally, pretty faithful to the way food is cooked in France.

USING FRESH OR DRIED HERBS

Both dried and fresh herbs are used in cooking. The rule of thumb is ½ teaspoon dried herb equals the flavoring capacity of 1 teaspoon of the minced and packed fresh herb. The cook, however, must taste the dish to be certain the flavor meets expectations. Strength of flavor in herbs varies according to how long it has been dried (when dried), and it is affected by soil, weather, and even the time of day the herb was picked (when fresh). Herb flavor is best in sprig tips picked before the heat of the sun reaches them in midmorning: The heat disperses the volatile oils that are the source of the herb flavor.

THE FASCINATING SPICES

Herbs are old familiars to most American cooks, but spices can still seem exotic. The following are some of the most commonly used spices in the western cook's repertoire.

CARDAMOM

Cardamom is a round, fragrant, buff-colored little spice that costs almost as much as saffron to harvest. It yields only a few hundred pounds per cultivated acre and must be picked by hand. In *The Cook's Companion* (Crown,

1978), Doris McFerran Townsend says the Vikings discovered it on a voyage to India and brought it home, where it has been part of Scandanavian cuisine ever since. It is used in many Indian and Middle Eastern dishes, gives a special flavor to pea and lentil soups, and is a delightful addition to a cup of black coffee.

Cardamom is sold in its pod and ground, and is a native of India.

CINNAMON

One of the most popular of spices in America, cinnamon goes into any number of desserts, pastries, baked cakes, and candies. In its earliest days, it was also used as a perfume and an incense. The Romans used it in their baths, and it often turned up in love potions in the Middle Ages. Cinnamon is the bark of certain evergreens, *Cinnamomum zeylanicum*, native to Sri Lanka and India. An oil is extracted which is used to flavor medicines and is thought to have some medicinal properties.

SIMPLE CURRY POWDER	*Makes 1¼ cups*

½ cup ground coriander
¼ cup ground cumin
¼ cup ground turmeric
¼ cup ground ginger

Mix well and store in bottle with a tight-fitting lid.

CLOVES

Cloves are the unopened buds of an evergreen tree called *Eugenia caryophyllata* which grows in the East Indies and Mauritius. Oil of cloves was once used to flavor toothache remedies, and it still goes into some toothpastes. Cloves have been considered both a pain killer and an antiseptic, and were once among the costliest of herbs. Today they are imported by every land from Madagascar (the Malagasy Republic) and Tanzania (Zanzibar). Cloves are used extensively in flavoring stocks (usually stuck into a whole small onion) and stews, in pork products of the delicatessen types, and in baked goods, candies, and cookies. Cloves and cinnamon were among the favorite spices of New England cooks during colonial days, and still go into many old recipes including apple and pumpkin pies.

CORIANDER

Coriander (*Coriandrum sativum*) seeds and leaves are used. The leaves are sometimes offered as Chinese parsley in Oriental food shops, and as *cilantro*, in Spanish food shops. When I lived in areas where I couldn't buy Chinese parsley (and was doing a lot of Oriental cooking), I planted coriander seeds in

my indoor flower pots and had all I needed. The seeds, whole or ground, are used in dried bean dishes, Indian and Spanish cooking, stews, and boiled fresh vegetables. One half teaspoon of ground coriander gives a unique flavor to homemade brown bread or baked apples. Place one crushed seed of coriander in *demitasse* coffee, top with whipped cream, and serve for gala occasions. Use fresh coriander leaves in salads. Coriander is also used in potpourris.

Coriander has been used along the Mediterranean since prehistoric times. Seeds have been found in tombs in Egypt, and it is believed to have grown in the hanging gardens of Babylon. It is referred to in the Bible, and the herbalists of the Middle Ages recommended it highly for worms and other ailments. Medicinally, it was often mixed with honey.

CURRY POWDER *Makes ⅓ to ½ cup*

¼ cup coriander seeds
2 tablespoons saffron threads
1 tablespoon cumin seeds
1 tablespoon mustard seeds
1½ teaspoons crushed red
   pepper
1 tablespoon poppy seeds

Grind all the ingredients together in a pepper mill, and bottle tightly.

CUMIN

Cumin seeds come from *Cuminum cyminum*, a small, slender herb of the *Umbelliferae* group, that has white or rose flowers. It grows in India, China, Mexico, and along the Mediterranean, and has been used to distill an oil for perfume, for medicine, and to flavor curries, chilies, and other Latin American and Middle Eastern dishes. Though it is relatively unknown in traditional American cooking, it flavors sauerkraut and some Dutch cheeses.

GINGERROOT

Gingerroot *(Zingiber officinale)* is essential to Oriental cuisine, in which it is used fresh, frozen, and ground. Ground, the dried root is the basic flavor in gingerbread, spice cakes, and cookies. A pinch of ground ginger perks up chicken casseroles and almost any sauce. It is part of a good curry and is used in pickles and conserves, with baked or stewed fruits, on vegetables, fish, lamb, beef, pork, veal, and in soups. Add a little ground ginger to plain commercial mayonnaise and it improves the flavor greatly. The leaves of the ginger plant are sometimes used to flavor soups.

For ages, ginger was called a rich man's spice and rivaled black pepper—the most valuable of spices—in price. Ginger was used in England before the eleventh century, and fancy gingerbread was a favorite of Elizabeth I's court. Spanish ships took gingerroot to the Caribbean, and it is now grown in Jamaica as an export crop. And in American and English homes in the last century, ginger was not only used in potpourris, but also to make the forerunner of one of today's favorite drinks—ginger ale.

MUSTARD

Mustard comes in light and dark types, and is one of the oldest spices known to man. It grows in the temperate countries, including the United States and Canada, whose fields are often yellow with wild mustard in summer, and Denmark and Britain, where it has been one of the most popular condiments for centuries. It generates a heat which made it sought after for medicinal uses. It is still used to make "mustard plasters," stinging poultices meant to relieve congestion. It is used for pickling, in salads, to flavor ground meats, egg dishes, cheeses, to base fresh mayonnaise, and in sauces and casseroles.

NUTMEG (MACE)

Nutmeg grows in the Moluccas (also Maluku, or Spice Islands), a group of fertile volcanic islands in Eastern Indonesia near New Guinea. These islands are the center of the nutmeg and clove trade. Nutmeg is the pit of the fruit of *Myristica fragrans* and mace is the thin lacy network that surrounds it. Nutmeg was once sold by traveling vendors and was so popular in Connecticut cooking it was named the Nutmeg State. In those days little graters, like miniature cheese graters, were sold specially for nutmeg. They had a containerlike top where the whole nutmeg could be stored so you wouldn't lose it. Today, most cooks buy nutmeg, and the brighter, orangy mace, ground and bottled. Nutmeg is used in all sorts of baked goods, puddings, sauces, vegetables, and mulled drinks—egg nog, for instance. A pinch of it was the secret to the superb white sauces of the Boston School of Cooking and was used in England and northern France in the same way. Mace is considered a better selection for pound cakes, cherry pie, and fish sauces. If you are out of one, you can use the other without changing the dish.

PAPRIKA

The paprika of Hungarian cooking is a mild flavorful powder ground from the fruit of *Capsicum annuum*, an annual pepper introduced to Europe by the Turks who occupied Hungary. Hungarian paprika has a special, fragrant taste that can't be replaced by paprikas that come from elsewhere, and this is essential to a real *paprikash*. Other varieties, almost as good but not quite the same, come from Spain and are used in cooking there. For a time paprika was called "Turkish pepper." Some of these are grown in California. There are many *Capsicum* varieties and species. Some give us cayenne, which is hot compared to paprika. Ordinary paprika became popular in the last century to add a dash of color to pale dishes and cream sauces without changing the flavor too much.

PEPPER

Pepper, at one time the most valuable spice in the world, is the ground seed of *Piper nigrum*, which grows in India and southwest Asia. The world uses about 175 million pounds of pepper a year, and Americans use more pepper than they use of all the other spices put together. Black pepper and white pepper come from the same plant. Black peppercorns are picked while still green and then dried in the sun. White peppercorns are mature before they are picked. Mignonette pepper is made by coarsely grinding and sieving either black or white peppercorns.

FRANCESCA BOSETTI MORRIS' PASTA AL PESTO　　　　　*Serves 4*

---

2 cups firmly packed fresh sweet basil leaves
Freshly ground black pepper to taste
3 cloves garlic, peeled and minced
1 teaspoon salt
2 tablespoons pine nuts (pignoli) or walnut meats
½ cup olive oil
½ cup grated Parmesan or Pecorino Sardo cheese
Hot spaghetti for 4

1. Put all the ingredients, except the cheese, into the blender. Blend at high speed, pushing the basil leaves down from time to time. Add more olive oil if the contents stick. When the sauce has the consistency of whipped butter, transfer it to a bowl and beat in the cheese with a fork.

2. Mix the pesto thoroughly into hot spaghetti. (Leftover pesto can be frozen and used later to flavor soups.)

SAFFRON

Saffron is still harvested, by women in baggy pants, from seas of purple crocus in India's northern state of Kashmir, and it is the world's most expensive

legal crop. Almost as valuable as opium, Indian exporters sell saffron for $450 a pound to countries in western Europe and America.

The cost is the result of the painstaking labor required to separate the threads of saffron from the flower petals. It takes an estimated 4,000 flowers to produce just one ounce of saffron, and the crocus plants take three years to reach their prime. So treasured has it been in the past that the Mogul Emperor Akbar the Great (1556-1605) ordered restriction of the use of saffron to ointment for the royal beards. During the days of the moguls, saffron-making was an imperial monopoly.

Saffron was harvested in the earliest days of India in the Indus Valley and has been prized for use in soups and stews, for flavoring yogurt, desserts, curries, and a thousand and one dishes since time began.

LIST OF FAVORITE HERBS

	Other Uses	Height	Perennial	Annual	Culinary	Fragrance
Anise (*Pimpinella anisum*)		2'-3'		✔	✔	✔
Basil (*Ocimum basilicum*)		1'-2'		✔	✔	✔
Bay Laurel (*Laurus nobilis*)		tree			✔	✔
Borage (*Borago officinalis*)	dried bouquets	1½'-3'		✔	✔	
Caraway (*Carum carvi*)		2½'		biennial	✔	
Catnip (*Nepeta cataria*)	for cats	3'-4'	✔			
Chamomile (*Anthemis nobilis*)	ground cover, hair rinse	3"-12"	✔			
Chervil (*Anthriscus cerefolium*)		6"-12"		✔	✔	
Chives (*Allium schoenoprasum*)	edible flowers	12"-15"	✔		✔	
Coriander (*Coriandrum sativum*)		18"		✔		✔

	Other Uses	Height	Perennial	Annual	Culinary	Fragrance
Costmary (*Chrysanthemum balsamita*)		5'-6'	✓		✓	✓
Cumin (*Cuminum cyminum*)		6"		✓	✓	✓
Dill (*Anethum graveolens*)		2'-3'		✓	✓	
Fennel (*Foeniculum*, all species)		2'-4'	✓	✓	✓	
Garlic (*Allium sativum*)		18"-24"		✓	✓	
Geranium (*Pelargonium*, all scented species)		2'-4'	✓		✓	✓
Gingerroot (*Zingiber officinale*)		18"-24"	✓		✓	✓
Lavender (*Lavandula*, all species)	hedge	3'-4'	✓			✓
Lavender Cotton (*Santolina chamaecyparissus*)	dried bouquets, hedge	1'-2'	✓			✓
Lemon Balm (*Melissa officinalis*)		24"	✓		✓	✓
Lemon Verbena (*Lippia citriodorata*)		3'-10'	✓		✓	✓
Marjoram (*Majorana hortensis*)		8"-12"	✓	✓	✓	✓
Mint (*Mentha*, all species)		18"-24"	✓		✓	✓
Moneywort (*Lysimachia nummularia*)	ground cover	1"-2"	✓			✓
Nasturtium (*Tropaeolum*, all species)		12"-18"	✓	✓	✓	
Oregano (*Origanum vulgare*)		24"-30"	✓		✓	
Parsley (*Petroselinum crispum*)		12"		biennial	✓	
Pennyroyal (*Mentha pulegium*)	ground cover	4"-6"	✓			
Peppers (*Capsicum annuum*)		18"-24"		✓	✓	
Rose (*Rosa*, all species)	edible flowers	3'-10'	✓		✓	✓
Rosemary (*Rosmarinus officinalis*)	ground cover, hedge	2'-6'	✓		✓	✓
Rue (*Ruta graveolens*)		2'-3'	✓			✓
Sage (*Salvia*, all species)		2'-3'	✓		✓	
Savory (*Satureja*, all species)		12"-18"	✓	✓	✓	
Shallots (*Allium ascalonicum*)		12"		✓	✓	
Sorrel (*Rumex*, all species)		2'-3'	✓	✓	✓	
Southernwood (*Artemisia abrotanum*)		3'-5'	✓			✓
Sweet Woodruff (*Asperula odorata*)	ground cover	8"	✓		✓	✓
Tansy (*Tanacetum vulgare*)		2'-3'	✓			✓
Tarragon (*Artemisia dracunculus*)		20"	✓		✓	✓

	Other Uses	Height	Perennial	Annual	Culinary	Fragrance
Thyme (*Thymus*, all species)	ground cover	4''-10''	✓		✓	✓
Violet (*Viola*, all species)	edible flowers	8''-12''	✓		✓	✓
Wormwood (*Artemisia*, all species)	ground cover	2'-4'	✓			✓

MARINADE WITH TARRAGON FOR VEGETABLES   *Makes ¾ cup*

½ cup olive oil
3 tablespoons strained lemon juice
3 tablespoons cider vinegar
⅛ teaspoon freshly ground black pepper
1 teaspoon salt
1 clove garlic, peeled and minced
2 tablespoons minced, fresh tarragon or 1 tablespoon dried

Combine all the ingredients and beat for 2 minutes, or process in a blender at low speed for 1 minute. Pour over warm vegetables and allow to marinate for several hours before serving.

2 FOODS AROUND THE WORLD

A GEOGRAPHIC VIEW OF COOKING

Cuisines around the world may be divided into eight basic groups. Moving, as history has moved, from East to West, I classify them as:

Soy-sauce flavored wok cookery (China, Japan, and their neighbors)

Curry cooking (India and its neighbors)

Kebab and sweetmeats (Persia and Arabia)

Couscous cookery (North Africa)

Hot foods and bean dishes (the lands of West Africa)

The European tradition of courses (France and Germany)

The New World foods (based on tomatoes, pineapples, and corn, all the foods discovered in the southern and island reaches of the New World)

The fast foods (evolving from the needs and technology of North America)

These are great oversimplifications, but they give us a way of thinking about who may be eating what kind of food tonight. Increasingly, the cuisines of the world, like the cultures of the world, are overlapping, borrowing from each other to the enrichment of all.

CHINA

The cuisine of China is divided by some into three regions of influence, and by others into five or six regions of influence. Schools of Chinese cooking known in the West are Szechwan, which is fiery; Cantonese, which is a little coarse; Shanghai; Peking; and Fukien, which is of the north and the most subtle. In the south and central regions, rice is the staple starch. In the north, millet is used. Pig is the word for "meat" in China, and is used as a flavoring agent as well as a protein. Fish is also used as a flavoring, as well as a main dish.

The Chinese cuisine familiar to Americans has its roots in peasant cooking. The focus of the meal is a bowl of rice, placed before each diner, along with chopsticks. Large dishes of meats or fish, usually in stewlike sauces rich in vegetables, are set in the center of the table. The rice, which is rather sticky, is scooped up with the chopsticks, and tidbits are selected from the shared dishes in the center of the table. How many common dishes there will be depends on the occasion, the number of diners, and the pocketbook.

Meals are extraordinarily flexible and the Chinese sense of variety and good taste makes their cooking perhaps the most interesting and the most subtle in the world. Banquets in the Orient are lengthy, and multitudes of dishes are served in constant procession, but without rigid "course" sequences familiar in the West. Soups may appear first, last, or in between, and numerous *dim sum*, savory fried or steamed salty or sweet tidbits, are offered throughout the meal to excite flagging appetites. Wine—especially warmed—is offered in thimble-size glasses.

Tea is the everyday drink, a pale "green" tea drunk without sugar or milk. (In India the tea is "black," and it is Indian tea that is most commonly served in America with sugar and milk or lemon.)

WINE'S UNIQUE FUNCTION

Wine in Chinese cooking is not used to enhance the flavor of a delicate sauce or a hearty stew. Although a small amount is always added to meat and seafood dishes, it serves only to neutralize any strong odors that may be emitted by these foods.

In earlier times, the game in Chinese meals included deer kidneys, birds' tongues, wild horse, camel, tiger, elephant, monkey, and porcupine, as well as every sort of fish and shellfish, including tiny snails in piquant sauces.

There are some curried dishes in Chinese cuisine, but the main accents come from soy sauce (fermented beans), oyster sauce, fish sauce, and Hoysin, a red bean sauce. Black beans, which are preserved soybeans, Chinese parsley (coriander greens), dried shrimp, five spice powder (anise, fennel, clove, Szechwan pepper, cinnamon), star anise which is licorice flavored, tiger lily buds or golden needles, and clouds ears (small gelatinous dried fungus) are only a few of hundreds of flavorings used. There is preserved lotus, fresh bamboo shoots, lily roots, shark fins, dried prawn eggs, dried ink fish, dried cuttlefish, edible seaweeds, duck tongues, pickled pine cones, etc. Almost every supermarket in America today carries common Chinese-American staples, such as bean sprouts, soy sauce, snow peas, gingerroot, sweet and sour sauce (duck sauce), crisp water chestnuts, sesame oil, and sesame seeds.

Milk is not used in Chinese cooking. To people who stop drinking it as infants, it becomes indigestible. A milk substitute is made from soy beans, and it

2 cups milk
1 cup grated fresh or packaged unsweetened coconut
3 medium onions, peeled
1 tablespoon ground coriander
1 teaspoon ground anise
½ teaspoon saffron threads
1 teaspoon ground ginger
1 teaspoon chili powder
2 cloves garlic, peeled and minced
2 tablespoons grated lemon rind
3 tablespoons lemon juice
2 tablespoons Damson plum preserves or other plum jam
1 teaspoon sugar
1 teaspoon salt
1 teaspoon vegetable oil
3 tablespoons butter or margarine
1 3-pound chicken, skinned, boned, and cut into 1-inch cubes
1 cup peeled whole almonds
6 cups hot cooked rice
Chutney

1. Bring the milk to a boil and add the coconut. Turn off the heat and let the coconut soak for 30 minutes. Drain, reserving the liquid. Squeeze the coconut dry and set it aside.

2. Slice the onions into rings and put them in a medium bowl. Toss with the coriander, anise, saffron, ginger, chili, garlic, lemon rind, lemon juice, preserves, sugar, and salt.

3. Set a wok over medium heat for 30 seconds. Swirl in the oil and add the butter. When the butter is completely melted, add the coconut shreds and sauté, stirring constantly, until lightly browned. Remove and toss with the onion and spice mixture. Add the chicken to the wok and toss to coat with the oil and butter. Add the onion mixture and toss. Add the coconut milk and almonds. Bring to a rapid boil, lower the heat, and simmer, stirring occasionally, for 10 minutes, or until the chicken is tender and the sauce is thick. Serve at once with warmed rice and chutney.

is the base of milk-like dishes, such as *tofu*, the bean curd sold in specialty shops.

A Chinese diplomat once boasted that in the Middle Kingdom there were 150 sorts of vegetables, that cabbage has "fifteen cousins," zucchini twenty, garlic ten. A delight in the Chinese way of handling of vegetables has swept the Western world, and it is interesting to note that a surprising number of the vegetables that turn up in good Chinese restaurants in New York, for instance, are familiar ones, such as celery and carrots, cut and cooked in unfamiliar ways.

What people usually mean when they say they love "Chinese vegetables" is that they love the Chinese way of flash-cooking, or stir-frying, many vegetables and serving them in a sauce made of their juices seasoned with salt, pepper, a bit of sugar, perhaps a few drops of sherry, soy sauce, and thickened with cornstarch and water. Cooking is oil-based.

Flash-cooking, or stir-frying, is accomplished by means of a Chinese utensil called a *wok*, which looks like an inverted coolie hat. It is set over a small cylindrical stove that focuses the heat on its bottom and sides. Shreds of precut meat and vegetables are added to a bit of oil heated almost to smoking in the bottom of the wok and are stirred and sautéed in carefully timed sequences until barely tender—*al dente*. A flash-cooked dish takes an average of 5 to 10 minutes to cook, but longer to cut sliver-thin. Since each dish moves very quickly through the cooking process and requires intense personal attention, far more chefs are required to produce a formal Chinese meal than a French meal of any scope.

JAPAN

Japanese cooking is of the same school as Chinese, but broiling and baking are popular, and foods are served somewhat more plainly with fewer sauces. Predominant in this island culture is fish. *Shoyu* sauce, like Chinese soy sauce, is the "salt" of the kitchen and goes into everything including salad dressings. Small side dishes of variations on this sauce are offered with many foods. Two very popular Japanese foods in the West are *tempura*, in which meat and vegetables are batter-coated and fried crisp, and *sukiyaki*, which consists of beef and vegetables, cut into thin strips, cooked on the table over a brazier, in a broth and served with sauce.

Japanese tea—green tea as in China—is drunk with all meals. *Sake*, a fermented rice wine, is the alcoholic beverage, and it is served warm in small cups. Utensils are chopsticks.

A major difference between Chinese and Japanese cooking is the popularity in Japan of raw fish and rice foods—*sushi* and *sashimi*—and the exquisite presentation which is a part of every Japanese meal.

The wok way of cooking is common to China's neighbors, the other rice-eating nations, such as Korea and Vietnam.

INDIA

West of China rice is still the common starch. The flat bread of the Arab lands appears in flexible tough little cakes that, along with fingers, were, and in some places are still, the dining utensils of the Middle East. In India, as in China, everything comes to the table pretty much at the same time. The main dish is a casserole, or there may be several meat and vegetable casseroles, one of them a curry. Many little side dishes are offered—chutney with its spiced fruits, grated coconut, diced apples, and chopped plantain, the small red banana of the area. There may or may not be rice. Food is cooked in *ghee*, a clarified butter, rather than in oil, and yogurt creams some of the best mutton casseroles. Mutton

and chicken and fish are the protein staples. Stews begin much as they do in Europe, with the frying of a handful of chopped onion and, sometimes, garlic. *Kebabs* are spit-roasted, a gift of the Turks.

LAMB KORMA

Serves 4 to 6

1 pound lamb from the leg, cut into 1-inch cubes
½ teaspoon salt
1 pint plain yogurt
1 tablespoon ground coriander
1 tablespoon ground cumin
2 cardamom seeds, peeled
½ teaspoon ground ginger
6 whole cloves
¼ teaspoon red pepper flakes
1 8-ounce can tomato sauce
1 tablespoon vegetable oil
3 tablespoons butter
1 large onion, peeled and sliced
1 clove garlic, peeled and minced

1. Marinate the lamb with the salt and yogurt for 15 minutes. Mix the coriander, cumin, cardamom seeds, ginger, cloves, and red pepper flakes in the tomato sauce.

2. Set a large heavy skilled over medium heat for 30 seconds. Swirl in the oil and add the butter. When the butter is completely melted, add the onion and garlic and sauté, tossing, until the onion is golden, 3 to 5 minutes. Add the lamb and yogurt, and the tomato sauce with spices. Stir well, cover, lower the heat and simmer until the meat is tender, about 20 to 30 minutes. Remove the cover for the last few minutes of cooking so that the sauce reduces.

Indian curries do not have to be hot to be good. Some of the best are fragrant but mild. The quality of the curry, and its aroma depend on the freshness of the spices used. Very common in Indian dishes are cumin, coriander, cardamom, turmeric, fenugreek, and aniseed. Saffron is common as well.

Flavored rice dishes, *pilafs* or *pulao*, are classic. A *pilaf* begins with the sautéing of a little minced onion in *ghee*, rice is added and a few minutes later, liquid, followed by meat, chicken, or fish, and condiments. Another classic dish is *kedgeree*, made of lentils cooked with fresh ginger, peppercorns, cloves, bay leaves, and salt. Mangoe chutney is served with it. *Kedgeree* may be offered alone, or as an accompaniment for a vegetable curry. Elaborate *kedgerees* include onions, cinnamon, saffron, or turmeric. Lentils also go into thick stewy soups. One the British adapted is mulligatawny. There are "mashes," called *bhurthas*, made of blended creamy vegetables, meat, or dry fish. *Chapati* is a bread made from whole meal flour and water, worked into a stiff dough, divided into lumps the size of a large egg and baked like a pancake on a hot griddle. *Paratha* is an Indian bread rolled out and buttered, then fried. Fritters are made with a yeast dough. Semolina is cooked with raisins, sugar, blanched almonds, cinnamon, and cardamom. *Khoa* is a sour milk dish of curds drained and fried in butter. *Dahi* is a dish of curds soured with vinegar or tartaric acid, drained and served with sugar, or with salt and rice. Minced fresh mint is used as we use minced parsley, as a flavoring and a garnish.

Bombay duck is an Indian delicacy famous for its aroma. It is a small gelatinous fish dried and salted, which is soaked in asafetida, a gum resin that smells of garlic or onions. The duck is served toasted and crisp as an appetizer, or is crumbled over curry.

AVGOLEMONO (LEMON SOUP) *Serves 10 to 12*

8 cups chicken broth, or 8 chicken
   bouillon cubes and 8 cups water
3 ounces converted white rice
4 large eggs
Juice of 1 large lemon, strained
1 teaspoon salt
¼ teaspoon freshly ground black pepper

1. Bring the chicken stock and rice to a boil in a large saucepan. Cover and simmer until the rice is tender, about 15 to 20 minutes. Remove the rice and reserve; keep the stock hot.

2. With an electric beater set at high speed, beat the eggs until thick and lemon colored. Than beat in the strained lemon juice a little at a time. Mixing with a spoon until blended, very slowly add 2 cups of the hot stock to the beaten eggs. (If the broth is too hot, or if you add it too quickly, you will curdle the eggs and ruin the soup—so add the broth very slowly.) When mixed, beat the eggs into the balance of the broth. Taste, then season with salt and pepper and add the rice.

3. Bring to simmer over very low heat and serve at once.

FOODS OF THE MIDDLE EAST

The food of the Middle East, permeated with exotic flavors and scents, has changed little over the centuries: ancient, sophisticated blends of herbs, spices, and tropical fruits, influenced by the more recent tastes and taboos of Islam and the Turks.

Pulao turns up here as *pilaf*, rice dishes flavored with mutton and spices, sweetened with dates and served with fat pieces of mutton roasted on skewers. There are *kebabs*, familiar and unfamiliar, like *salonique toti* which features livers and other meats dipped in batter. There's chicken with saffron in a stew; *dolmas*, forcemeat wrapped in vine leaves; *buerrek*, little cheese fingers. Over the street vendors' charcoal grills in Istanbul, pans of white and green beans simmer in a garlic-flavored herb sauce. Eggplant is stuffed with tomatoes and served with a yogurt sauce. Stews and soups of meat, dried fruits, spices, and, sometimes, mint, are served.

A great delicacy is *doner kebab*, in which lamb, seasoned with herbs including oregano and thyme, is cooked to sizzling crispness on a vertical grill—the gyro of American Greek fast-food restaurants. The cooked crust is cut off and served with onions, cucumber, salad, and tomatoes, while the grill cooks the crust for the next snack.

In the Istanbul region, and other areas bordering the Bosporus, a formal dinner for tourists includes a selection of appetizers—small roasted fish, stuffed mussels, shrimp, beans in sauces, meat-wrapped hot peppers, little stuffed toma-

BULGUR

Bulgur is simply whole wheat berries that have been cooked, dried, and ground. In Middle Eastern cuisines bulgar is often eaten in place of other starches, such as rice and potatoes, and is mixed with many dishes including salads.

To make bulgur: Rinse whole wheat berries in cold running water. Then put them in a pot and add cold water just to cover. Bring to a boil and lower the heat immediately. Simmer over low heat for about 40 minutes, or until most of the water has been absorbed by the berries. Drain the berries and put on a shallow baking sheet in 200-degree oven. Check to see if done by wetting several berries slightly and rubbing them between the palms of your hands. If the chaff is loose enough to remove, the berries are done. Grind the berries in a mill or grinder to a medium fine texture. Store in a tightly covered container.

To cook as a rice substitute: Bring 2 cups of water to a boil and stir in 1 cup of bulgur. As soon as the water returns to a boil, lower the heat and simmer for about 30 minutes, or until all the water has been absorbed.

toes, goat and sheep cheeses, and salted nuts. *Raki*, an anise liqueur, is served. Main dishes include lobster, broiled fish, roast chicken, cucumber and yogurt sauce, rice pilaf seasoned with saffron and cinnamon. Puff pastry cakes and cakes filled with chopped nuts, raisins, honey, rose jelly, and other delights are offered to the Western traveler as dessert, followed by Turkish coffee. The taboos of Islam still make wine a rarity, but fruit juice is sold everywhere.

SYRIA AND LEBANON

The national cooking of Syria and Lebanon includes the dishes of Persia and Turkey and the other Arab lands, and adds their own national dish, *kibbe*. This is raw ground lamb mixed with cracked wheat to make a creamy thick mixture eaten raw with accompaniments of basil, garlic, onions, or it is fried with pine nuts and seasoned with fresh mint. It is eaten with a flat Arab bread made from dough pressed by hand into thin sheets and stretched around hot stones to bake for a few minutes.

At a formal meal, dozens of the little appetizers are served, followed by mutton or chicken cooked in butter with coarsely ground wheat seasoned with saffron.

Desserts are exotic, including such elaborate preparations as pastries made with honey and rose syrup and filled with candied orange blossoms.

ISRAEL

A land composed of recent immigrants from Europe, Israeli cuisine is a melting pot that includes the best dishes from Yiddish *gefillte fish* to Hungarian goulash, combined with the ancient Hebrew dietary laws and the local Arabian-Turkish flavorings. The government has sponsored awards to encourage the development of dishes using the produce of Israel: lamb, fish, citrus fruits, avocados. The foods evolving are lightened by the use of grains and fruits. Something of a national dish is *falafel*, a spicy snack of *pita* bread, the flat bread pocket of the desert people, stuffed with spicy chick-pea mixtures. Breakfast, considered by tourists to be one of the best meals, brings a big assortment of fresh fruits, breads, and salads to the cool of the day.

FOODS OF NORTH AFRICA

The major influence in North Africa since the seventh century A.D. has been Turkish. Under the Ottoman Empire, Muhammedan Turks conquered the Balkans and threatened Vienna in the sixteenth century. Southward they ruled all the land to the Persian Gulf, and to the west conquered even the Berbers in Morocco. With the Berbers, they overwhelmed Spain in the eighth century. These were the Moors who dominated that land until the Spanish drove them out in 1492.

With that in mind, it's easy to guess the dominant foods along the shores of the Mediterranean. Herbs and spices from the Far East play their part in sheep-based stews. The main starch is semolina (wheat) steamed into a tasty *couscous*, and served with mutton or chicken broth and the vegetables that flavored the broth.

In Morocco, stuffed pimientos are a delicacy, grilled lamb cutlets are served with chopped mint, and there are banana cakes and coconut fritters. *Thetchouka* is an Algerian dish with tomatoes and pimientos, and cuttlefish (inksquid) is popular. In Tunisia, *chakchouka* is made with onions and tomatoes.

The Algerian *couscous* is different from the Moroccan. It is made of fresh-ground millet instead of semolina. Sweet manioc, yams, and leaves of the baobab tree go into it as well, reflecting the influence of West African ingredients and cooking tastes.

FOODS OF WEST AFRICA

The foods of West Africa are the least known to Americans, and yet they should be familiar. The cooks of the southern states came from West Africa, bringing with them knowledge of vegetables that have become part of the American cooking scene—for instance, peanuts and yams.

These are lands with an extraordinary diversity of peoples and rich cooking traditions. In rural areas women do the cooking over small open fires.

The major dish is a peppery stew, served with a starchy food, such as a small mound of cassava (manioc, or breadfruit), or a porridge of grains, loaves of bread, or steamed and fried cakes. Where westerners put a pinch of pepper into a sauce, West Africans put a teaspoonful. There's liberal use of peanut oil and also the orange-colored oil of the palm. Seeds and vegetables are used as thickeners. Okra, the "gumbo" of the southern United States, baobab, cotton tree, and jute leaves are sources that cook a slickness into the stews and soups. The flavor combinations are exotic to Western palates: meat and fish together, fish and bananas, bananas and tomatoes, salted, smoked, dried fish together. Stewing, simmering, and deep-frying are the common methods of preparation.

The main meat here is beef, with some pork, goat, lamb, duck, chicken, goose, pidgeon, and wild creatures, such as porcupine, opossums, turtles, caterpillars, and large snails. Fish and shrimp are often available as dried powdered flavorings. Home gardens produce the vegetables we are familiar with, and, in addition, bananas and plantains, eggplant, okra, and sweet potatoes, which are staples with yams and cassavas. There are taboos in many regions associated with some foods, for instance, eggs, which are thought to make childbirth difficult.

Among the classic dishes are *jollof* of rice, a stew of chicken, beef, pork, pigs feet and tails, white potatoes, yams, smoked fish, peas, pumpkin, eggplant, thyme, mint, bay, nutmeg, cloves, curry, parsley, garlic, brown sugar, and lots of tomato paste.

Another classic is peanut (groundnut) stew, which includes beef or chicken, and is served with several side dishes containing sliced oranges or bananas, tomatoes, peppers, fried onion rings, grated coconut, diced pineapple, roasted peanuts, boiled eggplant, diced papaya, and other foods.

In her *West African Cookbook* (M. Evans & Co., 1971), Ellen Gibson Wilson describes some of the foods that went from America to Africa and became staples: peppers, tomatoes, pineapples, sweet potatoes, corn, cassava, avocados, papayas. They were brought to Africa by Portuguese and Spanish traders.

Indigenous African foods that traveled to our shores include sesame seeds, pumpkins, melons, okra, eggplant, palm oil, mangoes, yellow plums, and cashew nuts.

FRANCE

The cuisine of France has been the most influential in the Western world for at least three centuries. Good cooks still treat Escoffier's turn-of-century recipes as gospel and insiders still consider Brillat-Savarin's 1825 *Physiology of Taste* as perhaps the best book ever published on the art of living. Most real initiates have at least one antique French cookbook dedicated to Marie-Antonin Carême, the Paris cook who turned down King George IV of England's offer at triple his salary because he feared London might not be inspiring.

Wave after wave of the world's wealthy and chef after chef from other lands have been seduced by the way of life in this small jewel of a land whose hills and valleys, rivers and coasts seem to have been created to bring together fine wines, tangy oysters, creamy cheeses, and the most exquisite sun-warmed, vine-ripened fruit and vegetables.

The average meal in France has a minimum of four courses, and more often, six or seven. Not much more food is served than in America—it's just that the French think in terms of courses.

There's a beginning course, usually something light and tangy. This is followed by soup; meat or fish with perhaps a vegetable; salad; cheese; fruit. A *demitasse* of bitter coffee taken with a lot of sugar, and, among sophisticates, a zest of lemon. The trimmed-down version would be a first course, meat, salad, and cheese. If the first course is a vegetable—artichokes, for instance, or asparagus in a *béarnaise* sauce—the meat or fish course may be served without an accompaniment, other than the bread which is eaten with every course—sometimes even with cake.

PÂTÉ RIDDLE

When is a *pâté* a *terrine*? When it is baked in a *terrine*. The word *pâté* means paste, and, originally, the dishes that became the famous first-course *pâtés* were pounded or mashed and spiced meats that were then baked—some in *terrines*.

The drink is wine. The rule of thumb is that the wine is served after the soup course. A sherry may be served before or with the soup, but mostly isn't. The French equivalent of cocktails is an *apéritif*, served with or without ice, and without the snacks prevalent at the American cocktail hour. *Apéritif* wines are cooked wines, with more body than dinner wines. Sherry is a type of *apéritif*. Vermouth is another. People serious about food don't have cocktails or liquor before dining. It numbs the taste buds. Gin makes even the best *pâté* taste like soap. The palate can be compared to a little chemical laboratory. Everything that goes onto it affects everything that comes after.

Since this is something the French are very much aware of, as much thought is put into how a meal is orchestrated as goes into acquiring perfect ingredients, and cooking them exquisitely. There are some rules: Cold precedes hot; tart precedes creamy; light precedes heavy; sour comes before sweet; fish precedes meat. Contrast is the name of the game that keeps appetites intrigued and enhances pleasure in a good meal.

In the days of the great Escoffier banquets, a *trou Normand*—a slug of apple brandy—was swallowed neat after the first three or four courses to make a "hole" in one's sense of satiation. In Victorian England, a tart sherbet followed the second or third course to clear the palate, much as crispy little *dim sum* are served at a Chinese banquet. At everyday meals, salad is served after the meat or fish main course to revive the sense of hunger and ready the stomach for more.

A glance at some old Escoffier menus shows why a *trou Normand* was helpful. The strong demitasse coffee and brandy and liqueurs served at the end of the meal helped create the illusion that you had not overeaten.

French flavors are dryish, rather tart. Meat is cooked pink, for the most part, pork and chicken a little more. Roasted meats are done simply, sometimes stuck with slivers of garlic (pork and lamb), sometimes cooked with sprigs of fresh tyme or tarragon. Fish is sautéed or baked with butter, dredged with lemon, and sometimes sauced with *beurre noire*. Soups are clear broths, which also make stock, white or brown, to base the many sauces and the great casserole dishes— *boeuf bourguignon, blanquette de veau, coq au vin, poule au pot, cassoulet*. Where roasts and vegetables are cooked rather simply, casseroles and stocks, salads and sauces display the European heritage of herb lore, knowledge they attained by scouring woods and hills for replacements for the spices and flavorings lost while the Turks dominated the routes to the East and the spice trade.

A *bouquet garni*—parsley, bay leaf, and thyme—goes into the pot the minute you put it on to boil. Onion is added to almost everything, as are peppercorns and salt. A few whole cloves are added to the bouillon of casseroles or sauces including chicken and veal. Lemon flavors veal as well as fish, and vinegar, wine, and mustard add substance to many casseroles. In the south and along the Mediterranean, garlic is common, along with marjoram, rosemary, fennel, and anise, the herbs used in Italy.

For a time, truffles—lemon-scented pungent mushrooms that grow underground and sell for $50 and more a pound—went into everything.

In addition, each region of France has specialties in flavor: Normandy is known for thick glorious cream and apples and apple cider and apple brandy. Britanny is known for the salty tang of its seafoods. In the Vendee, particular varieties of bay and thyme are prized. *Foie gras,* goose liver, comes from the southwest and turns up sliced on steaks, baked in crusts, and as a flavoring in casseroles. Marseilles, once a Greek posession, uses a pinch of saffron in its *bouillabaisse.* In the region of Cannes, a few drops of Pernod add a licorice flavor to foods and to after-dinner coffee. In contrast to the rest of France, where fresh butter is used for all cooking, in the south olive oil is the base, and the closer you get to Italy, the more tomatoes go into most everything, and sweet peppers, and *courges,* a squash, and black olives.

NAVARIN PRINTANIER *Serves 6*

This classical French casserole illustrates how stews are made.

¾ cup butter
3 pounds lamb for stewing (neck, breast, or chops) in 2-inch pieces
¼ teaspoon freshly ground black pepper
3 tablespoons all-purpose flour
4 cups chicken broth
¼ teaspoon dried thyme
½ medium bay leaf
Pinch of dried rosemary
8 baby turnips, peeled, or 4 medium, peeled and quartered
16 pearl onions, peeled
16 baby carrots, ends trimmed,
16 baby carrots, ends trimmed, scrubbed
Salt and freshly ground black pepper
¼ cup fresh or frozen peas

1. Melt the butter in a small saucepan over low heat, and skim into large sauté pan (preferably cast iron) 4 tablespoons of the clarified butter (the portion without milky residue). Set the sauté pan over high heat, sprinkle the lamb pieces with pepper, and sauté them on all sides until very well browned. As some brown, pile them on the coolest side of the pan. Remove the pan from the heat, tilt the pan, and remove 8 or 9 tablespoons of the grease, leaving about 3 tablespoons in the pan. Stir the flour into the remaining grease, return the pan to low heat and use a fork to work the flour into the browned-on drippings adhering to the bottom of the pan. This should take 3 or 4 minutes. Pour in the chicken broth and scrape up the pan drippings. Smooth the sauce, add the seasonings, and turn the contents into an enamel casserole with a lid.

2. Preheat the oven to 375 degrees. Cover the casserole and bake for 1 hour. Uncover the casserole. The sauce should be reduced and quite thick. Press the vegetables down into the sauce, adding a little water if needed to cover them. Cover and return to the oven and bake for 1 hour longer. Salt and pepper to taste. Add the peas for the last 15 minutes of cooking.

French table service is simpler than American, which is based in more formal British manners. The French napkin is huge, a good 18 or 20 inches square. At Escoffier Society banquets, part of the ritual is to tie the napkin around one's neck; it is supposed to be long enough to protect the lap so you can dig in wholeheartedly. In the country, bread is used as a resting place for used utensils, because you only get one set even if you have several courses. Unless there's fish—then you might, even in the country, be given a fish fork to protect the dishes that come after the fish from a fishy accent.

CHARLOTTE WITH FRUIT   *Serves 8 to 10*

12 ladyfingers
2 envelopes plain gelatin
1 cup milk
4 egg yolks
½ cup sugar
Pinch of salt
1 teaspoon vanilla extract
2 tablespoons light rum
1 cup heavy cream, whipped
4 slices canned pineapple, drained and diced, or other fruit
2 bananas, peeled and cubed

1. Split the ladyfingers. Cut a sliver from one end of each to square it and stand the fingers upright around the sides of an 8-inch springform pan.

2. In a medium-sized saucepan, dissolve the gelatin in ½ cup of scalded milk. Remove from the heat and let stand for 10 minutes.

3. Beat the egg yolks with the sugar, salt, vanilla, and remaining milk, and add to the gelatin mixture. Return to low heat, stirring constantly, until the cream thickens enough to coat a spoon. Don't boil. Remove from the heat and cool completely.

4. Add the rum and whipped cream to the cooled cream. Fold in the fruits and pour into the springform pan. Refrigerate overnight, or until firm. Unmold by releasing the sides of the pan carefully.

Butter generally is not offered with bread, so there's no need for a bread and butter plate—and salad goes onto the plate on which the main course was served, unless it was fish. In that case, you get a plate for the salad. Cheese, if it is going to be eaten with the salad, may go onto the dinner plate, too, but usually there is a fresh plate offered for cheese if it is going to be eaten with fruit.

One reason the dinner plate can serve so many purposes is that the French clean it up after each course with a chunk of bread. Sopping up the gravy in France is good form unless you are at a formal dinner. The dinner plate also serves as a sauceboat; artichokes are served with their lemon butter sauce in a deep dinner plate, which is then rested at a tilt against a spoon so all the sauce gathers in a convenient-for-dipping little pool at the bottom of the plate.

Breakfast in France is crusty fresh bread or a *croissant*, sweet butter, fruit jam, and *café au lait*, coffee and heated milk poured simultaneously into a large bowl, like a cereal bowl, or into really oversized cups. The *café au lait* is sweetened, and children drink it as well as adults, since it is half milk.

Farmers and workmen usually have a *casse croûte* ("break bread," literally) around ten o'clock in the morning, which might be sausage or shellfish, and a glass of white wine. Dinner used to be served at midday, and lasted a good two or three hours. Supper—*souper*—in the country then was soup, salad, cheese, maybe a little fruit, a *demitasse* of coffee with a few drops of *eau-de-vie* and sugar in it.

In the cities many stop in the late afternoon for coffee and cakes at the pastry shop, but on the whole the French are not big on desserts. For children at four o'clock, there is *le goûte*, a big crusty slab of bread with butter and jam, or with chocolate and a banana.

Cheese and fruit is the usual ending to a family meal. In the city, a cookie or a sweet wafer might appear with the *demitasse*. That hankering for a sweet after dinner is filled by the sugar that goes into the bitter black coffee of the *demitasse*, or by brandy or a liqueur, or a drop of an *eau-de-vie*. Special, homemade desserts mark holidays and celebrations. There are custards on which cooks pride themselves: caramel custard, which may be the world's best dessert, served with *crème brûlee*, and *ile flottante*, mounds of cloudy meringue floating on chilled custard; mousses such as *pot de crème, mousse au chocolat*, and sweetened cheese specialties, such as *coeur à la crème* and *petit-suisse*.

The French eat a great deal of cheese, and use a lot of butter in cooking, but they do not drink much milk. They don't drink water, either, as a rule, perhaps because water wasn't very wholesome at one time. The preference for those who do not drink wine is mineral water—Vichy water, Perrier, and others—or a combination of wine and mineral water. That's what young children are given until it is felt they are old enough to drink wine—usually at some point in their teens. Beer is weak and not very good.

The wines of France are famous. There are some general rules governing what kind with which food, but generally, it is left up to individual taste. The rule of thumb is that light wines are served before heavy wines. For instance, dry white wine with a fish course is served before a rich Burgundy offered with a roast of beef. There's a reason: A rich wine will overpower the taste buds, and a light white coming behind it will be tasteless, or maybe tinny.

Sweet wines are served with sweets, not with meat or fish. Really special bottles of wine are sometimes treated as *apéritifs*, so that the focus is entirely on the wine. At formal meals, there is a glass for the red wine, and another for the white, and others for the Champagne and liqueur.

In France, tea is a *tissane*, a distillation of leaves, usually herbs, mint for instance, for those who aren't feeling well.

ITALY

Food in Italy has much in common with French food. *Caffe a latte* is served with bread and often cheese for breakfast. The main meal of the day has one major difference. It includes a *pasta*, *polenta* (cornmeal), or a *risotto*. The *hors d'oeuvres*, or a first course, is called *antipasto*, meaning "before the pasta" course, and it will be a little more strongly flavored than in France—garlic sausage, *prosciutto*, anchovies, black olives, cheese, sardines. *Minestra* is the wonderful vegetable soup of Italy, thick and rich in dried beans and fresh legumes.

Seasonings include those used in France, and a number more. Garlic and tomato is characteristic of Neopolitan cooking. Basil flavors foods in the north, along with marjoram and oregano. Saffron, borage, and fennel are more popular in Italian cuisine than in French. Cooking is oil-based in the south, butter-based in parts of the north.

POLENTA (CORNMEAL CAKE)   *Serves 6 to 10*

8 ½ cups water
1 teaspoon salt
2 cups yellow cornmeal
1 tablespoon olive oil

1. Bring the water with the salt to a rapid boil in a medium-sized saucepan over high heat. Lower the heat to medium, and, stirring constantly, pour the cornmeal in a steady stream into the boiling water. Continue to stir for another 5 minutes, then reduce the heat to the point where the meal is simmering slowly. Stir occasionally, and cook for another 15 to 20 minutes, or until a crust starts to form on the bottom and sides of the pan. Add the olive oil, stir, and cook for another 5 minutes.

2. Invert the pan, and turn the polenta out onto a large, slightly concave dish. Serve at once, as you would rice, as an accompaniment for a savory Italian stew; or chill, slice thinly, and fry; or bake, topped with cheese.

Wine and coffee are the main drinks.

There are many famous Italian wines, other than Chianti, which is known in America. From Piedmont come Barolo, Barbera, and Freisa. From Venetia, Valpolicella. From Emilia-Romagna, Lambrusco. From Umbria, Orvieto. From Rome, Frascati. From Naples, Lacryma Christi. From Sicily, Marsala which is used in preparing many casseroles and desserts. It also flavors *zabaione*, a mousselike sweet of beaten eggs that is a famous Italian dessert. In Northern Italy sparkling wines comparable to Champagne—*spumanti*—are produced.

As in France, an *apéritif* is served before dinner, and after dinner, there are liqueurs, such as *amaretto* and *anisette*, which is Italy's licorice-flavored drink comparable to the Greek ouzo, the French Pernod, and North Africa's *raki*.

ITALIAN COFFEE

If you do not own an expresso machine, it is possible to serve an excellent coffee by brewing Italian-roast coffee in the Italian drip-pot which is called a *macchinetta* (pronounced "mock'-e-netta"). The *macchinetta* consists of two cylinders, one with a spout and one without, and a two-piece coffee "basket" which fits between the cylinders.

The correct coffee-to-water proportions are 3 ounces of cold water to each 2 tablespoons of drip-grind coffee. Pour the water into the lower cylinder (the one that does not have a spout). Put the coffee into the coffee compartment. Assemble the parts according to directions that come with the machine. Place on the heat. When steam emerges from the small hole in the lower cylinder, remove from the heat and turn the *macchinetta* upside down. When all the brew has dripped through, remove the two upper parts; the coffee is ready. Serve in demitasse cups or in glasses, with a twist of lemon peel and sugar.

Information from the Pan-American Coffee Bureau.

SPAIN

In Spain there are departures from French and Italian ways of dining. The memory of the Moors still lingers here. Dishes combine many more ingredients, a Middle Eastern heritage—*paella*, for example, with which the brandy-spiked fruit-laden wine drink *sangria* is served. The cooking fat is oil, and food is seasoned with garlic, onions, saffron, cloves, cinnamon, chili peppers, and paprika. Spanish paprika is mild, like Hungarian. There are more bean dishes than in France, a greater emphasis on sausages. There are *aperitivos* (*apéritifs*) and some fine Spanish wines.

Breakfast is coffee and a sweet cake. The midday meal is served between two and three o'clock, and includes several courses: eggs, a salad or *hors d'oeuvres*, soup, a fish dish, steak and potatoes, rabbit, chicken or pork, cheese or a sweet, fruit, almonds, or biscuits, followed by coffee. There's a long siesta; coffee and a pastry at five o'clock; dinner between ten and eleven o'clock, another several-course meal; then a stop at a café for coffee and liqueur.

Portuguese dining is very similar to Spanish.

GERMANY

Germany, like France, has had a major influence on international cuisine. A colder country than France, the food is heavier. This is meat and potato land. There's a strong interest in sugar and starch, sweet and sour. Sauer-kraut is one of Germany's gifts to world cuisine, sausages another. And excellent beer. To many Americans, this food is a little more familiar than that of France and southern Europe.

The day may start with a breakfast of milk rolls served with honey, coffee, and eggs. In southern Germany the drink may be tea. A second breakfast is taken around eleven o'clock. It used to be a grand meal with stuffed goose, smoked salmon, oysters, and a bottle of Rhine wine or the sparkling wine *Sekt*. Common folk might have potatoes, sausages, and beer, while the farmer would have thick slices of dark bread, ham, and *schnapps*—an *eau-de-vie*, gin, or *Kirschwasser* which is distilled from cherries.

Lunch comes next—with a hearty, typically German soup including noodles or dumplings, followed by a roast, potatoes, vegetable, salad, or a thick casserole, or *sauerkraut* with several kinds of sausage.

At five there is coffee with cakes—*kuchen*. Years ago this meal was like a British high tea. The table was set with the best silver and china, and there were homemade tarts. Cafés in Germany still fill up for this meal—which is rich in sweet German pastries, cakes, fruit pies, cream pies, and chocolate tarts.

The last meal of the day is a few hours later, more or less depending on whether you live in the country or the city. It consists of cold cuts, sausages, cheeses, several wonderful heavy breads—and beer.

Germany, of course, is the source of the rich array of delicatessen foods so popular in America. The American hot dog began here among the deliciously aromatic cold meats and sausages, and so did a number of Yiddish specialties: smoked salmon, Bismarck herring, rollmops (sour herring wrapped around sour pickles), and smoked trout.

Germany is also the originator of many sweet breads and peasant loaves. Honeybread is part of the rich German Christmas tradition adopted by America, and there are special cookies made with honey and spices to be given to each child who goes to market with his mother—and worn home around the neck.

The white wines from the Rhine are considered as appealing as some of the best French whites—and so are the delicious Mosels.

This was called "curry soup" when first brought to Britain from its native land, India. *Mulegoo thani* means "pepper-water," and depending on the heat in your curry powder, the soup may or may not justify its name. There are three main versions. One is made like a mutton curry, but it simmers for 3 hours. The luxury version is made with a stewing hen or fowl, enriched with a *roux* and with cream. The Indian version is a curry made just with lentils. Mulligatawny is served with a bowl of rice on the side. To eat the soup, take a little rice on your soup spoon, and dip up a little broth and chicken.

> 3 pounds breast of lamb or mutton
> 1 tablespoon butter
> 2 medium onions, peeled and minced
> 1 medium carrot, scraped and chopped
> ¼ small yellow turnip, scraped and chopped
> 2 tablespoons flour
> 1 tablespoon curry powder
> 2 ½ quarts chicken broth or water
> 2 tablespoons chopped parsley
> ½ teaspoon dried thyme
> 1 small bay leaf
> 1 large clove garlic, peeled and minced
> 2 teaspoons salt
> 2 tablespoons lemon juice
> Salt and freshly ground black pepper
> 4 cups hot cooked rice

1. Sauté the meat in the butter until brown. Add the onions, carrot, and turnip, and sauté for 8 minutes. Sprinkle with flour and curry powder, and stir in the broth. Scrape up the browned-on bits from the bottom of pot. Add the parsley, thyme, bay leaf, garlic, and salt. Bring to a boil, cover, reduce the heat, and simmer for 3 hours.

2. Lift out the bones, strip them of meat, and return the meat to the pot. Discard the bones and bay leaf. Add the lemon juice and cook for 5 minutes. Add salt and pepper to taste.

To serve, ladle into bowls and serve plain boiled rice in a small bowl on the side.

From *A Feast of Soups*, Heriteau (New York: The Dial Press, 1982).

NORTHERN EUROPE AND THE BRITISH ISLES

The Germans, Scandinavians, Dutch, English, Irish, and Scots have forebears, climates, and terrains that have much in common, so it isn't surprising to find that the food these people enjoy share certain similarities.

The Swedish still love dill, potatoes, *schnapps*, herring, and sausages; only its city restaurants have adopted French ways. *Smorgasbord*—those magnificent arrays of buffet-style dishes including everything desirable from cold lobster with

fresh mayonnaise to the best cheeses—are a legacy of the Northlands. They share origins with French *hors d'oeuvres Russes*, and may be at their best in Copenhagen, the capital of Denmark. Denmark copies, and often bests, French cheeses.

Holland produces the finest hard cheeses in the world, and perhaps the nicest smoked baby eel.

Belgium has some interesting dishes of great antiquity—*hochepot*, a wonderful old recipe including farmers' treasures such as pigs' feet, ears, tails, and *waterzooi*, which turns up in modern cookbooks as chicken soup, but can be a fish soup at home.

Britain, as the center of the colonial empire, was a melting pot for cookery, as well as the home of mutton dinners, well-cooked meats, fruit fools, and Yorkshire pudding. From China they took tea, and from Japan, the tea ceremony. A great old Scottish recipe is for cockaleekie, which combines fowl with leeks, barley, and prunes.

The Irish adopted the white potato, which originated in the Andes in South America, and gave the world Irish stew.

In these countries, as in the United States until wine began to find a place here, beer has been the people's drink, potatoes, the starch, and tea shared much of the popularity of coffee.

BRITISH HERITAGE

Larder in England is pantry in America. Loaf sugar in England is lump sugar in America. Grilled in England is broiled in America. Rump in England is sirloin in America. Undercut or fillet in England is tenderloin in America. Sirloin in England is porterhouse in America. Kipper in England is smoked herring in America. Tunny in England is tuna in America.

AUSTRIA AND HUNGARY

Once provinces of Rome, and in the last century a joint empire, Austria and Hungary eat French-style, with a lot of German cooking basics, Turkish touches and Magyar flourishes. The Magyars were people from the Urals who conquered Hungary in the late 800s and early 900s; the Turks conquered Hungary in the 1500s. The paprika that for many Westerners symbolizes Hungarian cooking and must flavor a *paprikash*, was introduced to Hungary by the Turks. Even the coffee and pastry fantasies of Vienna can be considered a spoil of their wars with the Turks, perhaps. For centuries, Vienna was the European bastion the Turks attacked, but could never breach.

Austria and Russia on occasion were allies against the Turks—a fact forgotten by the average cook until you take a look at the famous wine of Hungary—Tokay. Made in Hungary since the days of the Crusades, this wine is a product of the mountainous region whose center is Tokay. The grapes are allowed to remain on the vine until they are dried almost to raisins. Then they are mixed with fresh grapes, to produce the soft almost liqueurlike wine so delicious with dishes like apricot-flavored *crêpes suzettes*. In the old days, Tokay was kept for the Austrian Emperor and a few nobles. From the reign of Tsarina Catherine of Russia until 1840, a Cossak detachment was stationed at Tokay to guard the wines purchased by the Imperial Russian household, a reminder, perhaps of the days when Eastern Europe was a favorite target of the fearless Turks.

FOODS IN THE AMERICAS

The cuisines of the Americas are rooted in the produce of the land, the cultures that had evolved here before Europeans came, and in the traditions of the European settlers. New World foods have had perhaps more influence on the cooking of Mexico and Latin America than on North America. On the other hand, the technologies and fast pace of life that developed through the Europeans who came to North America have had a tremendous influence on the way the world eats. They are responsible for such innovations as refrigerated railway cars that transport fresh produce over great distances and methods of conservation that keep produce from one season to the next, for ideas such as frozen foods, freeze-drying, commercial dehydration, and other wonders of this century.

MEXICO

The influences in Mexico are Aztec, Spanish, and, to some extent, French. The *conquistadores* were amazed and delighted by the native dishes, and noted foods unknown to them, such as chocolate, vanilla, corn, chiles, peanuts, tomatoes, avocados, squash, beans, sweet potatoes, pineapples, and papaya. To this native wealth, Spain brought rice and wheat, and the spices of the East, in particular cinnamon and cloves. Today, Mexico is known for its uses of corn, chiles, tomatoes, and beans which are the basis of regional cooking. *Tortillas, tacos*, and *tamales* are Aztec in origin. *Tortillas* are the bread of ancient Mexico. Traditionally each bread was made by patting a ball of boiled corn dough until it was very thin, and then cooking it on a hot flat stone or griddle. There are sweet and non-sweet *tortillas. Tacos* are small (4-inch) *tortillas* stuffed with various mixtures and fastened with a toothpick. *Tostadas* are *tortillas* that have been fried in hot lard until golden brown, then covered with various combinations of meats, poultry, fish, sauces, chiles, and so on. *Quesadillas* are turnovers made by stuffing unbaked *tortillas* with a filling, pinching the edges together, and frying them in lard or oil. The peppers, hot and sometimes sweet, that base the *moles*— Aztec sauces made with chilis and the forebears of the chilis popular in America—are numerous, and colorful. Elizabeth Lambert Ortiz, *The Complete Book of Mexican Cooking* (M. Evans, 1967), speaks of sixty-one classified varieties. Beans are served at almost every meal in Mexico, either cooked and served separately, as a vegetable, or mashed and fried (*refritos*). The black bean is one of the most popular, along with the California pink, which is red but cooks more quickly than the real red bean. The aroma that makes your mouth water as you wander through a small Mexican town near the Californian border is that of a pot of chili with red beans cooking ever so slowly over fires in a hundred small homes.

CHILI POWDER

Chili powder is a combination of spices and herbs—cayenne pepper, with ground cumin and oregano. Authentic Latin American chili recipes include a little chocolate.

Nuts are used as thickening agents in Mexico, rather than flour or egg yolks and cream. Peanuts, pecans, and pumpkin seeds give flavoring and texture, and the herbs and spices preferred include anise, allspice, bay leaf, cinnamon, cloves, cumin, coriander seed, marjoram, oregano, sesame, saffron, mint, and parsley. *Cilantro*, which is the green leaf of coriander is also used. In America it is known as Chinese parsley. *Epazote* is used in many of the *tortilla* dishes.

It is the chilis that give Mexican cooking a reputation for being hot, but there are regional variations that are cooler, and many that are subtle enough to enchant a European epicure.

Mexican eating hours resemble those of Spain. The heat makes a midday siesta attractive, and that means dinner is well after eight o'clock.

SEVICHE
Serves 8

Seviche is as Peruvian as apple pie is American. The story goes that *seviche* was invented by hungry Peruvian fishermen stranded on the country's desert coast. There were some fresh caught fish and a basket of limes, but no wood to make a fire. So they "cooked" the fish in the juice of the lime. The word also is spelled *cebiche*.

A variation on the presentation of raw fish. The acid in the lime translates gelatinous fish into morsels with a firm texture. Originally, the fish was corvina, a white sea bass, but any firm white sea fish will do. Variations are made with shellfish and shrimp, flounder, bass, and conch. In New Zealand, a similar dish is eaten by the Maori.

The length of time the fish is to be marinated depends on the size of the pieces into which it is cut. The average is 2 hours, but some marinate *seviche* for as long as 4 hours. The fish is "done" when it turns from the translucent look of raw fish to that cooked look that is a dull white. Key lime may be used. Lemon doesn't seem as successful.

> 2 pounds white fish, filleted
> 8 to 10 key limes
> 2 large onion, peeled and finely sliced
> 2 yellow or red hot peppers, cut into small strips
> Salt and freshly ground black pepper
> 8 lettuce leaves
> 1 pound hot, boiled, sweet potatoes
> 2 ears corn, boiled

1. Cut the filleted fish into small pieces and wash in cold water. Drain and place in a shallow glass container. Cover completely with the strained lime juice. Break up and rinse and drain the onion slices. Add to the fish with the pepper strips. Add salt and pepper to taste. Cover and refrigerate for 4 hours.

2. Before serving, mix the fish with marinade ingredients, and serve in lettuce leaves with hot boiled sweet potatoes and chunks of corn.

South of Mexico, in the great southern continent, fish is a staple along the coasts. *Seviche*, which "cooks" raw fish with lime juice, is a Peruvian dish becoming popular in New York. The clambake is a common way of cooking in South America. The Spanish introduced domestic animals and adopted native foods, sometimes transforming them into new dishes. There are fascinating bean dishes—*feijoada completa*, for instance, a Brazilian stew that combines beef tongues, black beans, dried beef, various pork products, tomatoes and oranges. There are wonderful uses of coconuts—*mae bentas*, coconut pastries, *cocadas*, coconut candies. *Beignets de bananes*, banana fritters, speak of a French influence, and the same French influence is seen in some good red wines made in Argentina.

BAKED BEANS THE NEW ENGLAND WAY *Serves 6*

---

2 cups navy or pea beans
12 cups water
1 small onion, peeled
⅓ cup lightly packed dark brown sugar
1 teaspoon salt
1 ½ teaspoons dry mustard
½ teaspoon freshly ground black pepper
¼ cup dark molasses
3 tablespoons ketchup
¼ cup maple syrup
¼ pound fat salt pork, sliced
Boiling water

1. Wash the beans and soak them overnight in cold water to cover.

2. Drain the beans and put them into a heavy kettle. Cover them with 12 cups of fresh water. Bring to a boil, then simmer, uncovered, until the skins split when blown upon, about 30 to 40 minutes.

3. Preheat the oven to 250 degrees.

4. Drain the beans and put them into a bean crock or a small heavy casserole. Bury the onion in the center of the beans. Mix all the remaining ingredients, except the pork, and pour the mixture over the beans. Insert the slices of salt pork just below the surface. Add sufficient boiling water to cover the beans. Cover the crock or casserole and bake for 8 hours, adding a small amount of boiling water from time to time so the beans do not become dry. Uncover during last 30 minutes of baking.

UNITED STATES

The United States and Canada have been most influenced by Northern Europe, rather than by Spain and Portugal. There's a touch of Oriental cookery on the West Coast and some French, Spanish, and African ideas in the South, but most of the land goes the way of meat and potatoes, which is Germanic.

The traffic was far from one-sided. The Italians got corn from the West by way of the East, called it *polenta*, and thought it came from Turkey. The turkey, the big American Thanksgiving bird, is native to North America. It was named by Europeans who were accustomed to the idea that anything exotic came from the East—the land called Turkey. Peanuts traveled from America to Africa and came back again as an African food. White potatoes, which became a staple in Ireland, are South American, as are many of the drying beans, including limas, snap beans, and those that go into Boston baked beans. The Indians taught settlers to make beans. In colonial America, the bean pot was sent to the bakery on Saturday night—since no cooking was done on the Sabbath—to simmer on the baker's stove until Sunday morning, when the pot was returned to the owner, complete with Boston brown bread. But despite native influences, the American way of eating was imposed by the settlers, though the availability of ingredients had everything to do with what happened next.

In the southern United States, black women from Africa grafted foods from their homelands onto the French/Spanish/Indian traditions, spawning dishes such as crawfish bisque, pompano fries, gumbos with the slippery feel of cooked okra, *coupe de milieu*, borrowed from the *trou Normand*, *café brûlot* to end big

LOVE AFFAIR WITH KETCHUP

Nearly 3 pounds of tomato ketchup is consumed by the average American each year, more than 650 million bottles. One million tons of tomatoes are processed annually for this popular all-American product.

Actually it's the tomato that makes ketchup American. The Orient first produced ketchup, called *ketsiap*, *koeshiap*, or *kechap*, but it was far from the tomato product we know today. The Oriental variety, made from a brine of pickled fish, was used as an all-purpose seasoning.

In the seventeenth and eighteenth centuries, English traders brought the sauce home from the Orient. It became an English favorite by 1841.

By the nineteenth century, Maine sea captains circling the globe acquired a taste for *ketsiap* and introduced it to America. Exotic Eastern ingredients were not available to early America, so new recipes were developed. Eighteenth- and nineteenth-century cookbooks list a dozen recipes including ingredients such as mushrooms, grapes, gooseberries, walnuts, cucumbers, lobsters, and oysters. Ketchup became an important contribution to gravies and sauces and gained popularity as a condiment with meats.

How and when tomatoes became the main ingredient in America's ketchup is a mystery since tomatoes were considered poison until the early 1800s. Today more than 97 percent of all American households have ketchup in the kitchen.

meals, *jambalaya* to feed big crowds, and many Creole and Acadian dishes based on long-cooking brown *roux*—not to mention corn bread, corn pone, hush puppies, hominy grits, and cherries jubilee.

Filé powder, made from the dried leaves of sassafras trees that grow wild in the South along the Gulf coast, was discovered and used by the Choctaw Indians long before the Acadians were exiled from Nova Scotia by the conquering British. *Filé* imparts a flavor like that of a fragrant thyme, and a spoonful or so thickens stock into a rich gravy that is the heart of many great southern dishes.

Elsewhere in the United States, cooking influences are regional. There's the Pennsylvania Dutch (Deutsch) school, which is German, and the Shaker way with preserves. After 1870, when the shining rails had spanned the continent, the Chinese and Japanese who built the Western portion of the rails made their influence felt. By the same token, the railroads brought industrializing America westward and spread ways of eating that belonged to the wealthy of Europe.

Diamond Jim Brady is a symbol of the dining of that day. Born James Brady Buchanan in 1856, he made a fortune selling and later making railroad equipment and was a lavish spender. His favorite restaurant in New York was Rector's, and here he and his cronies would dine on several dozen oysters each, half a dozen crabs each, two bowls of turtle soup, half a dozen lobsters each, a pair of ducks, steak, vegetables, a plateful of pastries, and a box of chocolates each. According to the legend, they ate that way several times a day. Diamond Jim's frequent companion was singer Lillian Russell, who, no one will be surprised to learn, weighed 200 pounds.

Here's how Oliver Wendell Holmes (1809—1894), author of *The Autocrat at the Breakfast Table*, liked to start the day:

Littleneck Clams	Potatoes
Cucumbers, Sautéed	Ice Cream Grilled Plover
Strawberries Grilled Trout	Cakes Omelette with Mushrooms in Cream
Coffee	Fillet Mignon

Mrs. Rorer's *Everyday Menu Book*, 1905, suggested a breakfast of:

	Or:	
Baked Apples		Oranges
Minced Beef		Chops
Granoise		Toast
Toast		Oatmeal with Cream
Coffee		Stewed Potatoes
		Coffee

PASS THE CORN FLAKES

The favorite American breakfast food is cereal, and the United States is the only country where cold grain is eaten first thing in the morning.

One hundred years ago, an English listing of breakfast foods included Finnan Haddie, smoked haddock fillets, sausage, Sally Lunns (which are rather like English muffins), squab pie, and sheep's head with potatoes as typical morning fare. The French offered frogs' legs, and pickled herring pleased the Dutch. The Tartars ate raw horse flesh, dog meat was breakfast for the Northwest Indians, and curry for East Indians. Hungarians had a cold breakfast early and a hot breakfast later.

The Japanese came to work in America's Hawaiian plantations where they ate a breakfast of unpolished steamed rice. On the mainland, the average folk ate slightly stale bread and slabs of cold bacon.

In the 1830s, Rev. Sylvester Graham developed a flour retaining the bran in wheat, which was traditionally removed to make fashionably white bread. By 1840, Graham boarding houses had been set up to serve health foods, including Graham's bread, served slightly stale (eventually becoming the Graham Cracker.) Health spas flourished after the Civil War, and a famous vegetarian, James Caleb Jackson, baked and ground up zwieback which he called granola, to be eaten with a sweetener and milk for breakfast. Dr. John Harvey Kellogg took this idea to Battle Creek, Michigan. He wanted something that encouraged his jaws to chew. There, Kellogg's brother developed corn flakes. Charles W. Post picked up on the Kellogg brothers' idea and called his variation on chewable breakfast food Grape Nuts, which remains today as the hardest of the morning cereals. Post made a corn flake, too, and called it Post Toasties. Farther west, Dr. Henry Perky developed the process that made shredded wheat. Within the next 100 years cereals proliferated, but corn flakes still holds 10 percent of the market.

Contemporary cereals are less nutritious than the early varieties developed by health food buffs, but the bran and other B-complex carrying layers removed as part of the processing of the grain is compensated for by the addition of enough vitamins so that a serving provides the daily minimum required. The instant hot cereals are also fortified, so that even though they are easier to prepare, they are designed to be as nutritious as those of the last century.

Many of the dishes we think of as American began in the last century. Beth Tartan, in *The Good Old Days Cookbook* (Westover Publishing Company, 1971), says the Club Sandwich was started by a chef of the period who composed sandwiches in layers. She reports that a tea room started the Marshall Field Special, and a St. Louis physician is credited with the 1890 invention of peanut butter (for patients needing easily digested protein). She says the Reuben sandwich was conceived by Mrs. Fern Snider, chef at the Rose Bowl Restaurant, Omaha, Nebraska. Both Beth Tartan and James Traeger attribute the first hot dogs to the delicatessen counters of Germany, but specifically credit Charles Feltman, a German butcher who started a beer garden in Coney Island in the late 1800s.

Since the hot dog and the hamburger have become symbols of the fast foods that seem to be sweeping the world, their heritage is worth a glance. Antoine Ludwig Feuchtwanger, a Bavarian sausage salesman, is said to have put the first bun to a weiner at the St. Louis exposition in 1904. He had been, it is said, providing gloves to eat his hot sausages with, and not getting his gloves back. The bun saved his gloves and launched a tradition. One Nathan Handwerker and his wife, Ida, employed by Feltman, left his establishment in 1916 to start Nathan's Famous, Inc. The weiners first were called "hot dogs," according to James Traeger, in 1906, when cartoonist T. A. Dorgan drew a dachshund inside a long bun, and Harry M. Stevens, a concessionaire at New York's Polo Grounds, is said to have been the first to shout "Get yer red hots!"

Traeger says hamburgers are named for Hamburg, Germany, where round beef patties, like our Tartar steaks were served. Cooked, and wrapped in a bun at the St. Louis exposition, they became an American heritage.

America today is beginning to recognize some of its own ways with food as exceptional. The West Coast foods that put together, Chinese-style, asparagus and artichokes, black olives and fish in one dish, are catching on here and there, and some of the fish stews and soups in San Francisco restaurants are hard to beat. From the West Coast, the East is adopting little scrubbed-wood restaurants with foods based on crisp wholesome fresh fruits and vegetables, combined in fast-food ways.

While there is no pie in the world like Mom's Apple Pie, *à la mode* (especially if a hint of canned peach is combined with very tart apples, and the sugar is brown), at this point in time, fast-food cookery probably is the item perceived as specially American by the rest of the world. We are not alone.

Today there is a restlessness in the kitchens where once Curnonsky, Prince of Gastronomes, ruled. When Escoffier was *Chef*, and Carême, *Maître*, fat was good. Cold castles burned calories, and the candles alone waxed warm at tables where twelve-course dinners were set. With neither jets nor television sets to make accessible the sands of Samarkand, an imaginative cook was worth his or her weight in courtesans to while away the nights.

Interest in food may not have diminished all that much in Europe, but the store of time has shrunk. With servants replaced by dishwashing machines, wives

working, with the intense life of the blue-jean set, time savers are coming into being everywhere. There are plastic corks for some wines, chestnuts and snails come in cans, and *supermarchés* carry frozen foods to the heart of Paris. Under the influence of a group of Oriental *aides de cuisines*, France's sometimes over-cooked vegetables have become the pureed sauces of *cuisine nouvelle*, sometimes hardly cooked at all. Tall, slender-waisted girls and boys shudder at the *avoirdupois* of their grandparents, wanting light wines, light dishes, lighter lives.

Neither the French, who consider their food as something of a national treasure, nor anyone else would compare fine cuisine with hamburgers, but France, along with the rest of Europe, has of late been importing the American way of life.

SAVING THE WORLD

"In contemplating the present opening prospects of human affairs, I am led to expect that a material part of the general happiness which heaven seems to have prepared for mankind, will be derived from the manufacture and general use of Maple Sugar."
   Letter to Thomas Jefferson from Benjamin Rush, Aug. 19, 1791
From the Vermont General Store and Grist Mill.

The new ways on both continents are a synthesis of old and new, East and West, moving with the speed of consciousness, propelled world wide by television. Meanwhile, technologies that will dramatically affect future ways of eating are evolving—spurred by a concern that all mankind be fed abundantly, spurred by the need for new ways with food that can be taken to the outer planets and the satellites we expect to build for our own planet.

In the Bay of Fundy, Nova Scotia, there are groups learning to farm the sea in its 60-foot-high tides. There are industries in Hawaii devoted to creating self-nourishing ecological cycles. At the Kahuku Seafood Plantation, an old landing strip grows oysters. In the warm effluvium of certain electrical plants, lobsters are farmed. Cloning opens unimaginable vistas. Working with cloned plants, scientists have been able to increase the sweet potato crop in Taiwan (one of that country's staples), by a third. A four-sided bean that grows in the tropics and withstands everything promises to solve food shortages for the third world. Big juicy gulf shrimp and delicious mushrooms have been freeze-dried as part of the meal-planning for the space shuttle. Astronauts go first class, and they are taking with them the beginnings of new ways with foods.

It's possible, even likely, that our century's ways with food, ways that seem so permanent to us, may already be fading into history, becoming the heritage we will take to the stars, the legends our great grandchildren will hear from people whose ways with food may be as different from ours as ours are from those of Diamond Jim Brady.

3 TALKING ABOUT COOKING: A glossary

TALKING ABOUT COOKING :

A Glossary

In a world where the cuisine of every country has expanded to encompass the cooking of many other nations, a glossary of cooking and food terms would have to be multivolumed and multilingual to be complete. In the space allotted here, the glossary has had to be restricted to an arbitrarily chosen selection answering the author's curiosity. The entries are meant to inform and or reassure the beginning to intermediate cook. In addition, a handful of the names of not-so-common ingredients, dishes, and cooking methods most often mentioned or written about by food buffs and found on the menus of good restaurants are included.

ACETIC ACID: Wine or cider, fermented beyond the stage of alcohol. In diluted form, it is vinegar. Also, acetic acid is used in preserving fruits to keep flesh from discoloring, and in freezing.

ACHAR/ACHARD: Pickles and salt relishes used in the cooking of India.

ACHIRA: South American plant used as is arrowroot.

ACID RINSE: A bath of acidulated water used to prevent discoloration of peeled fruits and vegetables that brown when exposed to air.

ACIDULATED WATER: Cold water with vinegar, lemon or lime juice added.

ACORN COFFEE: A drink made from ground acorns. Victorians recommended it for strengthening delicate children.

ACQUETTE: Aromatic liqueurs popular in southern Europe.

ACTINIA: Sea anemone prized for its crablike flavor.

ADE: A fruit drink made by combining water with sugar, boiling until the sugar dissolves, then adding a citrus juice and ice.

ADIRONDACK BREAD: Bread baked from coarsely ground flour; made in the Adirondack Mountains of New York State.

ADJUST: In cooking, the term means the cook must taste before serving, and add seasonings to suit his or her own sense of what the right flavor is.

ADOBO: A Philippine national dish of braised pork, chicken, or fish. Also, a seasoned Mexican sauce made with vinegar and chilies.

AEMONO: A Japanese salad served with dressing, or the dressing itself.

AFRICAN PEPPER: Red pepper; cayenne.

AGAR-AGAR: Seaweed used as a thickening agent, as is gelatin.

AGAVE: Century plant, a cactus. The fermented alcoholic drink called *pulque* is made in Mexico from this plant. The peyote button, a hallucinatory drug, comes from the agave.

AIGUILLETTES: Thin strips of meat or fish.

AIOLI: Rich mayonnaise served along the Mediterranean with a platter heaped with boiled white fish and another of potatoes. To make *aioli* follow the recipe for mayonnaise, but start by mashing in the bowl 3 or 4 large cloves of peeled, sliced garlic, with the salt to be used in the recipe, then proceed with the mayonnaise instructions.

AJI-NO-MOTTO: Japanese name for monosodium glutamate, MSG, used by Oriental cooks on occasion to revive a dish that has turned out tasteless.

AKAVIT/AQUAVIT: Scandanavian form of distilled alcohol made from grain or potatoes, and flavored with caraway seeds. See also *aqua vitae.*

À LA/À/L'AU: French, literally, "prepared in the style of."

À LA MODE: Literally, "following the fashion." In the United States, it describes pie topped with ice cream. In France it names braised meat smothered in sauce.

AL DENTE: Italian for, literally, "to the tooth." The term refers to pasta, rice, or vegetables, cooked only until slightly firm to the bite.

ALBONDIGAS: A Mexican dish of spiced meat balls. Also found in Spanish, Brazilian, and Scottish recipes.

ALBUMIN: A protein found in egg white, milk, green plants, seeds, and animal blood.

ALE: A fermented drink. The original term for beer, it is still used in England and in Scandanavia.

ALEWIFE: A fish of the shad family that is inexpensive and resembles herring. North American. Not used much currently as the flavor is inferior to shad.

ALGERIENNE: A garnish for meat of small tomatoes and sweet potatoes.

ALLIGATOR APPLE: Also known as custard apple. It is tropical, has something in common with a pineapple, and is related to sweetsop and soursop. Used mostly to make iced drinks.

ALLIGATOR PEAR: Another name for avocado.

ALLSPICE: The berry of a pimento tree found in Jamaica. This spice combines the taste of clove, nutmeg, and cinnamon. Used ground for desserts, sauces, picklings, and sometimes, in meats.

ALLUMETTES: Cut into matchstick sizes and shapes. Also, a puff pastry used for *hors d'oeuvres.*

ALUMINUM

Aluminum can change the flavor of acidic foods, such as tomatoes and rhubarb. Acidic foods, and very salty foods, will stain aluminum. Magnalite cookware avoids these problems, and so does aluminum cookware coated with Calphalon. To clean aluminum that has darkened, boil in it 3 tablespoons of cream of tartar for each quart of water needed to reach to the top of the stained portion—about 15 minutes will do the job. Then wash in hot soapy water, rinse well, and dry thoroughly.

ALMOND PASTE: A mixture of sugar, almonds, and rose water traditional among Christmas foods in Europe. Used to make marzipan, for decorations, and served in thin wedges with wine.

ALSACIENNE, À LA: Dishes that highlight a braised sauerkraut, boiled potatoes, ham, and/or Strasbourg sausage.

AMARETTO: Liqueur of almonds.

AMÉRICAINE, À LA: French. A sauce of olive oil and tomato used for lobster and shellfish.

AMANDINE: A dish garnished with sauteed almonds. For example, *sole amandine*.

ANADAMA BREAD: Yeast bread made of cornmeal and white flour with molasses.

ANCHOVY: A small fish usually cured in olive oil or salt. Anchovy is sold for flavoring. It is popular in Scandanavian meals and in Italian cooking on occasion. Herringlike.

ANCIENNE, À L': French. Literally, "old style." A method of cooking sauces and dishes that mixes ingredients more than in modern French cooking.

ANDALOUSE, À L': Dishes which feature sweet peppers, eggplant, tomatoes, and may include *chippolata* sausage and a rice pilaf.

ANGELICA: A sweet herb used to flavor a variety of liqueurs and drinks. Candied, it is used in baking, especially fruit cakes.

ANGLAISE, À L': "English style," literally. A dish cooked in water or a white stock. Usually rather insipid in flavor.

ANGOSTURA BITTERS: An aromatic liquid used to flavor cocktails, soft drinks, as well as soups and sweet dishes, such as ice cream.

ANISE: An herb of the carrot family that gives a licoricelike flavor.

ANTIPASTO: Assorted *hors d'oeuvres*, Italian style. Often included are ripe black olives, green stuffed olives, garlic sausage slices, salted anchovy curled on a sliced tomato, cooked dried beans in a *vinaigrette* dressing, *prosciutto* (thinly sliced fat ham) with cantaloupe. Bread and butter is served with *antipasto*.

APÉRITIF: A cooked, usually sweet, wine, taken before a meal to stimulate the appetite. *Lillet* is an example. In France, "*prennons l'apéritif*" is the equivalent of "let's have a drink."

APPETIZER: A snack served before a meal, often with cocktails, in the United States. Also sometimes a first course.

APPLE BUTTER: A very thick preserve of cooked apples.

AQUA VITAE: Latin, "water of life," a term now used to describe clear distilled liquors and brandies.

ARAB BREAD: Leavened and unleavened breads of the Arab countries. *Pita*, an envelope used for sandwich fillings, is very popular now.

ARAB COFFEE: Thick, black, bitter coffee, served in tiny cups and often flavored with cardamom or cloves, and a lot of sugar.

ARCHIDUC, À L': A dish that highlights the use of paprika and cream.

ARECA NUT: Betel nut, East India pepper plant. It is chewed in Asia to aid digestion.

ARGENTEUIL: A dish featuring asparagus. Geographically, it is a region in France where asparagus are grown.

ARLESIENNE, À L': A dish with a garnish that contains tomato with a variety of other vegetables.

ARMORICAINE: A dish originating in the region of Armorici, now called Britanny, in France.

AROMA: Describes flavor and fragrance, both closely related. A significant portion of what we "taste" is actually what we are sniffing in the air.

ARRACK/ARAK/RAKI: Strong liquor distilled in North Africa and in Arab lands. It is drunk in very small portions.

ARROWROOT: A flour used to thicken clear liquids because it does not cloud. Use half as much arrowroot as flour, and the same amount as you would use of cornstarch.

ATHOL BROSE: A popular Scottish drink made of whisky, oatmeal, and cream, sweetened with honey.

ASPIC: A jelly produced from the stock of meat, fish, or fowl.

AUBERGINE: French for eggplant.

AU BEURRE: Cooked or served in or with butter.

AU GRATIN: Dishes browned under the broiler after baking with a topping of bread crumbs or cheese.

AU JUS: Served in its own juice. Most often this refers to meat.

AU NATUREL: Also *nature*. Dishes cooked as simply as possible and served with a minimum of accompaniments.

AVOCADO: Also known as alligator pear and love fruit, this is the fruit of the Cacti varieties native to Mexico and Guatamala. Color can be green, maroon, purple, black. In season from February to April.

BABA: A molded yeast-raised *brioche*, often served in a rum or liqueur sauce. *Baba au rhum* is a very popular French dessert.

BACON: Whole side of select pork, cured in dry salt or brine, and sold as bacon.

BAGNA CAUDA: Italian sauce for *crudités*, raw vegetable appetizers. It includes anchovies and olive oil, and is served hot.

BAGNA CAUDA AND CRUDITÉS	*Serves 10 to 12*

6 cloves garlic, peeled
12 anchovy fillets in oil
½ pound butter
1 cup light olive oil
Freshly ground black pepper
6 cups cut-up fresh vegetables, such as green peppers,
    cauliflower, etc.

Mash the garlic in a mortar or a small wooden bowl, and add the anchovies a little at a time to make a thick paste. Turn into a fondue dish and place over heat, stirring until the mixture thickens. Stir in the butter and the oil a little at a time, and cook for 3 minutes. Season with salt and pepper to taste. Lower the flame, but keep the mixture hot. Serve with the cut-up vegetables.

BAGUETTE: A long, thin, crisp loaf of French bread.

BAIN-MARIE: French version of the double boiler.

BAKE: To cook surrounded by dry heat, as in an oven.

BAKING POWDER: A powder used to leaven (raise) baked foods. It contains sodium bicarbonate and an acid that releases gas when combined with liquid and heated.

BAKLAVA: A Middle Eastern sweet rich with honey and nuts and made from *filo*, a paper-thin pastry in many flaky layers.

BAMBOO SHOOT: The crunchy tip of a young bamboo tree. It is served as a salad and as an appetizer and is used in Oriental dishes.

BANANA FLOUR: Flour made from bananas, nutritious and easily digested.

BANNOCK: Scottish round cake that is served in Great Britain.

BARBECUE SAUCE: Spicy American sauce used to baste meat or poultry while it is cooking in a broiler or on a grill.

BARDING: A thin piece of fatty bacon or lard used to cover too-lean meat while it roasts. See also *larding*.

BAR-LE-DUC: An elegant French preserve based on currants.

BARLEY: A cereal with less gluten and protein than wheat. Served in Eastern Europe in the manner rice is used elsewhere, and popular in soups.

BARLEY SUGAR: Sugar boiled in a barley water until brittle. It was once used medicinally for digestion and mild travel sickness.

BARLEY WATER: Ground barley boiled in lightly salted water.

BARLEY WINE: Another name for malt liquor.

BARON (OF BEEF): A double sirloin roast from 50 to 100 pounds; (of lamb) the hindquarters, both legs and loins.

BAVARIAN FRUIT CREAM
Serves 8

Berries and pineapple are most often used in this recipe

2 envelopes unflavored gelatin
½ cup pineapple juice, from a 16-ounce can
5 egg yolks
1 cup sugar
2 teaspoon cornstarch
1 ½ cups boiling milk
5 egg whites
1/16 teaspoon salt
1 tablespoon sugar
2 cups pineapple chunks, strained
1 cup whipping cream, sweetened to taste

1. Dissolve the gelatin in the juice and set aside. Beat the egg yolks until thick, and beat in sugar a little at a time. Add the cornstarch. Beat the milk into the egg mixture and set over medium-low heat. Stir until the mixture is thick enough to coat a spoon. Remove from the heat at once. Beat the pineapple gelatin into the custard, then return the custard to the bowl the pineapple was in.

2. Beat the egg whites with the salt until thick enough to stand in soft peaks. Add the sugar a little at a time, beating constantly until dry peaks are formed. Fold in the hot custard, and mix gently with a spatula once or twice as the mixture cools.

3. When the mixture has cooled, fold in the pineapple chunks and the whipped cream. Turn into a 2-quart mold rinsed in cold water. Chill for 4 hours, or overnight, before serving.

BASTE: To moisten and flavor meat while roasting with melted fat, butter, liquid, or pan juices.

BATTER: A liquid-flour mixture used to coat foods before frying, usually in deep fat.

BAVARIAN CREAM: A soft, sweet egg custard mixed with gelatin and whipped cream, then flavored with fruit. A delicious old-fashioned recipe.

BAVEUX: Omelettes and other egg dishes removed from the heat while still soft and runny. French.

BEAN CURD: A soybean custard used in Oriental dishes.

BEEF OLIVES: Rump steak sliced thin, stuffed, and cooked in a rich brown sauce.

BEEF TEA: Beef broth or essence once used to sustain invalids.

BEER: Mildly alcoholic drink made by boiling malted barley with hops and then fermenting. There are a number of related beers, such as ginger beer and dandelion beer, made in essentially the same way.

BEET ROOT: Root vegetable of beets. To prevent bleeding, do not cut before cooking.

BELUGA STURGEON: A fish whose roe is the source of the finest caviar.

BEURRE MANIÉ: Thickener made by combining 2 tablespoons butter with 2 tablespoons all-purpose flour. Form into small balls. A thick, buttery paste will result. *Beurre manié* is beaten into the cooking liquid of casseroles or soups or sauces that are too thin, or that are meant to be thickened after the cooking is almost complete.

BEURRE NOIR: Also, *beurre noisette,* a butter sauce for meat and fish dishes. To make it, melt over medium to low heat a stick of butter, cut into pieces. Skim off the foam and pour only the clear oily butter into a bowl. Discard the milky residue, and return the oily butter (clarified butter) to the pan and the heat. Over moderate heat, warm until the butter turns a nut brown, then remove at once. To this brown (not really black as the literal translation of the name implies) butter, you may add seasonings, such as vinegar, strained lemon juice, salt, and pepper to taste.

BILBERRY: A berry of the blueberry species, which grows wild in America.

BIND: To cause a mixture to hold together by beating in an egg, sauce, or some other thickening agent.

BIRDS' NESTS: Used in Chinese cookery, these are swift's nests from the South Seas. They are high in protein and gelatinous when cooked. Of the many grades, manilla yellow is considered the finest.

BISHOP: A mulled port wine drink served hot or cold, flavored with orange, cinnamon, star anise, and cloves.

BISQUE: A thick creamy soup which has been thickened with flour and pureed shellfish. The name originally described a shellfish dish, but today it is used to describe vegetable soups as well.

BITKI: Russian-style hamburger.

BITTERS: Highly scented flavoring for drinks.

BLACK PUDDING: Also, blood pudding and blood sausage. There are French, Scottish, and Canadian versions of this dish, and probably more. All have a base of pork or other meat blood, fat, seasonings, including onion and garlic. The sausage is fried, usually in slices. Excellent.

BLACKSTRAP: Dark cane syrup.

BLANCH: To immerse briefly in boiling water, then plunge into cold water. The process firms flesh, heightens and sets color and flavor, and also loosens skin, as in tomatoes intended for peeling.

BLANCMANGE: A sweet pudding made with milk and cornstarch flavored with almonds, vanilla, rum, or brandy.

BLEND: To mix ingredients until well-combined and smooth.

BLENDER: Pitcher-shaped kitchen accessory with rotary blades that chop, grind, whip, grate, puree, blend, or liquefy.

BLEU, AU: A method of cooking fish, particularly trout, by plunging fresh-killed fish into boiling *court bouillon* (broth). Vinegar often is added to create a bluer tinge. French, meaning "done in blue fashion."

BLINI: Russian buckwheat pancakes served with a variety of spreads, notably, sour cream and caviar.

BLOATER: A herring cured with salt and smoked; also, the base of a popular British sandwich spread.

BOAR: Still hunted occasionally in Europe, this is a wild pig.

BOCKBEER: A beer brewed to celebrate the coming of spring. It is dark, strong, and sweet.

BODY: Describes a characteristic of wines. A "full bodied" wine is rich without bitterness, when it is a good one.

BONE, TO: To remove bones.

BONE MARROW: An opaque, jellylike substance in the center of marrow bones. It is a delicacy considered highly nutritious. Sometimes (withdrawn from cooked bones), it is served on toast.

BONNE FEMME, À LA: Food cooked in a home-style fashion.

BORSCHT: Russian and Polish beet soup or beet and vegetable soup, thick or thin, served with sour cream.

BORSCHT   *Serves 10*
_____

2 16-ounce cans whole beets, or 6 large cooked beets, peeled
8 cups beef stock or canned broth
1 tablespoon butter
1 teaspoon salt
1 teaspoon light brown sugar
1 tablespoon white vinegar
10 tablespoons sour cream

1. Grate the cooked beets into the stock. Place in a large saucepan and simmer for 5 minutes. Add the butter, salt, sugar, vinegar, and simmer for 10 minutes. Blend 2 cups at a time, or put through a food processor. Return to the pan and reheat.

To serve, ladle into bowls and garnish with sour cream.

BOSTON BAKED BEANS: American bean dish often made in a crock. These are small white beans (navy beans) cooked with salt pork and a sweetener such as molasses or maple syrup.

BOSTON BROWN BREAD: Moist American brown bread cooked in round tins. Served with beans.

BOUQUET: Aroma, a term used to describe the fragrance of wines and other foods.

BOQUET GARNI: A group of herbs. Tied together in a cheesecloth bag, or by the stems, they are used to flavor stocks and stews.

BOURGEOISE, À LA: Braised meat prepared with carrots, turnips, button onions, and glazed lean cubes of bacon, all in uniform sizes.

BOURGUIGNONNE, À LA: Braised meat in a sauce based on red wine with small onions, mushrooms, and grilled bacon bits or salt pork.

BOURRIDE: A Mediterranean fish dish, rather like *bouillabaisse* but with fewer fish.

BRAISING: To brown in fat slowly, then slowly cook in a covered casserole, such as a Dutch oven. If not browned, then placed on a bed of vegetables and seasonings, covered, and cooked very slowly.

BREADFRUIT: *Artocarpus* and its fruit, common in Indonesia as a staple foodstuff. The fruits are about 6 inches long and starchy. They are cooked before using.

BRINE: A solution of salt and water used in pickling, for instance. Brine draws natural sugars and moisture from foods and forms lactic acids which protects them against spoilage. Usually the strongest brine used in food processing is a 10 percent solution, made by dissolving 1½ cups of salt in 1 gallon of liquid, or 6 tablespoons of salt for each quart of liquid. A rule of thumb is that 10 percent brine will float a 2-ounce egg.

BRIOCHE: A yeast-raised cake baked to a rich brown usually circular in shape, with a smaller round on top. It is different from other raised doughs in that eggs are added, giving it a characteristic golden tinge, and also it is raised in the refrigerator, overnight.

BRISLING: A small herring from Norway which is familiar in America as brisling sardines, the finest small sardines sold in tins.

BROTH: A thin soup of fish, meat, or poultry, or the water in which they have cooked.

BRUNOISE: Finely diced or shredded vegetables, usually cooked in butter or stock, and used to flavor soups and sauces.

BUBBLE AND SQUEAK: A British dish of meat and greens which first "bubbles" in water, then "squeaks" in a frying pan, and finishes as fried, cold, boiled meat and greens.

BUFFALO BERRY: Also, buffalo currant. A currantlike fruit of the Western plains of the United States.

BULB BASTER: A suction instrument that is used in basting food, and in removing fat from the surface of drippings and sauces.

BULLY BEEF: From French *bouilli* (boiled), it is now called corned beef after an English word, corned, meaning "cured."

BURRIDA: A specialty of Genoa, this fish stew is cooked and served in the same dish.

BURRITO: A flour tortilla made with a filling.

BUTTER, BLACK: See *beurre noir*. This is butter melted, clarified, and cooked until it is nut brown.

BUTTER CREAM: A rich, smooth cake filling and icing made of butter and confectioners' or icing sugar, flavored with vanilla and other essences.

BUTTER, SAVORY: Butter whipped with a variety of flavorings, used as a spread for canapés (anchovy butter, for instance), a sauce for grilled fish or meat (tarragon butter), or to flavor sauces (shrimp butter).

BUTTERFLY: To cut food almost in half so that when flattened the two halves resemble butterfly wings, as is done with shrimp.

CABBAGE PALM: A member of the palm group which has edible bulbs. Found in the West Indies, the southern coastal United States, and Bermuda, the vegetablelike bud may be eaten raw, as endive, or cooked, as cabbage.

CACAO: Native South American tree whose seeds are fermented and processed to make cocoa and chocolate.

CHOCOLATE LOVERS ONLY

Chocolate and cocoa come from the same source, the kernels inside the bean of the *Theobroma* cacao plant, but there's a difference in the amount of fat they contain. Even high-fat cocoa contains only half the calories in chocolate, about 75 an ounce. Semisweet and milk chocolate contain between 135 and 150 calories an ounce. Chocolate was discovered in the Americas.

CALAMARI: Small squid considered a delicacy along the Mediterranean, in particular in Italy.

CALAMONDIN: A citrus tree cultivated for its naturally high concentration of vitamin C. It also is used as a base for artificial flavorings. Calamondin oranges are small, bitter, and make good marmalade. They are grown as houseplants, too, and will produce oranges indoors.

CALF: Young of a cow, but specifically, the word calf designates a cow less than one year old.

CALF FOOT: Foot of a calf, and the source for gelatin used in soups and to make stock for *galantines*.

CALORIE: A measure of heat required to produce energy. The fuel derived from food stored by the body is measured in units of calories.

CANAPÉS: Garnished bite-sized rounds of bread or vegetables (cucumber, zucchini) served with cocktails and at buffets.

CANDIED PEEL: Usually a citrus peel, cooked in sugar syrup and sugared.

CANDY THERMOMETER: A kitchen tool used to determine heat levels in the cooking of candy, jams, and preserves.

CANETON À L'ORANGE, OR À LA BIGARDE: Braised duck served with an orange sauce.

CAPERS: The flower buds of the caper plant. A condiment salted and processed in vinegar. Used generally with fish dishes and in *vinaigrettes*.

CAPON: A male chicken gelded when young and fattened to 6 or more pounds. Exceptionally tender for a large bird, and considered a luxury item.

CARBOHYDRATES: The food group containing sugars, starches, and cellulose as well as carbon, hydrogen, and oxygen.

CARBONNADES: A French beef stew cooked with beer.

CARRAGEEN OR CARRAGHEN MOSS: An edible seaweed; Irish moss.

CARTE, À LA: A term used for restaurant dishes priced individually, rather than as part of a complete one-price meal. *Prix-fixe* is the opposite.

CASSAVA CAKES: A Jamaican specialty served toasted, hot, and buttered.

CASSOULET: A fine French stew of white beans baked for hours with meats, onions, and garlic sausage.

CASTOR, OR CASTOR SUGAR: English term for superfine granulated sugar.

CAVIAR: The salted roe of sturgeon. Red caviar is the salted roe of salmon, and considered a less desirable substitute.

CELERY SALT: Salt flavored with ground celery seed.

WHIPPING CREAM

If you encounter heavy cream that won't whip, even in a chilled bowl with chilled beaters, set the bowl in a larger bowl of cracked ice while you whip. And if it still won't whip, gradually add a few drops of strained lemon juice to the cream while you beat it. (Egg whites, on the contrary, whip best at room temperature, with a pinch of cream of tartar or salt added to them.)

CÈPE: A delicious mushroom.

CHAFING DISH: A metal pan heated by a spirit flame, or charcoal, or electricity, for quick cooking at the table or with a water basin underneath for longer cooking or keeping of food.

CHAMBRER: A French term used to describe the gradual raising of the temperature of wines from the cool wine "cellar" to room temperature. Slightly warmer, the wine flavor is more pungent.

CHANTILLY: Heavy cream whipped then sweetened and flavored with vanilla. Also, a sauce with whipped cream added.

CHARLOTTES: Mold of biscuits, sponge cake, ladyfingers, etc., or sliced bread, filled with a custard cream and fruit.

CHASSEUR: Game or poultry served "hunter style," with a rich red wine sauce, or a white wine sauce, including mushrooms and shallots.

CHÂTEAU BOTTLED: Wine bottled at the *château* where it was grown and made. Usually this means a superior wine, one with a distinct flavor of its own. Other wines are the result of grapes grown in a region and brought together at the vintner's for handling. The results are less distinguished, though these regional wines may be very good.

CHÂTEAUBRIAND: An exceptionally good, thick steak from the fillet, usually grilled and served with a *béarnaise* sauce. French.

CHERRYSTONE CLAM: Clams 3 inches long.

CHICORY, CULTIVATED: A salad known in the United States as French endive or witloof-chicory. Chicory root is roasted and mixed with coffee to give it a rich bitter flavor. This is the source of the chicory in chicory-flavored coffee.

CHIFFONADE: Finely cut vegetable strips used to garnish soups, raw, or simmered in butter. Lettuce and sorrel often are used in this manner. French.

CHILES RELLENOS: Hot green peppers stuffed with cheese and dipped in batter and fried.

CHINOIS: French for a conical strainer with fine mesh.

CHIPPOLATA: Common name for a tiny sausage, this originally described a garnish of chestnuts, glazed vegetables, and small sausages.

CHIPS: British chips are American french fried potatoes; American chips are what the British called "crisps."

CHITTERLINGS: Part of the small intestine of a pig, cooked.

CHOCOLATE: The liquid product of grinding, fermented, dried, and roasted cacao beans. The liquid is then cooled into slabs or powdered.

WHITE CHOCOLATE

Cocoa beans are machine processed to obtain a chocolate liquor which is further processed to obtain cocoa butter. The butter is ivory colored and has a chocolate flavor. To this, whole milk and sugar cooked to a thick paste is added—and that's what white chocolate is. Dark chocolate is chocolate made with the whole of the chocolate liquor.

CHOP: Cut into small pieces. Also, rib section of beef, lamb, pork, or other animals, including a piece of rib and a nut of meat.

CHUTNEY: A relish used in Indian meals with curry, and usually including a fruit, particularly mango. Spicy or sweet, or both. The most famous chutney in America is Major Grey's.

CIDER VINEGAR: Vinegar of unprocessed apple cider.

CITRIC ACID: An organic acid common to citrus fruits and used in preserving, retaining color, or flavoring drinks.

CITRON: A fruit likened to an overgrown knobbly lemon, it is famed for its peel, which is used in marmalades, candies and fruit cakes.

CIVET: A stew of furred game cooked in red wine, garnished with mushrooms, small onions, and cardoons. A sauce is made with the blood.

CLARIFIED BUTTER: The fat in butter, obtained by melting butter and spooning off the oily portion and discarding the milky residue. See *beurre noir.* Akin to *ghee.* It is excellent for browning meats as it will not burn.

CLARIFY: To make a liquid clear and free of sediment. Coffee can be clarified by adding raw egg whites, or crushed egg shells, which are then strained out. Frying fat is clarified by adding water: The water and sediment will settle at the bottom, and the clarified fat can then be strained off.

CLOTTED CREAM: An English version of the French *crème fraîche.*

COBBLER: A deep-dish fruit pie with a top crust of biscuit dough. Also, a tall drink made of rum, whiskey, or claret and garnished with citrus slices or mint or fennel.

COCKLE: A small mollusk related to the oyster, usually eaten boiled with condiments or in a sauce.

COCOTTE: French, a cooking pot or oval made of cast iron, or enameled cast iron, with a heavy, tightly fitting lid, used for cooking braised dishes and casseroles. The equivalent of a Dutch oven.

CODDLE: To poach in slowly simmering liquid.

COEUR À LA CRÈME: One of the world's more exquisite cream desserts made of cream cheese combined with cream (16 ounces of cream cheese to 1½ cups heavy cream) drained and chilled in a cheesecloth-lined wicker basket overnight. The heart is then turned out onto a dish, and served with crushed very ripe berries, usually strawberries.

COLLOPS: Slices or chunks of meat or bacon; an archaic term, today translated to steaks and chops.

COMFITS: Small sweets or vegetables preserved in vinegar, sugar, or brandy. Archaic.

CONSOMMÉ: French, for hot or cold (usually jellied) broth or stock, made by simmering meat, vegetables, or fish. A "simple" *consommé* is the broth produced by recipes such as for beef stock (*le fond brun*); a double *consommé* is the heartier broth produced by recipes such as that for *petite marmite*. Double *consommé* will jell, since it is full of the gelatin that is drawn from meat and fish bones by long cooking. The jelling capacity of a *consommé* can be increased by adding gelatin.

CONVECTION OVEN: An electric oven in which heat is circulated rapidly around the cooking foods by means of a fan, resulting in fast crisping and browning. See also "Microwave and Convection Ovens," Section V.

COQ AU VIN: Classic French casserole of chicken cooked in red wine.

COQUILLE ST. JACQUES: Scallops in a cream sauce served in scallop shells.

CORAL: The roe of female lobsters. It turns bright red when cooked and is used in sauces. Considered a delicacy.

CORDON BLEU: Means, literally, blue ribbon in French, and it is a prize of note rewarding gastronomical excellence in France. It has also come to mean a school of French cooking rich in sauces and ingredients. The Cordon Bleu school itself was founded by Madame de Maintenon, Louis XIV's last mistress and then his wife, for the orphaned daughters of titled army officers. It attracts many Americans interested in fine food.

CORKED, OR CORKY: Description of wine whose flavor has been tainted by the odor of the cork. Corked also means a wine bottle with the cork in.

CORN, INDIAN CORN, SWEET CORN, MAIZE: Corn originally meant any grain, but has come to designate the maize of America, sweet corn. Indian corn is colored or multicolored and is used as an ornament, though it is edible.

CORN: FADES FAST

The sugars (carbohydrates) in corn start to convert to starch the minute the corn is picked, faster than in any other vegetable. That's why just-picked corn is so much better than even day-old corn.

CORN FLOUR: Flour made from ground corn, used in baking, sauces, and sausages.

CORNSTARCH: Corn milled to an extremely fine white powder and used to thicken sauces and stews; it is a common practice to thicken the juices in a flash-cooked Chinese dish with a solution of 1 tablespoon cornstarch to 1 or 2 tablespoons water. Cornstarch clouds a liquid when it is added, but it quickly clears as it cooks.

INDIAN PUDDING
Serves 8

2 cups whole milk
2 cups light cream
¼ cup yellow or white cornmeal
2 eggs
2 tablespoons dark molasses
½ cup firmly packed light brown sugar
½ teaspoon salt
½ teaspoon ground ginger
1 teaspoon ground cinnamon
4 tablespoons butter or margarine
¾ cup dark raisins
½ pint heavy cream

1. Heat the milk and half the cream. Combine the remaining cream with the cornmeal and add to the saucepan. Stir constantly until the mixture begins to simmer. Cover, and cook over very low heat, stirring occasionally, 20 minutes.

2. Preheat the oven to 325 degrees.

3. Beat the eggs to a froth in a small bowl, and stir in the molasses, sugar, salt, ginger, and cinnamon.

4. When the cream mixture is finished, remove from the heat. Cut the butter into the mixture, and stir in the raisins. Add the egg mixture, whipping quickly, and pour into a 2-quart mold. Bake for 1 hour and 15 minutes. Test by inserting silver knife in the center. If it comes out clean, the custard is done.

5. Cool and unmold, and serve with cream. Or serve lukewarm from the baking dish.

CORNMEAL: A flour used as a hot creal or in baking muffins, for instance. Cornmeal can be either yellow or white and can be purchased in fine, medium, or coarse grinds.

CORN SYRUP: A nutritious syrup obtained as cornstarch is processed with acid. Used as a binding sweet (in candy making, for instance).

COULIS: Another word for *bisque*, a thick fish soup. An older meaning implies juices from cooked meat.

COURT BOUILLON: A seasoned broth for the cooking of fish and sometimes vegetables or veal.

COUSCOUS: A fine semolina wheat steamed over a pot in which chicken or mutton is cooking with vegetables, then served with the soup and the meat and vegetables. This is an ancient dish of Arabian lands, and a staple of North African cooking. A red pepper sauce may be served as an accompaniment.

CRADLE: A wicker basket used to decant wine.

CRAYFISH: A freshwater crustacean similar to lobster but smaller. The salt water variety is known as spiny lobster.

CREAM(ING): To beat a mixture until it is soft, smooth, and creamlike, usually butter or lard. This used to be a tedious operation but a food processor or an electric beater will do the job in no time.

CREAM OF TARTAR: Potassium bitartrate, a main ingredient of some baking powders. It is refined from the substance deposited by grapes after they are fermented for wine.

CRÉCY: Dishes cooked with carrots.

CRÈME FRAÎCHE: French. Often compared to British clotted cream, this is cream so thick it is a solid. Sold by some specialty shops in the United States, it can be thinned with large amounts of heavy cream and still remain relatively thick. It is served in France, thinned, with berries, particularly wild strawberries, and with other desserts. A substitute is whipping cream mixed with an equal volume of sour cream and allowed to thicken at room temperature for a few hours.

CRÊPE: A French pancake, much thinner than American versions. The basic batter calls for ¾ cup milk, ¾ cup cold water, 3 egg yolks, 1 tablespoon sugar, 3 tablespoons of liqueur such as Grand Marnier, 1½ cups sifted all-purpose flour, 5 tablespoons melted butter. Beat, chill for several hours overnight, cook on a griddle as an American pancake, stuff with a sweet preserve, apricot for instance, and *flambée* with heated liqueur just before serving. Powder with confectioner's sugar.

CROISSANT: French breakfast bread pastry, delicate, flaky, and rich. The dough is yeast-raised, then rolled out, spread with soft butter, folded into thirds, rolled out again and buttered, then rolled out yet again, to make a layered puff pastry. In France it may be served with butter and preserves.

CROQUETTES: A fried dish of ground or finely minced poultry, meat, or fish bound together with a thick white sauce, seasoned, shaped into balls or ovals, coated with flour, egg, and bread crumbs then cooked in hot fat until golden.

CRUDITÉS: French word for an American cocktail appetizer of raw vegetables served with a dip, such as *bagna cauda*.

CRUMB: To moisten food with an adhesive liquid such as milk, beaten egg, or batter, then roll it in bread or cracker crumbs.

CRUMPET: The original English muffin.

CRUSTACEAN: A shellfish, for instance, shrimp, lobster, crab, crayfish.

CRYSTALIZE: To preserve fruit, fondant, and edible flowers with a boiled sugar.

CUBE: To cut into squares; to dice.

CUBE STEAK: Meat tenderized by scoring the surface with a pattern of squares or cubes.

CURD: A solid milk product that develops as milk sours and separates into solids (curds) and liquid (whey). In cheesemaking, it is induced by the addition of acid or rennet.

CURING: To preserve meat, fish, or cheese with salt or by drying and or smoking.

CURRY POWDER: As old as civilization, this is a blending of spices and herbs that comes from India. Curry powders are mostly deep yellow, a color they get from turmeric, one of the spices added, but they are a blending of usually four, five and more spices; as many as twenty-eight substances are common. Each Indian household grinds its own daily to suit recipes undertaken, and in addition, may have a "house blend" made up somewhat in advance of use.

CUSTARD APPLE: See alligator apple.

CUSTARD, EGG: An egg and milk combination, cooked, to a thick sauce or firm pudding. Custard-making is an important part of cooking lore, since there are a great many dishes that begin with custard. The use of custard-based dishes is somewhat less than it was in Victorian times when almost everything cooked began with cream and eggs. The best custards are made with eggs and milk or cream, but today it is common practice to include a little cornstarch in a custard to keep it from curdling if the heat becomes a little too intense.

CUTLET: A chop from the prime end of the neck of pork, mutton, lamb, or veal. Fry, grill, or braise.

DAIKON: A Japanese radish.

DAMSON: A type of plum best used in cooking or for jams and jellies.

DANDELION: Field weed and lawn pest with bright yellow flowers which used to be commonly used in the kitchen to make salads, wines, beets, and for medicinal effects. A French dressing rich in minced garlic makes salads of this rather bitter green delicious. Usually they are served with hot, cooked, diced lean bacon as well.

DANISH PASTRY: A rich and flaky sweet butter pastry filled with fruit or custard.

DASH: A seasoning measure indicating a scant ⅛ teaspoon or less.

DASHI: A clear fish stock which is the basis of Japanese dishes.

DAUBIERE: A cooking pot with a tight-fitting lid used for braising.

DECANT: To pour a liquid, generally wine, from one container to another. Red wine is decanted to remove the sediment deposited during the aging process.

DEEP-FAT FRYING: To cook in hot fat (about 360 degrees) that is deep enough for food to float—usually a minimum of 3 inches.

DEGLAZE: To pour hot stock, wine, or water on the degreased sediment left in the

roasting or frying pan in which meat has cooked. The purpose of deglazing is to dissolve the caramelized juices of meats dropped during the cooking process. This process is the secret of rich gravies, and a vital step in making good casseroles and soups.

DEHYDRATION: A process that removes the water content from food.

DEMI-GLAZE: A rich brown sauce or gravy made by reducing meat stock.

DEMIJOHN: A large glass wine container which can hold up to 10 gallons.

DEMI-SEC: A distinctive type of sweet champagne.

DEMITASSE: A small cup (half cup, literally) of bitter black coffee served after lunch or dinner in Europe. In addition to quite a lot of sugar, lemon zest may be added.

DESSERT WINE: Any sweet wine, or a wine that has been fortified by the addition of brandy.

DEVIL: This is a verb, and it means to chop and combine with hot seasonings or sauce, commonly mustard and cayenne.

DEVONSHIRE CREAM: A smooth English clotted cream, akin to *crème fraîche*.

DEVONSHIRE CREAM

Thick clotted cream and the French *crème fraîche* are easy to make. Pour heavy cream (whipping cream) into a saucepan and warm over low heat, stirring, until the cream is reduced by more than half. Then refrigerate overnight in a tightly covered jar. You'll have cream almost stiff enough to stand a spoon in. Especially nice with berries.

DHAL: The Indian name for lentils.

DICE: To cut into small cubes, ⅛ to ¼ inch.

DIGESTER: The pressure cooker of the seventeenth and eighteenth centuries.

DIGESTIVES: Liqueurs or cordials often made with herbs and said to aid digestion. Usually drunk at the end of a meal.

DILUTE: To thin or reduce in strength by adding liquid.

DIP: An *hors d'oeuvres* that is a soft savory mixture and served with crackers, vegetables, shrimp, potato chips, or other dipping food. A popular dip can be made by combining 1 cup of sour cream, a small slice of crushed onion, and a small clove of crushed garlic. The mixture is chilled for several hours before serving with potato chips. Another popular dip with corn chips is *guacamole*.

DISTILLED WATER: Water from which all gases and minerals have been removed.

DIVINITIES: Fudge, made with brown or white sugar. Southern United States.

DIVINITY CARAMEL CREAM   *Makes 2 pounds*

---

2 cups heavy cream
3 cups light brown sugar
Pinch of salt
1 cup light corn syrup
1 cup pecan meats, broken

1. In a heavy saucepan over medium heat, simmer the cream, sugar and salt, and corn syrup without stirring, to the softball stage, 238 degrees on the candy thermometer.

2. Remove from the heat and cool to 110 degrees. Then beat until very stiff. Just before you turn the candy out onto a buttered dish, add the nutmeats. When the candy stiffens, cut it into squares, then allow it to cool until firm.

DOBOS TORTE: A layer cake rich with chocolate cream and caramel.

DOGFISH: A common name for a species of small shark valuable for vitamin C in its liver oil.

DOLCI: Italian for sweet dishes.

DOUGHNUTS: A sweet cake fried in deep fat, and made of yeast-leavened or baking powder-raised dough. Fried cakes are a holiday tradition in most European countries and generally celebrate the name day or birthday of various Christian saints. The Dutch are generally credited with introducing doughnuts to the United States. Traditionally, they are served in America on the Tuesday before Lent begins, a day called *Mardi Gras* by the French, meaning a day when meat and other luxuries are eaten, before the lean season begins.

DOUBLE BOILER: Two saucepans, one of which fits into the top of the other. The lower pan is partially filled with water kept boiling or near boiling to keep the food in the upper pan cooking without excessive or uneven heat.

DRAGÉE: Colored sugar-coated nuts or candies.

DRAW: To remove the entrails of poultry, game.

DRAWN BUTTER: Melted butter, sometimes clarified butter.

DREDGE: To coat lightly with a dry ingredient, for instance, flour, sugar, bread crumbs, or cornmeal. Fish is often dredged in flour and seasonings before it is fried. A common method is to place half a cup of seasoned flour in a large paper bag, and to shake the fish in it gently until all the parts are coated. Also a good way to coat chicken parts with bread crumbs.

DRESS: To draw and clean a fowl for cooking. Also, to add dressing to a salad; to garnish.

DRIPPINGS: The fat, juices, and other residues separated from meat during cooking and left in the pan, or crusted onto the bottom of the pan. What actually happens is that the substance in the animal juices caramelizes, just as sugar does, on the bottom of a hot pan. Diluting and scraping these up, the cook creates the basis for the flavor of the best stews and soups and gravies. Drippings from roasts or sautéed meats in cast iron utensils caramelize exceptionally well, and make possible tastier casseroles and gravies. Traditionally, Yorkshire pudding is cooked in drippings that include a lot of fat.

DRY ICE: Used for long-term refrigeration, this crystalized carbon dioxide is ice that does not produce water when melted. Don't touch with bare hands and avoid prolonged breathing in an atmosphere saturated by melting dry ice.

DUCHESSE: A term for potatoes pureed with milk and butter.

DUCK PRESS: A device used to extract juices from a duck carcass to make pressed duck. Various gourmet duck recipes call for the extraction of the blood from the duck.

DULCE: Another name for carragheen moss which is an edible seaweed used for its gelatinous properties.

DUMPLING: A small ball of dough or bread or potatoes, steamed, or simmered in a stew or soup. Sweet dumplings are usually baked and contain fruit.

DUNDEE CAKE: A rich fruitcake covered with blanched almonds.

DURUM WHEAT: A variety of hard wheat used for making pasta.

DUST: To powder food very lightly with a dry ingredient.

DUTCH OVEN: A cast iron pot with a tightly fitting lid used to braise and sometimes to bake, meat puddings, for instance.

DUXELLES: A hash of minced mushrooms, shallots, and herbs simmered in butter, used to flavor soups, sauces, and stuffings or to garnish.

EAU-DE-VIE: Also *aqua vitae*, or "water of life" literally. A term commonly applied to homemade brandies and distilled white spirits, made from the lees of wine.

ÉCLAIR: A pastry cake shaped like a long finger. *Éclairs* can be filled with custard or cream and are usually glazed with chocolate.

EGGNOG: A frothy drink made from cream or milk, egg yolks, sugar, and flavorings, such as rum or brandy. A typical recipe calls for blending 1 cup of heavy cream with 1 egg, 2 teaspoons of honey, a dash of nutmeg or grated orange rind, and brandy or rum. Add milk to taste and chill. Eggnog is a traditional Christmas Eve drink in America.

EGG ROLL: Chinese pastry stuffed with a mixture of shredded meats, shrimp, cabbage or lettuce, and vegetables, then deep-fried.

EGG TIMER: A small, hourglass-shaped container that holds a fixed amount of sand. When the timer is turned upside down, the sand moves from one half to another in a three-minute period, the time required to cook a medium-sized fresh egg to the soft-boiled stage.

SOAK EGG-COVERED UTENSILS IN COLD WATER

Hot water sets egg and makes it harder to clean off. Always rinse utensils used in egg cookery in cold water, then wash in hot.

ELIXIRS: Cordials or essences that are said to be life-prolonging.

EMINCÉ: A term used to describe meat, vegetables, or fish sliced very thinly, placed in an earthenware dish and simmered in added sauce.

ENTRECÔTE: A cut of beef taken from between the ribs. Sometimes the term refers to a rumpsteak or sirloin.

ENTRÉE: Today the term refers to the main course of a meal, but originally it was the second course of many. French, meaning "entrance."

ENTREMETS: Side dishes, literally "between dishes"; can be a savory or sweet.

EPERGNE: A serving dish of numerous separate bowls attached to one main stem.

EPICURE: A gourmet who gives special attention to the knowledge of food and wine.

ESCALOPE: Refers to a thin slice of meat or fish, without bones, gristle, or skin.

ESPRESSO: An Italian way of preparing coffee using steam. Like the French *demitasse*, it is served in a small cup and is very strong.

ESSENCES: Condensed flavors made as their source is distilled or pressed, then mixed with liquid. Examples are almond extract, rose water, etc.

ESTAMINET: In France, those restaurants or cafes that allowed smoking were called *estaminets*. Today it can refer to a basement tavern.

FARCE: Stuffing.

FARFEL: A soup garnish made of minced noodle dough.

FELL: A thin, papery tissue found on the outside of the surface of a leg of lamb.

FENUGREEK: An Asiatic herb with a bitter celery-like flavor. Its chief use is in curry powders and stews.

FIDDLEHEAD FERN: A wild or cultivated fern such as *Osmunda cinnamome* (cinnamon fern). Pick in early spring before the asparaguslike fronds grow leafy. Cook as asparagus. In cooler climates, the ostrich fern, *Matteucia struthiopteris*, is called fiddlehead. The term comes from the appearance of the tightly curled fronds. In some states (Connecticut is one), the ostrich fern is protected and may not be gathered.

FILÉ: A powder made from dried sassafras leaves, *filé* thickens and binds gumbos and other Southern United States dishes.

FILET MIGNON: A small cut of beef taken from the end of the fillet, considered by many to be the most elegant steak of all. It is very tender and sweet, but lacks the flavor of a steak with bone in.

FILLET, FILET: To remove the bone; also, a piece of meat or fish without bones.

FILO: In Greek *philo*, this is the very flaky, buttery pastry made by layering dough with shortening and rolling it and rerolling it. *Filo* is usually purchased in a roll (like tissue paper).

FINE: Term for good brandy.

FINES HERBES: French, "fine herbs," usually a mixture of parsley, chives, tarragon, and chervil used to flavor omelettes and in casseroles and soups.

FINNOCHIO: Also, Florence fennel; an herb with a licorice flavor, used as is celery and in Mediterranean cooking.

FINGER BOWLS: Bowls half-filled with warm water which may be scented with roses or a slice of lemon. served to diners to rinse their hands in after a course in which the fingers were used to eat (lobster, oysters, or artichokes, for example).

FIZZ: A sweet effervescent summer drink made of gin and a carbonated beverage.

BURN OUT

Brandy should be warmed before you light it—it is easier this way. The pretty blue flames that rise above the flaming brandy use up the alcohol content of the liquor, and, therefore, there is little or no alcohol in a flambéed dish—only the flavor of the brandy remains.

FLAMBER: To cover or combine food with heated liquor, then set alight, and serve flaming. It also means to singe. Heating the liquor first is the secret to keeping the flame going.

FLAN: A pastry shell filled with fruit, cream, or custard. Also, a set custard usually served with a caramel sauce.

FLATBROD: Flat bread of Norwegian origin, it is wafer-thin, and made from whole grain and served with salad, cheese, or soup.

FLIP: A sweet drink containing alcohol and eggs. Originally, it was a heated drink but a cold flip is more common today.

FLORENTINE: Food set on a bed of cooked spinach and usually covered with a cream sauce and baked. From Florence, Italy.

FLUTE: To cut vegetables, fruit, or other foods in a decorative manner. Also, to make a decorative edge on a pastry shell. Also, a long loaf of French bread.

FOIE GRAS: An *hors d'oeuvres* of seasoned livers of geese, duck, chicken, or veal made into a *pâté*.

FOLD: To combine, usually mixtures, turning over and over gently to prevent air from escaping. The term often is used in instructions relating to whipped cream and beaten egg whites.

FONDANT: A sugar paste used as a candy stuffing or icing.

FONDUE: A melted sauce, usually with cheese, served with crisp bread rounds or as a filling. These are sauces kept hot in a chaffing dish into which crisp chunks of bread, vegetables, meat, or fruits are dipped before eating. Chocolate fondue with fruit chunks and berries is a sweet fondue that is excellent. Fondue means melted.

FONDUE CHEESE   *Serves 6 to 8*

---

1 tablespoon cornstarch
2 tablespoons Kirsch, or fragrant gin
1 medium clove garlic
2 cups Neichatel or other dry white wine
1 pound Swiss or Gruyère cheese, shredded
Salt and freshly ground black pepper
Pinch of ground nutmeg, optional
Slightly stale, or very crusty French bread, cut into chunks

Mix the cornstarch and liquor together in a small bowl. Halve the garlic and rub it around the inside of a chafing dish. Pour in the wine, and heat to simmer, but do not boil. Add the shredded cheese in small amounts, stirring constantly until the cheese is melted. Stir in the cornstarch mixture and continue stirring while cooking for 5 minutes. Add salt and pepper to taste and nutmeg, if you wish. Serve at once, offering each guest crusty chunks of bread, and a small two-pronged fondue fork with which to spear the bread and hold it while dipping it into the fondue.

FOOD CHOPPER: A knife created for efficiency. It is double-handled and crescent-

shaped, used with a rocking motion to rapidly chop and dice. In Italy it is known as a *mezzaluna*. Less useful today, since food processors do much of this work.

FOOD MILL: Used to puree or rice food by forcing the food through tiny holes.

FOOL: An English dessert of stewed and pureed fruit combined with a sweet cream.

FRUIT FOOL   *Serves 6*

1 heaping cup fresh raspberries, or 1 10-ounce package frozen
   whole berries, thawed.
1 package unflavored gelatin
2 teaspoons imported raspberry liqueur, optional
2 cups heavy cream, whipped with 2 teaspoons granulated sugar
6 fresh flowers of *Violata odorata*, or African violet
6 pairs baby mint leaves

1. If the berries are fresh, crush them slightly to obtain ⅔ cup of juice. If frozen, thaw, and drain the juice into a small saucepan. Bring the juice to a boil over medium heat, and stir in the unflavored gelatin at once. Remove from the heat and stir until the gelatin has dissolved. Then stir in the berries. Put into the freezer, and remove when almost jelled.

2. Combine the liqueur, if you wish, with the fruit, whipping slightly with a fork, then fold the cream into the fruit.

To serve, heap into stemmed goblets and freeze for 20 to 30 minutes before serving. Garnish with a flower and a pair of mint leaves.

FORCEMEAT: Finely ground meat often combined with ground vegetables to make a stuffing or combined with stiffly beaten egg whites to make delicate *quenelles* for poaching and serving with sauce. Also, combined with custardlike sauce to make souffles.

FRANGIPANI: A rich, sweet cream named for a tropical flower with a sweet scent.

FRAPPÉ: An iced drink made from sweetened fruit juices barely frozen. Also, liqueur served over shaved ice.

FRENCH FRY: To cook food in deep hot fat.

FRENCH TOAST: American breakfast dish of sliced bread dipped into beaten eggs and milk then fried.

FRIJOLES: Mexican beans.

FRITTER: Food coated in batter then fried in deep fat, usually.

FRUIT BUTTER: A sweet spread made of fruit cooked to a paste then lightly sweetened. Apple butter is a common example.

FRUMENTY: A popular food in English history, it is a rich, sweet porridge high in vitamins A and B.

FUMET: A concentrated stock used to give body to sauces.

GALANTINE: A cold jellied dish of boned chicken, veal, game, or fish.

GAME: Wild animals and birds hunted for sport. Cooked, they are leaner and less fat-sweetened than domestic animals.

GAMMON: The same cut of pork as ham, though cured differently.

GARBURE: A casserole or stew made of cabbage, beans, potatoes, and pork or bacon.

GARLIC SALT: Commercially prepared garlic-flavored salt. It can be made at home by mashing 1 peeled, sliced clove of garlic with 1 tablespoon of salt in the bottom of a wooden bowl.

GARLIC READY!

To have peeled cloves of garlic ready to make salad dressing or for cooking, put the peeled garlic in oil in a small jar with a tight-fitting lid. They will keep for weeks in the refrigerator. If you want, you can just use the oil in your salad dressing, because the garlic will flavor the oil as it sits.

GARNISH: The term used to define any addition to a dish that improves the appearance and/or flavor.

GAZPACHO: An iced soup made with fresh ripe tomatoes, cucumbers, sweet peppers, onions, and seasonings, marinated overnight. Mexican in origin.

GEFILTE FISH: A traditional Jewish dish of poached stuffed fish, whole or in balls, served hot or cold.

GELATIN: The by-product of boiling bones, cartilage and tendons of meat. Gelatin is transparent and tasteless unless flavored and colored. It is sold packaged either in granules or thin strips. When softened in cold water and added to a hot broth, it dissolves and when cooled, forms a gel. Commercial packages of gelatin generally contain 1 ounce or 1 tablespoon, and this will jell 2 cups of liquid.

GENOESE: A light cake made of eggs, sugar, butter, and cake flour (6 eggs to each cup of flour). *Genoese* is known for its versatility. It can be used for baked alaska, lady fingers, an iced birthday cake.

GHEE: Clarified butter used in Asian cooking. See *clarified butter*.

GHERKIN: Small cucumber species 1½ inches long, for pickling.

GIBLETS: The heart, liver, gizzard, and neck of fowl and small game, used to make soups, stews, and specialty dishes such as chopped chicken livers.

GIGOT: French term for a leg of lamb.

GINGER BEER: A mildly alcoholic drink that is effervescent and ginger flavored. Made with gingerroot.

GIZZARD: Part of the alimentary canal of fowl, whose function is to "grind" food, sometimes with pebbles swallowed for this purpose.

GLACÉ: To glaze with sugar syrup; also, to serve iced.

GLAZE: To make food shiny or glossy usually with aspic, sugar, or fruit syrup, or to brush with an egg mixed with a little milk or water.

GLOGG: Hot wine cup Swedes serve at Christmas.

GLUCOSE: Also, dextrose. A natural sugar found in fruits, vegetables, honey, and other products. Commercially produced, it is used in candy, jams, syrups, and wine.

GLUTEN: A water-soluble protein found in flour. Kneading flour in breadmaking brings out the smooth elastic qualities of the gluten content.

GNOCCHI: Dumplings made from a paste of flour or potatoes and egg.

GOULASH: Also, *gulyas*, a rich Hungarian stew made of meat, highly seasoned with paprika.

GOURD: A squashlike vegetable, usually dried and used as a fall decoration.

GRAHAM FLOUR: A wheat flour similar to wholemeal flour, ground from the whole grain.

GRAPPA: A brandy distilled from the stalks and grape skins that remain after the wine has been pressed. See *eau-de-vie*.

GRATE, TO: Reduce foods to smaller particles by rubbing through a grater by hand or in a food processor.

GRATER: A square metal or plastic instrument with perforations stamped in it against which goods can be rubbed to break off particles.

GREASE: To rub a pan with shortening to prevent food from sticking. Shortening may be butter, lard, bacon drippings, etc.

GRECQUE, À LA: Vegetables *à la Grecque* are cooked in seasoned oil and water.

GRENADIN: Thin slices of fillet of veal, larded and braised.

GRENADINE: A red sugar syrup made from pomegranate juice, and used to flavor drinks (usually for children) and to sweeten food.

GRIDDLE: A flat pan, often of cast iron, used for cooking pancakes, omelettes, or steaks on top of the stove.

GRIDDLE CAKES: In the United States and Canada, another word for pancakes. In England and Scotland, a name for drop scones.

GRIDIRON: A metal frame used to hold meat or fish as it cooks over a flame.

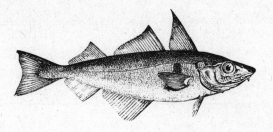

GRILL: Similar to the term "broil."

GRITS/OATS: Oats or corn with the husk removed and ground to a coarse meal.

GROUND CHERRY: A berry sometimes called husk tomato, it is used to make preserves.

GROUNDNUT: A peanut.

GUM ARABIC: A preservative made of sugar, water, and powdered acacia. It is used with leaves such as mint and rose.

GUMBO: A dish or thick soup made with okra as a main ingredient. The term also describes the okra plant.

GUM TRAGACANTH: A gum from plants found in Iran, Turkey, and Greece, it is used as a thickener and a base for ice cream powders and gelatinous desserts.

HADDOCK: Of the cod family, this fish is white-fleshed and is good to use in any recipe calling for cod. Smoked, it is known as Finnan Haddie. Poached, and served with drawn butter, it has a faint hint of the flavor of lobster.

HAGGAMUGGIE (HAGGIS): The minced innards of an animal cooked with oatmeal and suet. Traditionally, a meat pudding or sausage was made then boiled in the cleaned stomach bag of the animal—sheep

HAGGIS: See *haggamuggie.*

HAKE: Of the cod family, this fish is easy to fillet and has soft white flesh.

HALF-AND-HALF: A mixture of cream and milk preferred in a day when less fattening and less rich foods are becoming popular. For recipes, where you read half-and-half, the term formerly would have been "rich milk."

CREAM UNCURDLER

To keep cream from curdling when you mix it with acidic fruits, such as strawberries, stir a small pinch of baking soda into the cream before you pour.

HALVA: A sweet dish or candy made from ground sesame seeds, fruit, or vegetables. Near Eastern in origin.

HANG: To tenderize game or meat by hanging in a cool, dry, well-ventilated place.

HARD SAUCE: A sweet liquor-flavored sauce traditionally served on hot puddings and cold cake. Often offered at Christmas with plum pudding.

HARDTACK: A sailor's name for sea biscuits.

HARE: A wild rabbit with a strong gamey flavor. This is not a wild version of the rabbits raised domestically for food in Europe and some parts of the United States, but another type. It may not be used in place of rabbit in a recipe. The best-known American way to use hare is for *hasenpfeffer*, a German dish.

HASH: A recipe using leftovers, this dish is made by dicing pre-cooked meats and/or vegetables, and cooking with seasonings, minced onions, herbs, or sauce in a frying pan until crisp. It can take as long as 40 minutes to reach the right degree of crispness.

HASLET: Country dish of pork sweetbreads, heart, and liver. It is cooked in a casserole, or fried, stewed, or ground with onions and prepared as a sausage.

HEADCHEESE: A molded jelly or sausage made from pig's or calf's head stewed with herbs and seasonings; it includes meat.

HEART: The heart of sheep, calf, ox, and pig is used as a variety meat in many popular dishes. It can be a main ingredient in soup and forcemeat, or used as a supplement.

HEARTHCAKES: The English name for a French round cake. Each region in France creates its own version. The first hearthcakes were baked on the hearth in hot ashes.

HEN: Female bird. Commercially raised hen-chickens are tender. Hen is also a term applied to the female of various aquatic creatures, lobster for one.

HERB: Plant or plant part strongly flavored and used to flavor foods.

HET PINT: A Scottish drink used for special occasions. It is a heated mixture of ale, eggs, whiskey, and nutmeg.

HIP: Bright reddish orange fruit of roses, particularly species roses, as *Rosa rugosa*. It contains Vitamin C and is used to make a tea, and for jams and syrups.

HOCHEPOT (HOTCHPOTCH): A Belgian dish of considerable antiquity, a very thick soup traditionally made with brisket of beef, shoulder and breast of mutton, shoulder of veal, pigs feet, ears and tails, *chippolata* sausages, onions, assorted vegetables, herbs, and condiments. The meat garnished with vegetables is served separately from the broth. Probably associated with the phrase, hodge-podge, which refers to a jumble of things all mixed together. England has a "hot pot" which probably is a version of the Belgian dish.

HOCK: British term for any white Rhine wine. Also, a cut of meat from the leg of an animal, valued for soups, stews, and jellies.

HOMINY: Hulled corn with the germ removed. Hominy grits are uniform granules that are boiled and served as a breakfast cereal or as an accompaniment to a main dish of fish, meat, or poultry.

HOMOGENIZED: Treatment for milk that breaks the fat into tiny particles that can remain suspended in liquid rather than rising to the top as cream in untreated milk.

HORS D'OEUVRES: A light food, hot or cold, prepared for small servings, to be

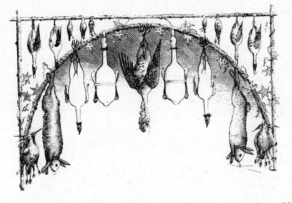

eaten before the main meal. The American equivalent is appetizer. *Hors d'oeuvres* were originally served on a sideboard apart from the dining table and before the meal.

HUMBLE PIE: "Umbles" are the heart, liver, kidney, and other innards of a deer. Servants once made this into a pie for themselves and coined the phrase "humble pie." Today the connotation is one who accepts a humble status or humiliating treatment voluntarily.

HUNDRED-YEAR-OLD EGGS: A Chinese delicacy, these are eggs preserved by wrapping in combinations of ashes, tea, lime and salt, covered with rice husks and buried for up to two months. Also, known as thousand-year-old-eggs, and Ming Dynasty eggs. They emerge from their aging process dark and with a particular flavor.

HUSH PUPPIES: A traditional dish of the southern United States, made of fried cornmeal batter. The term is said to have originated at a southern fish fry where the cooks fried extra bits of fish batter to throw to the noisy dogs to hush the puppies.

INDIAN PUDDING: A spicy cornmeal and molasses staple of early American colonists, the pudding varied with each day and according to the condiments available in the cook's larder. It was popular even in France in the seventeenth century.

INDIENNE, À L': Dishes containing curry and served with rice.

INFUSE: To steep herbs and other flavorings in boiling liquid. Coffee and tea are examples, and so is milk steeped with a vanilla bean.

IRISH STEW: A traditional mutton dish made by boiling well-salted and peppered chops with an equal quantity of onions and potatoes. After onions and chops have cooked for half an hour with enough water to cover, the broth is completely degreased, and cooking resumes for another three quarters of an hour with the potatoes. Modern versions add herbs and some cooks add carrots, but mutton, onions, and potatoes made up the original Irish stew.

JAM: Fresh whole fruit and sugar cooked into a spread that preserves well.

JAMBALAYA: A Creole dish that adds rice to any kind of meat, poultry, or seafood on hand. There are no two recipes alike for jambalaya.

2 cups dry white wine
3 cups chicken broth
1 large slice lemon
1 large bay leaf
1 large clove garlic, peeled and halved
6 whole black peppercorns
4 large sprigs parsley
1 small sprig celery leaves
1 small sliced peeled onion
1 small carrot, scraped and cut up
1 pinch cayenne pepper
2 pounds fresh shrimp, or thawed medium shrimp
6 slices bacon, chopped
1½ pound cooked ham, julienned
3 large onions, peeled and chopped
2 large cloves garlic, peeled and minced

1 28-ounce can whole tomatoes in puree
½ pound pepperoni sausage, sliced
3 whole green peppers, seeded and coarsely chopped
½ teaspoon dried thyme
Pinch of dried tarragon
¼ cup chopped celery leaves
¼ cup minced parsley
1 medium bay leaf
Pinch of cayenne pepper
2 cups converted white rice
3 tablespoons butter or margarine
1 pound scrubbed raw cherry-stone clams (1½ to 2 inches long)
Salt and freshly ground black pepper
½ cup minced parsley

1. The night before, combine the wine and the chicken broth with the next 9 ingredients in a large pot. Cover and bring to a boil over medium heat. Reduce the heat and simmer for 20 minutes. Bring back to a boil and add the shrimp. Return to a boil, reduce the heat, cover, and simmer for 5 minutes. Remove from the heat and allow to cool. Transfer to a glass bowl, cover, and refrigerate overnight.

2. In a big pot, sauté the bacon over medium heat for 1 to 2 minutes, then add the ham, onions, and garlic. Sauté, cooking and stirring, for 2 minutes longer. Add the next 9 ingredients, bring to a boil, reduce the heat, and simmer, uncovered, for 20 minutes, stirring occasionally while the sauce thickens. Remove the shrimp from the marinade, strain the marinade, and add it to the tomato sauce.

3. In a saucepan, sauté the rice in the butter over medium heat until the rice begins to brown. Add the rice to the tomato-marinade mixture. Bring to a boil, cover, reduce the heat, and simmer for 15 minutes.

4. Shell and devein the shrimp, and set them aside. Rinse the clams quickly under cold water, and bury them in the simmering sauce. Cover, and simmer for 5 minutes longer, or until all the clams are open. By that time, the rice should have absorbed most of the liquid. If you can still see liquid in the pan, spoon the excess liquid into a small saucepan and boil it rapidly to reduce it by more than half. Then return the reduced liquid to the rice mixture, add the shelled and deveined shrimp, and fork them in carefully. Taste the dish for salt and pepper, and add if necessary. Turn the jambalaya into a large deep platter and serve sprinkled with minced parsley.

JARDINIÈRE, À LA: Garnished with fresh vegetables.

JELLY: A clear preserve of strained fruit juice with sugar. Jelly of another sort is made by boiling animal or fish bones and tissue.

JELLY ROLL: A thin sponge cake spread with jelly and rolled up.

JEROBOAM: An oversize bottle, generally holding up to 4 quarts.

JIGGER: A liquid measure equal to 1½ fluid ounces.

JOHNNYCAKE: A classic corn bread unique because the meal is water-ground and made from white sweet corn.

JOINT: To cut; to cut into pieces at the joint. Also, a British cut of meat for roasting.

JUG: A stew made of game meat, particularly hare—jugged hare. The blood of the animal is used in the stew and it is cooked in a jug or an earthenware pot.

JUJUBE: The edible fruit of a tropical plant also known as the Chinese date. Also, a chewy gelatin candy.

JULIENNE: Finely cut matchlike strips of vegetables. Also, a *consommé* to which a mixture of julienned vegetables is added.

JUNKET: Milk which has been thickened with rennet, sweetened, and is served as dessert. Also, trade name for a flavored dessert mix including rennet.

KAKAVIA: A Greek fish soup.

KASHA: A side dish, like a pasta or rice side dish, served in Eastern Europe. It may be buckwheat, barley, or millet. Also, cooked buckwheat.

KEBAB: Grilled chunks of meat, fish, or vegetables. Usually threaded on a skewer, and broiled over charcoal, with or without being combined with onions and other foods.

KEDGEREE: An English breakfast dish brought from India, and made of leftover fish, rice, and hard-boiled eggs.

KETTLE: Pot for boiling liquids. In some regions the word has come to mean a pot with a handle and a spout for pouring, as a teakettle.

KIPPER: Fish cured by splitting, salting, and drying or smoking. A breakfast food in England, kippered herring is poached, grilled, or baked.

KIRSCH: Liqueur made of black cherries and their pits, used to flavor fruit compotes and salads.

KISSES: Meringues. Also, small candies rolled up in twists of silver paper.

KNEAD: Working dough ingredients with the hands by pressing, and folding, turning and smoothing until the dough becomes satiny and smooth. Some recipe instructions call for throwing the dough violently against the kneading surface dozens and even hundreds of times to knead, but that is not a common method.

KNUCKLE: The ankle joint of pork, veal, and other meat. It is used in stews and pies, and particularly in soups.

KOFTA: A meat ball popular in the Balkans, the Middle and Far East.

KORMA: Also, *quoorma*. A spicy Pakistani/Indian stew made of mutton and yogurt, and flavored with the spices that go into a curry.

KOSHER: Food that conforms to Jewish dietary laws, which were laid down by Moses, according to Biblical accounts of Hebrew history.

KULICH: A traditional Russian Easter cake. It is made of sweet bread dough and candied fruit, baked tall and round like the headgear of a Russian Orthodox priest.

KUMMEL: A sweet liqueur prepared with caraway seed and cumin, made in regions bordering the eastern coast of the Baltic sea.

LACTIC ACID: A colorless liquid produced as milk sugar ferments and milk sours. It is used to curdle milk in cheesemaking.

LADYFINGERS: A small finger-shaped sponge cake, like a cookie.

LAGER: Any light beer.

LAMB'S FRY: The heart, liver, sweetbread, and inside fat of the lamb.

LAMB'S LETTUCE: A hardy annual plant also known as corn salad. A salad green.

LAMB'S WOOL: A fancy hot alcoholic drink popular in Pepys' time. It is made of hot sweetened ale, roasted apples, and nutmeg or ginger.

LANGOUSTE: See *spiny lobster.*

LARD: Tenderized hog fat used in pie crusts and for deep-frying. Also, to insert strips of fat into meat to keep it moist and add flavor. See also *bard.*

LARDING NEEDLE: A long needle with a large eye, used to insert strips of fat into lean meats.

LASAGNE: Long wide noodles. Basis for the dish called lasagne in which the noodles are layered with cheeses and meat sauce or tomato sauce.

LAYER CAKE: Two, three, or more layers of cake with a filling between.

LAZY SUSAN: A revolving tray that sits in the middle of a dining table. Usually round.

LAUREL: Bay leaf.

LEAVEN: To lighten and increase the volume of bakery products. Leavening agents are yeast (which the Egyptians isolated from the sourdough bread the desert nomads made), baking powder, baking soda, and eggs.

LEES: The sediment or dregs left as wine or liquor ferments. Also, the settling of a liquid.

WHAT'S A LEGUME?

A legume is defined as a pod, or multi-seeded dry fruit that frees its fruit by splitting along two margins, as with peas and beans. Leguminous plants are members of the pea family, which includes soybeans, lentils, and peanuts (groundnuts and goobers are other names). They have the particular quality of being able to produce nodules containing nitrogen-fixing bacteria—which means that crops following leguminous crops will not require additional fertilizer containing nitrogen.

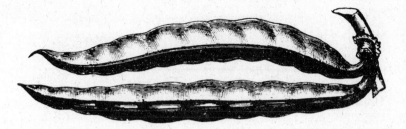

LEGUME: A family of plants with edible pods or seeds, which include peanuts, peas, beans, and lentils, among others.

LEMON SOLE: A particularly delicate flounder taken in the waters of Georges Bank, Cape Cod, Massachusetts.

LIAISON: A thickening or binding agent for soups, sauces, stuffings, and so on. Examples are flour, *beurre manié*, cornstarch, eggs, arrowroot, etc.

LIGHTS: The lungs of an animal.

LINZER TORTE: A double hazelnut cookie filled with jam and made famous in Vienna, Austria.

LIQUEUR: A sweet alcoholic drink also known as a cordial and as a *digestif*, to be drunk after meals and served in small glasses. Also used to flavor desserts and in pastry making.

LITTLENECK CLAMS: Clams 1½ inches long.

LOQUAT: A small citrus fruit that sweetens as it ripens. It is good peeled, stewed with sugar, and served with cream or combined with other fruits.

LOTUS ROOT: A water lily whose root is used as a vegetable. It is crisp when fresh. Sold dried, cut into rounds in Oriental markets.

LOTUS SEEDS: Small and nutlike, these can be eaten raw or cooked into a stuffing.

LUAU: A traditional Hawaiian feast featuring roast pig.

LYCHEE: A small fruit native to South China. It has a sweet-sour flavor and is considered as good canned as fresh.

LYONNAISE, À LA: "In the style of Lyons," literally, and usually featuring shredded fried onions as a garnish. Lyons is a city in central France famous for its cuisine.

MACADAMIA NUT: A round, costly, and delicious nut sold shelled and bottled. It is the fruit of a subtropical evergreen native to Australia but most that reach the market come from Hawaii (also grown in California). Seeds were brought to Hawaii in 1880, and the nuts first were offered on the market in the 1930s.

MACARONI: A general term for all pastas. Specifically, it refers to a tubular form of pasta.

MADELEINE: A small cake baked in a shell-shaped mold. Also, a garnish of artichoke bottoms, onions, and green beans.

MADRILÈNE: A *consommé* flavored with tomato, usually served cold.

MAGNUM: A single bottle with a capacity of two bottles or about ⅖ gallon, or 160 centilitres.

MAÎTRE D'HÔTEL: Head waiter, but on menus, a dish that is cooked quickly and simply with parsley as the featured flavor.

MAÎTRE D'HÔTEL BUTTER: A parsley butter excellent with grilled meats or fish and vegetables, especially carrots. The recipe calls for butter, minced parsley, lemon juice, salt, and pepper, blended. (Be wary of mincing the parsley in a blender: overblended in a blender or a processor, parsley releases a bitter juice that spoils the food it is combined with. You can avoid overblending by cutting only a small handful at a time in the machine.)

MAIZE BREAD: American corn bread, also known as corn pone, spoon bread, egg cake, and ash cake. Each of these is made by a somewhat different method, but all have cornmeal as the base.

MALT: Sprouted barley used to brew beer or distill spirits.

MALTED MILK: A popular drink some years ago, made from powdered wheat and malted barley extracts, mixed with milk and, sometimes, added flavorings—chocolate, strawberry, etc.

MANGO: A tropical fruit the size of a small pear, in its original species, but today mango hybrids are as large as small or medium grapefruits. From India, and a key ingredient in some of the best chutneys, notably Major Grey's. The fruit is yellow shaded red when ripe, and is peeled before eating. Best chilled, and ripe enough to be softly yielding. Delicious taste between a pineapple and a very ripe peach. Makes an attractive dessert peeled, sliced, chilled and garnished with blueberries.

MANIOC: Cassava, the source plant for tapioca.

MARASCHINO: A sweet liqueur made from cherries. Also, red cherries in maraschino syrup, which are used in mixed drinks and with desserts, such as fruit salad, and as a garnish on, for instance, grapefruit.

MARBLED: A term for meat streaked with fat. When cooked, marbled meat is juicy and exceptionally tender, so this is a mark of a high-quality piece, especially sought after in steaks and beef roasts.

MARC: *Eau-de-vie*, a spirit distilled from the residue of grapes or other fruit after wine has been pressed and strained. Calvados is the *marc* made of apples.

MARÉCHALE, À LA: Small cuts of meat and poultry which are breaded and fried in butter. Green asparagus tips and truffles are usual in the garnish.

MARENNES: A type of oyster found in French waters. Highly prized for flavor.

MARGARINE: A butter substitute made from animal or vegetable fat and butter flavored.

MARINADE: A seasoned and flavored liquid mixture containing a tenderizing acid, such as wine or vinegar, in which meat and fish are steeped before cooking. Game is usually marinated before cooking, as are *kebabs* of mutton and many other tougher cuts of meat.

MARINIÈRE: To cook shellfish with white wine. Also, a garnish with mussels.

MARMALADE: A fruit preserve made from citrus fruits. The rinds are sliced thinly and included.

MARMITE: A heavy metal or earthenware pot.

CARING FOR CLAY

Clay cooking equipment from France or Mexico, and elsewhere, is as fragile as glass, and if you think of it that way it will last longer. The main cause of damage is too-sudden changes in temperature. Don't pour cold water into a very hot earthenware casserole. And avoid using clay on the stove top unless you have a protective asbestos pad to place between the bottom of the clay pot and the heat.

MARMITE, PETITE: French dish. A rich broth called *consommé double*, it includes chicken and beef with vegetables and herbs and is a classic. The words mean "small pot."

MARROW: A squash. Also, the inner substance of meat bones, usually shin bones. These are cut across the grain by the butcher, and sold for the famous Italian dish, *ossobucco*, and also to make soup. After cooking, the marrow is drawn from the interior of the bone with a fork. It may be placed on a small crisp piece of bread and served as an appetizer.

MARZIPAN (also MARCHPANE): A combination of almond paste, sugar, and egg whites used in making pastry and small fruit shapes for holidays.

MASH: To reduce to pulp, with a fork or potato masher. Also, a mess of boiled grain, bran, and so on, fed to horses and cattle.

MATELOTE: A rich fish stew flavored with red or white wine, and herbs.

MATZO: A type of thin unleavened bread special to the Passover feast celebrated by the Jews. It resembles a cracker. Also, unleavened dumplings.

MAYONNAISE: The familiar white commercial mayonnaise is a product that is cooked. The mayonnaise called for in gourmet cookbooks, "fresh mayonnaise," is a thick sauce of yolks beaten with oil and vinegar. It is a staple of French home cooking, and one of the first kitchen secrets taught to young French girls and boys.

MEAD: An alcoholic drink of fermented honey and water.

MEDALLION: A small, coin-shaped slice of meat or fish.

MELBA TOAST: Thin slices of bread baked slowly until crisp. Named for the coloratura soprano, Dame Nellie Melba, who was the toast of international society early in this century.

MERINGUE: A mixture of egg whites beaten with sugar and baked into cookies or used as a pie topping. The addition of sugar to a meringue is critical; poured in too quickly, the meringue will fall and will not be usable.

MEUNIÈRE: French for, literally, "in the style of the miller's wife," dusted with flour and sautéed in butter.

MICROWAVE OVEN: A specially constructed and wired oven that cooks with microwaves, a form of electromagnetic radiation used in radar and telecommunications. Microwave ovens tenderize foods more rapidly than conventional cooking instruments. See also "Microwave and Convection Ovens," Section V.

MIGNONETTE: Coarsely ground white or black pepper.

MILANAISE, À LA: Food dipped in egg and bread crumbs and sauteed in butter. Named for Milan, a city in northern Italy known for elegant food.

MILLE-FEUILLES: Literally, "a thousand leaves," this is the flaky pastry the Middle East introduced into European cuisines, layered with cream, and topped with jam and icing.

MILT: The reproductive gland of a male fish, also known as soft roe.

MIMOSA: A garnish of grated hard-boiled egg yolks, named for the tree flower that is a spray of tiny yellow fluffy balls.

MINCE: To cut as finely as possible into small pieces. This is one step larger than ground, and smaller than "chop."

MINCEMEAT: A preserve of chopped apples, suet, dried fruits, candied peel, sugar, spices, and brandy or rum. It is matured for a month or more and used in holiday pies, and in some recipes for fruitcake.

CLEANING A MEAT GRINDER

A nifty way to quick-clean a meat grinder when you have finished with the meat is to run a piece of stale bread through it. Of course, this will also remove the last of the meat caught in the grinder, and, if you are going to mix the ground meat with bread, you can use this last bit, too. Then wash the grinder in hot soapy water and rinse very well in very hot water before drying thoroughly.

MINESTRA: Italian; a thick soup of meat and vegetables.

MINESTRONE: A *minestra* with pasta.

MINT: Herb used in Middle Eastern and Indian cooking. In the West, commonly used to make tea as well as a sauce served with lamb roasts.

MINUTE STEAK: A boneless steak cut one quarter inch thick, and criss-crossed with cuts for tenderizing. It is intended to be sautéed in 1 minute. To cook it longer is to toughen it.

MIREPOIX: A vegetable and herb seasoning the French use in flavoring sauces, fish, and meat dishes. The usual ingredients are 1 carrot and 1 onion, minced, plus 3 sprigs of parsley, a bay leaf, and a quarter teaspoon of dried thyme, all sauteed in butter for 5 minutes.

MIXED GRILL: A combination of grilled meats, such as liver, steak, and bacon, garnished with tomatoes and mushrooms. It is usually served with fried potatoes.

MOCHA: A rich coffee originally grown in Mocha, Yemen. The beans are almost without bitterness in the best grades. Mocha also describes a combination of chocolate and coffee used to flavor cakes and candies.

MODE, À LA: Literally, "in the mode." Meats à *la mode* are braised with vegetables and served with gravy. In the United States, à *la mode* usually refers to a pie or cake served with ice cream.

MOLASSES: A dark, sweet syrup that is the by-product of sugar refining. Used to flavor candy, puddings, baked goods, and other foods.

MONOSODIUM GLUTAMATE (MSG): An amino acid derived from gluten or soybeans. Used in Oriental cooking to improve the flavor of a dish that has not come up to par.

MOREL: A small, very tasty mushroom.

MOUSSAKA: A traditional dish of the Balkan peninsula, and generally known as Greek. There are many variations, but all are layered casseroles of vegetables and ground meat. The favorite is a combination of eggplant with tomatoes and lamb.

MOUSSE: A dish usually based on beaten egg whites and yolks, baked into a savory or a sweet. A mousse can be a puree of meat, poultry, fish, or vegetables, served hot or cold. As a dessert it is an extra-light pudding flavored with fruit, lemon, or chocolate, and served warm or cold with or without cream.

MOUSSELINE: A sauce with whipped cream added. The name for small molds of poultry, game, fish, and shellfish and cream, served hot or cold.

MUDDLER: A thick rod used to crush and mix fruit and sugar in drinks. Also, used to free the bubbles in champagne.

MUFFIN: A small, round, quick sweet bread raised with baking powder, and baked in small molds (muffin tins). In the United States these often are served as bread with a main course.

MULLED WINE: Wine, usually red, that is heated, but not boiled, with sugar and spices, such as cinnamon stick, ground mace, and whole cloves.

MULLIGATAWNY: English version of chicken or lamb soup served with rice. The original is Indian.

MUSH: A cooked cereal popular in the Southern United States, made by boiling cornmeal. Best served with melting butter and a little sweet syrup.

MUSSELS: Edible mollusks found under seaweed clinging to the rocks by the seashore, these are a staple of French shore meals, as clams are a staple of American shore meals. Mussels are generally less familiar than clams in the United States, but this delicious mollusk may still be gathered wild. However, like other shellfish, mussels are subject to a condition called "red tide," which occurs in some spring seasons and renders the shellfish poisonous. Therefore, before harvesting mussels, check with the local authorities to be sure they are safe.

MUTTON: Meat of the mature sheep, that is, 1 year to 18 months old. The meat is a darker color than lamb, and more strongly flavored.

NACHO: A Mexican appetizer made with chilies and melted cheese, and served on a tortilla.

NASTURTIUM: An edible flower. The young leaves and blooms are used in salads and sandwiches, and as garnishes for cold summer soups; the buds may be picked and pickled and used as substitute for capers.

NAVARIN: A French lamb stew.

NEOPOLITAN ICE CREAM: Ice cream brick. It is usually made up of layers of chocolate, strawberry, and vanilla.

NEAT: An undiluted alcohol.

NECTAR: Any delicious drink. In mythology, this was the drink of the Olympian gods. Also, the juice of plants collected for honey.

NESSELRODE: A mold of ice cream flavored with candied fruits and chestnut puree. Also, a Bavarian cream similarly flavored and used in a pie.

NEWBURG: Hot lobster or seafood cooked in a sherry sauce enriched with a thick cream sauce.

NIÇOISE, À LA: Dishes with black olives, tomatoes, garlic, anchovies, and olive oil, flavorings and ingredients found in the cooking of Nice, a city on the Mediterranean in southern France.

NOUGAT: A candy of boiled sugar and egg whites mixed with nuts and dried cherries. Or, a candy of caramelized sugar and browned almonds.

NOUVELLE CUISINE: Literally, "new cooking." Akin to *cuisine minceur*, or "thinning cookery." A new approach to cooking evolved in recent years in France, it avoids the rich ingredients of the Cordon Bleu recipes and uses a lot of vegetables and fruits in a somewhat Oriental manner to produce lean, light dishes.

ORANGE WATER, ORANGE FLOWER WATER: A liquid essence of distilled orange blossoms, once used for flavoring.

OSSOBUCCO: Literally, "hollow bone," this Italian specialty is made of veal marrow bones, usually shin bones, braised in wine with vegetables and seasonings.

OXTAIL SOUP: A popular winter soup in Europe made from oxtails and vegetables. The oxtail is the tail cut of beef, usually.

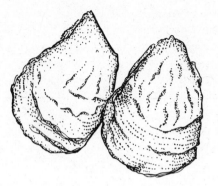

OYSTER, BLUE POINT: The name for an oyster found in the waters off Long Island Sound, New York. Also, term used to refer to any good-sized oyster.

OYSTERS ROCKEFELLER: Oysters which are topped with chopped spinach, bacon, and seasoned bread crumbs and baked.

PAELLA: Traditional Spanish one-pot dish of chicken, seafood, vegetables, rice, and garlic, flavored with saffron.

PAKORA: Small, deep-fried snacks of India with chick-pea flour as an ingredient in the mixture. Vegetables, fish, or chicken are spiced with ginger, cumin, chopped onion, and garlic, blended with the flour, shaped into small patties, and deep fried. An American version makes appetizers by dipping chunks of raw vegetables into a fritter batter, and deep frying.

PALMIER: Delicious flat flaky palm-shaped pastries made by layering puff pastry with sugar, rolling it, then slicing it thin and baking.

PAN-BROIL: To cook in hot, bare or lightly-greased pan, removing fat as it seeps out.

FRYING WITH FEWER CALORIES

Sprinkle the pan for sautéing steaks and other meats lightly with salt before adding the meat. The salt will keep the meat from sticking and adds nothing to the calorie content.

PAPER COOKERY: *En papillote* is the French term for this process of cooking food in a container made from heavy paper.

PAPILLOTE: French term for fancy paper shapes and ruffles used to hide the ends of chop bones. Also, see *paper cookery*.

PARFAIT: A French dessert of frozen pudding, either ice cream or mousse layered with fruits or syrups and whipped cream.

PARSLEY: Most-used herb in the world, it grows easily anywhere, including in window boxes and pots indoors. It is the mainstay of French seasonings.

PASHKA: A traditional Russian Easter cheesecake with nuts and candied fruit made in the form of a pyramid.

PASSOVER BREAD: See *matzo*.

PASTA: Flour, eggs, and water in various shapes from broad, flat, long lasagne, to the familiar thin spaghetti, including noodles, and so on.

PASTRAMI: Spicy smoked beef eaten hot or cold. Italian variation of corned beef.

PÂTÉ: A meatloaf of any variety of liver and/or finely ground meats blended together with herbs and spices and baked. *pâté maison* is a familiar item on French menus, and means *pâté* made in house. Most French households have a *pâté* recipe of their own. In America, it is often made in a blender by combining cooked meats, which later jell.

PAUPIETTES: Thin slices of meat or fish, stuffed, then rolled and cooked. Sometimes the meat is pounded to thin and enlarge it, before stuffing.

PECTIN: Substance that occurs in fruits or vegetables that acts as jelling agent in jams and other preserves. It is packed in bottles and sold commercially.

PEPITAS: Roasted pumpkin seeds.

PEPPERPOT: A spicy stew without much sauce.

PEPPER STEAK (STEAK AU POIVRE): A beefsteak dipped in crushed pepper and sautéed in butter, then flamed with brandy. A sauce is made from the pan drippings and red wine. Also, a Chinese dish made with green pepper strips and thin-sliced beef.

PERIWINKLE: A small sea snail served roasted, poached, or raw, with sauce.

PERSIMMON: Small acidulous plumlike orchard fruit that becomes sweet when soft and ripe.

PESTLE AND MORTAR: A pestle is a rodlike tool used to crush or pound food in a bowl with rough interior surface—the mortar.

PETIT FOUR: A bite-sized, usually square, decorated cake covered with colorful frosting and served in France at the end of formal meals.

PETIT SUISSE: An unsalted, very rich cream cheese rolled in paper in a cylindrical shape. In France, it is treated as a dessert, and served with sugar and cream.

PICKLE: To preserve in seasoned and/or flavored vinegar, brine, or oil. This is common for vegetables, especially cucumbers, fruits, and meats.

PIGNOLI: Pine nuts.

PILAF, PILAFF, PILAU: A rice dish in which the raw rice is first simmered in a shortening, then cooked with water or broth, and sometimes meat, poultry, fish, or shellfish.

PIMIENTO: A variety of sweet pepper, ripened to the red stage, and canned or bottled. It is used as a garnish for salads, sauces, rice dishes, or stews. Sometimes the word is mistakenly spelled "pimento," which is really allspice. One cannot be used as a substitute for the other.

PINCH: A measure of less than ⅛ teaspoon; an amount held between the thumb and forefinger.

PINE NUTS: A nut with a tangy flavor reminiscent of pine, used in Mediterranean dishes, and brought to attention recently by the spaghetti sauce called *pesto pignoli*.

PIPE: In cookery, this means to apply with a pastry tube.

PISSALADIÈRE: French. A tart, or pizza-type dish, made of baked dough with onions, tomatoes, garlic, anchovies, black olives, and/or other garnishes.

PISTACHIO: A flavorful nut used for snacking when roasted, and for flavoring sweets and ice cream. It has a high iron content and a characteristic greenish tinge.

PITA: Envelope of unleavened bread used for making sandwiches. Arab.

PIZZA: A yeast dough, sometimes thick, sometimes thin, baked with such toppings as pureed tomatoes, shredded mozzarella cheese, sausages, olives, anchovies, etc. Versions of this dish, which originated in Naples, Italy, vary throughout the world.

PLANKING: A style of baking or broiling meat or fish on a piece of hard wood. Plank also describes a wooden carving or serving platter with grooves that keep juices from spilling; used for serving roasts.

PLUM PUDDING: British holiday pudding made mostly of dried fruit, rarely with plums. It is steamed, then served with hard sauce.

POACH: To cook in liquid that is simmering at 185 degrees, or just below boiling, so gently the water scarcely bubbles.

PLUM PUDDING	*Yield: 4 puddings, each serving 8 to 10*
2 cups dark brown sugar	2 cups (1 pound) chopped suet
10 eggs	2 cups candied orange peel
1 ½ teaspoons salt	2 cups candied lemon peel
1 ½ teaspoons ground cinnamon	2 cups candied citron
1 teaspoon ground nutmeg	1 cup candied cherries
½ teaspoon ground cloves	2 cups dried currants
½ cup dark rum	2 cups seedless raisins
½ cup brandy	3 cups all-purpose flour
3 cups apple cider	½ cup brandy or rum
3 cups unflavored bread crumbs	Hard Sauce, optional

1. Put the sugar and eggs in a large bowl and beat at high speed with an electric mixer. Add the salt, cinnamon, nutmeg, cloves, rum, and brandy while still beating. Turn into a large jam kettle, or the biggest bowl you've got, mix in the cider and fold in the bread crumbs. Toss the suet and all of the fruits with the flour, and combine everything (including any excess flour) with the egg mixture.

2. Divide into four, and pack into greased molds. Seal the molds with foil and store in a cool place. The puddings will keep indefinitely.

3. To serve, steam over simmering water in a covered pot for 4 to 6 hours. Warm the brandy or rum, ignite it, and bring the pudding to the table, basting it with the flaming alcohol. When the flame dies, all the alcohol will have been consumed. Serve the pudding with the Hard Sauce, if you wish.

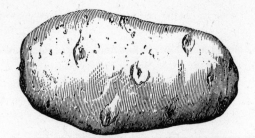

HARD SAUCE   *Serves 8 to 10*

6 tablespoons butter
1 cup confectioners' sugar
¼ teaspoon salt
1 teaspoon vanilla extract
2 tablespoons rum, brandy, bourbon, or similar liquor
¼ cup heavy cream

Put the butter in a food processor or the small bowl of an electric mixer and beat with the sugar and salt until creamy. Beat in the remaining ingredients. Turn into a serving dish, cover, and chill thoroughly before using.

POI: Hawaiian dish of cooked and pounded taro root.

POLENTA: Italian cornmeal pudding or mush, eaten hot or cold, usually with sauce and/or meats. It may be cooled and fried after cooking.

POPOVER: A batter muffin that is puffy and almost hollow, it has risen so high. The ingredients are about the same as for Yorkshire pudding, and like Yorkshire pudding, the batter is poured into already-heated containers. The beating period is critical and cannot be skimped on, as the leavening agent is egg, which must be thoroughly aerated.

PORRINGER: A child's dish used for porridge.

PORT: A grape wine fortified with brandy, which often is used to flavor casseroles and desserts. It may also be drunk after dinner as a *digestif*.

PORTERHOUSE STEAK: A thick steak of high quality cut from the wide end of the sirloin.

PORTMANTEAU: A French steak that has a pocket cut into the side into which oysters are placed. The pocket is sewn shut before the steak is cooked.

POTATO FLOUR: A flour made from potatoes. It is used as a thickening agent, like cornstarch.

POTATOES, STRAW: Potatoes grated or sliced into tiny sticks, and deep fried.

POT-AU-FEU: Literally, "pot on the fire," this is one of the oldest ways with food in

France—a thick soup, or thin stew. Often the cooked meat and vegetables are served with rock salt, after the soup has been drunk.

POT PIE: A pie of meat or poultry and vegetables in a thick gravy, topped with a short pastry crust.

POT-ROASTING: A phrase that describes braising, the process of browning meat and then cooking it in very little liquid.

POTTED MEAT: Cooked meat preserved in a jar.

POUND: In cooking, to flatten with a heavy tool. The process is intended to tenderize certain very tough or wiry fish (such as abalone), and to thin for fast cooking, and tenderize, cuts of meat—veal scallops, for instance, to make *scaloppine*, and *paupiettes*.

PRALINES: Candy-coated almonds in pastel colors given out as favors at French ceremonies, such as baptism.

PRALINE: A hard candy made of sugar cooked to 310 degrees on the candy thermometer, to which almonds or pecans are added. The candy is cooled in butter, then cracked and the confection is used as topping. It may also be poured directly onto a pudding or cake icing as a sweet garnish.

PRAWNS: Crustaceans like shrimp. In some areas of the United States, the term is applied to any large shrimp.

PREHEAT: To bring the oven to the temperature set required before baking.

PRESSED BEEF: The brisket which has been boned, salted, and pressed.

PRINTANIER, À LA: To be cooked or garnished with fresh spring vegetables. *Printemps* is the French word for spring.

PROFITEROLES: Cream puffs filled with a sweet or savory mixture.

PROOF: To allow a yeast mixture to rise in a warm, dry place. Also, to test yeast for potency.

PROVENÇALE, À LA: A dish including garlic, olive oil, tomatoes, and often black olives.

PRUNE: A dried plum.

PUDDING: A general name for many thick, rich dishes, both sweet and savory. Puddings are generally made of an ingredient that thickens, like cornmeal, or include a thickener, such as cornstarch.

PUFF PASTRY: Pastry that puffs when baked.

PULSES: The dried form of peas, beans, soybeans, peanuts, and other legumes.

PUREE: To grind or mash to a smooth paste in a blender or food processor, or by pushing through a sieve or food mill.

QUAHOG: A hardshell clam of excellent quality. Large sizes (4-5 inches), are called quahogs; smaller sizes are known as cherrystones (3 inches), and littlenecks (1½ inches). Quahogs are best for chowders.

QUAIL: A game bird sought for its fine flavor.

QUENELLES: Tiny mousses poached in broth, then drained and served with a savory sauce. Fish and poultry mousses are most popular.

QUESO: Creamy cheeses or cottage cheeses from Mexico or Argentina.

QUICHE: Savory custard baked in a pie shell.

QUOORMA: A spicy Pakistani or Indian stew of mutton and yogurt. See *Korma*.

RACLETTE   *Serves 1*

---

1 6-inch square (¼ inch thick) slice of natural Gruyère,
    Raclette des Bagnes, or Mutschli
1 boiled potato, peeled and halved
Pickled tiny onions or chopped gherkins

1. Set broiler on high.

2. Place the slice of cheese and the boiled potato halves on an ovenproof plate, and set it about 4 inches from the heat. As soon as the cheese begins to melt and has softened inside, place the ovenproof dish on a cold serving plate, and serve with the onions and gherkins on the side. To eat, scrape a bit of melted cheese onto the fork, mash into a little potato, and add a bit of onion or pickle.

RACK: A rib section of meat. Considered a luxury cut, rib ends may be decorated with *papillotes.*

RACLETTE: A cheese dish related to fondue, and perhaps its earliest form. A chunk of cheese that melts smoothly and easily is brought to the table melting under a broiler or in one of the *raclette* stoves for making the dish. It is served with a boiled potato for each diner and side dishes of tiny cocktail onions, dilled pickles, and gherkins. Diners scrape the melting portion of the cheese onto a bit of mashed potato, and add a spicy relish to each bite. The word *racler* means to scrape.

RAGOÛT: A stew made with meat, poultry, or fish, cooked simply with or without vegetables.

RAMEKIN: A small dish designed to both bake and serve individual portions. Also, a cheese dish with bread crumbs or pastry.

RAREBIT: Melted cheese poured onto toast. It is one of a group of dishes called "savory" sometimes served after the sweet at a formal English meal.

RASHER: British. The word "rash" means to slice. A rasher is a slice of bacon or raw ham, cut in any thickness.

RASPINGS: Very finely grated stale bread.

RATATOUILLE: A southern French dish of vegetables cooked together. Usually included are diced onion, sautéed in oil, eggplant, garlic, green peppers, tomatoes, zucchini, flavored with oregano, thyme, rosemary, and basil.

RAVIOLI: Small squares of pasta stuffed with various fillings and served with tomato sauce and grated Parmesan cheese.

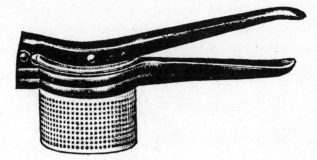

REFRESH: To immerse hot vegetables in ice water to set the color and flavor. The food is then drained and reheated in butter or sauce.

RELISH: A sweet-sour combination of pickled vegetables and fruit. Condiment.

RENDER: To make solid animal fat liquid by melting it slowly in a pan. Rendered lard is creamy and excellent for certain pastries, such as pie.

RENNET: A substance used to coagulate milk for cheese-making, or to set certain puddings, such as junket. See *junket*.

RICER: A colanderlike utensil that forces food through tiny holes, giving potatoes, for instance, the texture of cooked rice.

RICE VINEGAR: A mild white vinegar good for salads and used in Chinese cuisine.

RILLETTES: A *pâté* of pork that is somewhat coarser than liver *pâtés*.

RISOTTO: Italian rice dishes. A *risotto* is rather like a *pilaf*, and may have any number of flavorings.

ROAST: To cook in dry heat, as in an oven, or in a rotisserie.

ROE: Fish eggs. Caviar is the most famous use of roe.

ROLLMOP: A herring, particularly when marinated for a long period with gherkins or other pickles.

ROSE WATER: A liquid flavored with the oil of rose petals. It is used to flavor desserts in Balkan, Indian, and Middle Eastern cooking.

ROULADE: A food rolled around a stuffing. *Paupiettes* is one example. Peach *roulade*, and a stuffed *genoese* is another.

ROUX: This is a paste of butter and flour that is used to thicken almost everything in Western cooking. A white *roux* is the base for white, or cream sauces, such as *sauce béchamel*, used with chicken, vegetables, and fish. A brown *roux* is the base for much Cajun Creole cooking, and for many rich casseroles. The time allowed for the cooking determines the color of the *roux*.

ROYALE: A thin custard cooled and cut into decorative shapes. Used to garnish soups primarily.

RUMP ROAST: A boneless cut from the leg.

RUSKS: Twice-toasted bread or cake.

RUTABAGA: Also called Swede, this is a yellow winter turnip, more strongly flavored than the white and purple turnips of spring. It is excellent with turkey and duck, and in soups and stews.

SABAYON: A sweet egg dessert or sauce, flavored with wine. In Italy it is called *zabaione.*

SACCHARIN: A commercial synthetic sugar substitute. It is said to be 500 times sweeter than sugar.

SACHER TORTE: A famous Viennese cake made of chocolate with apricot filling and dark chocolate icing.

SADDLE: A cut of meat including both loins. In beef, this is considered the finest cut. Also used in reference to lamb and mutton.

SAFFLOWER: A major source of orange dye, oil, and polyunsaturated fat.

SAFFRON: Dried, yellow-orange stamens of the flower of *Crocus sativus.* Saffron is available as threads and as grains. The threads are considered best, though far more expensive.

SAINT-GERMAIN: A soup made of fresh green peas.

SAINT HONORÉ: An impressive dessert of caramel-glazed cream puffs circling cream filling.

SAKE: A wine made from rice.

SALAMI: A highly seasoned dried Italian sausage made of pork or beef.

SALMAGUNDI: A meat-salad dish with hard boiled eggs, beets, anchovies, and pickles.

SALMI: A stew made of leftover or precooked roast game.

SALTPETER: Potassium nitrate, a preservative used with salt for pickling and keeping meat. Said to inhibit sexuality, but this is considered to be a myth.

SANGRIA: A sweetened wine drink made with red wine and fruit and brandy, which is served traditionally with *paella*, in Spain.

SARSAPARILLA: A drink flavoring made with the dried roots of a plant of the *Smilax* genus.

SASHIMI: Raw saltwater fish and other foods sliced paper thin and served decoratively; a native Japanese dish.

SAUERKRAUT: White cabbage cut finely, salted, and fermented in its own liquid.

SAUTÉ: To brown food in a small quality of very hot fat, on top of the stove in a frying pan or sauté pan.

SAVARIN: A yeast-raised sweet cake soaked in Kirsch or rum. French.

SCALD: To heat a liquid, such as milk, to just below boiling so that tiny bubbles begin to rise around the edge of the pan. Also, to quickly dip and remove a solid food from boiling water in order to loosen the skin. Tomatoes are peeled easily when scalded first.

SCALLION: Also known as a green onion, it has a thin white bulb and a long green top. Can be substituted for shallots and for onions.

SCAMPI: Name for shrimp. Also, a dish of shrimp cooked in a rich garlic-butter sauce. Italian.

SCHNITZEL: A thin slice of veal; a cutlet. May be breaded and sauteed, as in *Wiener schnitzel.*

SCONE: A quick bread used as a tea biscuit served hot with butter and jam. British Isles.

SCORE: To make patterned shallow cuts on the surface of foods, either for decoration or to tenderize, or to prevent edges from curling.

SCOTCH WOODCOCK: Scrambled eggs on top of toast, spread with anchovy paste, and garnished with smoked anchovies. This is in the category of dishes called "savories" in Britain.

SEAR: To brown the outside of meat quickly in a hot oven, or in a hot pan on top of the stove.

SEASON: To add salt, pepper, herbs, and/or other seasonings. Seasoning is a critical aspect of food preparation. The best cookbooks instruct the cook to "season to taste," since no recipe can be more than a guideline.

SELF-RISING FLOUR: Flour that is premixed with salt and leavening.

SEMOLINA: A by-product of milled flour, these large wheat grains are used to make couscous, pasta, puddings, or as a thickening agent.

SEVICHE: White sea fish pickled in lime juice. South American.

SHAD: A seafish that spawns in fresh water. Most popular for its delicate roe, it can be used as is fresh herring or mackerel.

SHALLOTS: An herb with a garlic-onion flavor, smaller and milder than an onion, but resembling garlic cloves.

SHEEPSHEAD: A fish found along the Atlantic coast; it has white flesh that is well-flavored and lean.

SHEETING: Stage at which sugary jams, candies, and other preserves will jell; 220 to 222 degrees on a candy or jelly thermometer. Syrup falling from a spoon dipped into the boiling kettle will sheet at this stage, rather than run off the spoon in a stream or fall off in rapidly forming individual drops. This is the signal to remove the kettle from the heat. See also "About Preserving and Freezing," Section IV.

SHEPHERD'S PIE: A meat pie with a mashed potato crust.

SHERBET: A frozen sweet made with fruit juice that originated in the Middle East almost before recorded history.

SHIRR: Applies to eggs baked in buttered ramekins and usually topped with cream. Some versions also call for bread crumbs.

SHORT: The description of any pastry with a high content of fat. Fat makes pastry tender and flaky. Shortbread is a good example.

SHORTBREAD: A butter-rich crumbly cookie, Scottish, that breaks easily but keeps for weeks sealed into a cookie tin and stored in a cool place.

SHORTENING: A general name for all fats, especially solid vegetable fats.

SHRED: To cut into long narrow strips, usually with a grater or sharp knife. Today, shredding is often accomplished with the aid of a food processor.

SHORTBREAD

Yield: About 2 dozen

2 cups sifted all-purpose flour
¼ teaspoon baking powder
¼ teaspoon salt
1 cup butter
½ cup superfine sugar

1. Sift the dry ingredients together into a large bowl.
2. Cream the butter and the sugar in a food processor or with an electric mixer. Stir in the flour and chill for 30 minutes.
3. Preheat the oven to 350 degrees.
4. Turn the dough out onto a floured board, and pat it into a round about ¼ inch thick. Cut into 2-inch squares, or shape into rounds, and place on an ungreased cookie sheet. Bake for 20 to 25 minutes, or until golden brown.

SHRUB: An alcoholic drink made with rum or brandy and a sweetened fruit syrup.

SIEVE: To separate coarse particles by passing them through a wire screen.

SIFT: To lighten ingredients and remove lumps, by putting them through a fine sieve or sifter. In baking, all dry ingredients may be sifted together. Sifted flour is apt to be greater in volume, lighter in content, than unsifted.

SIMMER: To heat liquid to just below boiling, 195 degrees, where bubbles form on the sides of the pan and the liquid barely moves.

SIRLOIN: The front part of the loin of beef. This is near the hip, thus a little less tender but still excellent for roasting.

SKIM: To remove anything floating on top of a liquid, either fat or frothy scum, that forms in the early stages of boiling meats and vegetables.

SLOE: A wild plum used to flavor sloe gin, a Dutch alcohol. Also, a cultivated plum used for jams and jellies.

SMOKE: To preserve meat or fish by slowly drying in the smoke of a fragrant hardwood fire.

SMORGASBORD: A buffet meal with a variety of hot and cold dishes.

SNOW PEAS: The immature sugar pea which has a tender, edible pod in its early stages. Also called Chinese peas, or pod peas.

SOBA: Japanese buckwheat flour noodles.

SODA: Bicarbonate of soda; a leavening agent used in early baking recipes, particularly with buttermilk, sour milk, cream, fruits, or chocolate. Any of these, when heated with soda give off a gas that causes the dough to rise.

SODA WATER: A sparkling water produced by adding carbon dioxide, often in the form of bicarbonate of soda.

SOFT PEAKS: The term used to describe egg whites beaten to form peaks, but still soft enough so the peaks fold or curl over, not yet at the stage described as "stiff" or "dry."

SOUFFLÉ: A sweet or savory dish made with beaten egg whites. It is served hot or cold, and has innumerable variations, from chocolate to spinach.

STORING EGG YOLKS

Save unused egg yolks by putting them in a small glass jar with a tight-fitting lid and covering them with water or milk. They'll keep for a few days in the refrigerator and can be added to whole eggs when making scrambled eggs.

SOYBEAN CURD: See *tofu*.

SOYBEAN SAUCE: A sauce made of fermented soybeans and wheat. It is very salty and some form of it is used in the cooking of most Eastern countries.

SPAGHETTI: Long, thin strings of pasta. Specifically, it is of medium or thin dimension.

SPAGHETTI CARBONARA: Hot spaghetti noodles tossed with beaten eggs and a mixture of cream, grated cheese, bacon (or *pancetta*), salt, and pepper, which has been slightly thickened by cooking.

SPICE: An aromatic plant substance, generally bark or berry, used to flavor foods.

SPINY LOBSTER: Crustacean lacking claws, but otherwise like a large American lobster.

SPONGE CAKE: A cake made without shortening and leavened only with eggs.

SPRAT: A small herring found in European waters. It is served smoked but can be eaten fresh, grilled, or fried.

SPRING ONIONS: See *scallion*.

SPROUTS: The young growth of any seed. Certain sprouts make tasty and nutritious salads, for instance, bean sprouts or alfalfa sprouts.

SPROUTING: Sprouting is to cause seeds to germinate for use in cooking or salads.

SQUAB: Young commercially raised pigeons.

SQUID: A relative of the octopus, and a popular food in fish dishes in the Mediterranean.

STAR ANISE: A star-shaped spice used in Oriental cooking. It is used by some as a substitute for the bay leaf.

STEAM: To cook indirectly by setting food on top of boiling water in a covered pot.

STEEP: To let stand in boiling hot water so flavor may be extracted.

STEW: Long, slow cooking in liquid at low heat, an especially good way to cook tough cuts of meat.

STIFF PEAKS: Egg whites beaten until they are stiff enough to stand on their own. They have a glossy moist look when just right, and stand upright when the beater is lifted from the bowl.

STIR: To mix with a circular motion.

STIR-FRY: Flash-cooking method of the Far East, in which food cut into quick-cooking bite-sized pieces are put into a little hot oil in a concave-shaped, very hot utensil, usually a wok, and stirred until tender, which takes a matter of minutes.

STOCK: The liquid made from a simmering of water and meat, poultry, vegetables, or fish. In fine cuisine, good broth or stock is used instead of water in making casseroles and soups, to braise vegetables, and in preparing sauces and gravies. Meats most commonly used to make stocks are chicken, veal, and beef, and combinations of these.

STRUDEL: A German pastry of paper-thin flaky dough, filled with a sweet or savory mixture, often apple.

STUFFINGS: Seasoned filling for meat, poultry, fish, vegetables, or leaves.

SUET: The fat surrounding the kidneys and loin of an animal. It is used in stuffings, mincemeat, and plum pudding.

SUKIYAKI: Japanese dish of thinly sliced meat and vegetables, cooked quickly in a little broth, and heaped in a big plate in the center of the table. Diners help themselves with chopsticks.

SUPRÊME: A French term used to describe a boned chicken breast.

SUSHI-MESHI: Japanese vinegared rice, decorated beautifully, and served with slices of raw fish.

SWEAT: A method of cooking vegetables in simmering butter; also called "fat steaming."

SWEET AND SOUR: A term used to describe a dish or sauce combining sugar and vinegar. Used in Chinese, Jewish and German cooking, and sometimes in Italian.

SWEETBREADS: The glands of animals. Calf and lamb sweetbreads are preferred.

SYLLABUB: A drink made of frothy milk and alcohol, usually wine, served on festive occasions in the past.

TABASCO: A very small hot red pepper. Also, the sauce made from it.

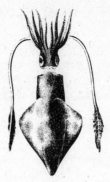

TABLE D'HÔTE: A complete meal of specific courses offered at one set price. Also, *prix fixe*.

TABOOLI/TABOULE: A Middle Eastern mint salad made with cracked wheat, tomatoes, parsley, lemon juice, onion, and olive oil.

TACO: A fried tortilla folded around a filling.

TAGIATELLE: Wide egg noodle.

TAHINA: A paste made from crushed sesame seeds and used to flavor Middle Eastern dishes. When combined with a little oil, it is used as a spread on bread.

TAMALE: A cornhusk spread with cornmeal and filled with chili-seasoned chicken, beef, or cheese, then rolled and steamed. This is a delicacy in the southwestern United States, exacting to prepare and very subtle and delicious.

TAMARI: A type of soy sauce.

TANGELO: A fruit that is a cross between a grapefruit and a tangerine.

TARO: A tropical food plant whose potatolike root is the basis for *poi*, a staple of Polynesian cooking.

TEMPURA: Japanese dish of vegetables and fish, including shrimp, dipped in batter, deep fried, and served with a sauce.

TERRINE: An earthenware covered dish often decorative or in animal shapes, used for cooking meatloaf or a *pâté* of minced meat, poultry, or liver.

THIMBLEBERRY: A wild raspberry.

TOAD IN THE HOLE: An English name for meat, sausage, or lamb cutlets baked in batter. Also, an egg, sautéed in a hole cut from a piece of bread.

TODDY: A hot alcoholic drink made of spirits, usually rum, hot water, sugar, and lemon.

TOFU: Smooth cakes of curds made from the milklike liquid of cooked soybeans and water.

TONKA BEAN: The fruit of a South American tree with a single seed that is dried and used to make bitters or as a substitute for vanilla. Also used in potpourris and sachets.

TORTILLA: A round flat Mexican corn or wheat flour bread.

TOSS: To turn food by tossing in the air in a saute pan (pancakes) or in a bowl (salad).

TOURNEDO: A small thick slice of beef fillet, considered of the choicest quality; often served with a sauce.

TREACLE: The British word for molasses.

TRIFLE: A sweet pudding made with leftover sponge cake moistened with sherry, topped with jam, almonds, and layered with custard and/or whipped cream. It may be decorated with angelica and candied cherries. Italian *zuppa inglese*, meaning, English soup.

TRUFFLE: Any of the subterranean edible fungi of the genus *Tuber*. Prized in French cooking for its aroma, and used in luxury dishes, particularly *pates* of goose liver.

TRUFFLE, CHOCOLATE: A sweet chocolate specialty from Flanders made with hot melted bittersweet chocolate mixed with beaten egg yolks, butter, rum, and cream. The mixture is cooled, then rolled in cocoa powder.

TRUSS: To tie poultry, game or meat together firmly with string to keep extremeties from burning or drying out, or portions of meat from separating from the main body of the roast during cooking.

TUREEN: A large, deep bowl with a lid, used to serve soup.

TURN-OVER: A circle or square of pastry folded over to encase a sweet or savory filling. Apple turnovers are a popular example.

TUTTI-FRUTTI: A preserve of sweet fruits. It is made in a crock where layers of fruit, covered with sugar are laid down as they ripen during the season, stirred daily, and covered with brandy. Tutti-frutti is used to make puddings, ice cream, and as a topping for some desserts.

UNMOLD: To remove food from its container, usually a decorative mold. Gelatin and fatty dishes can be unmolded by setting briefly in hot water, then reversing over the serving dish.

UPSIDE-DOWN CAKE: A cake with fruit placed on the bottom of the pan, topped by batter. After baking, the cake is turned upside down, and served with the fruit on top.

VANILLA: An essential flavoring that comes from the pod of a tropical vine, an orchid that climbs, *Vanilla planifolia*. It is commonly used in the United States as vanilla extract; it is also sold powdered or by the whole pod. In Europe, the pod is used to flavor sugar which is then used in baking.

VANILLA SUGAR: Sugar flavored by vanilla beans. To make vanilla sugar, fill a large jar with sugar, break a vanilla bean in three pieces, press it into the sugar, and leave for several weeks.

VEAL: The meat of a two- or three-month-old beef calf. The meat is finer grained than beef, and pink where beef is red. A popular meat in Italy.

VEGETABLE OR SPAGHETTI SQUASH: A winter squash, 4 to 7 pounds, whose inner flesh, when cooked, is very like spaghetti. Pierce the skin, and boil 20 to 30 minutes, or bake at 350 degrees for 1 to 1¼ hours, depending on the size. Then break

the squash open, draw out the spaghettilike strands, and season and sauce as you would spaghetti.

USE REAL VANILLA

Experts agree that real vanilla is worth the price you pay. The seemingly high cost is due to the fermentation and curing required. Green vanilla beans are dried in the sun, turned, brought inside to cure, and returned to the outdoors in a process that takes six months to complete. The extract is made by macerating the beans in a solution of 35 percent alcohol.

Most of the world's vanilla is exported from Madagascar, Java, and Tahiti. Madagascar exports 80 percent while Java exports about 19 percent and Tahiti only 1 percent. Mexico produces beans, but does not export them.

Beans from Madagascar are preferred by some as those from Java are picked and cured differently. Java beans are picked before they have ripened and are then cured over a fire, lending a slightly smoky taste and a somewhat thinner flavor.

The dark bottle is a custom and is not essential to preservation. The glass is important, however. Vanilla will keep indefinitely when stored in glass as long as it is not exposed to extreme cold or heat.

VENISON: Meat of deer. The most popular game meat in America.

VERMICELLI: A very thin pasta, often packaged in loops.

VERMOUTH: A white *apéritif* wine of France, sweet or dry.

VERONIQUE: Usually means garnished with white grapes.

VERT-PRE: A green herb sauce; also, a garnish of straw potatoes and watercress served with grilled meat.

VICHISSOISE: A cold soup made with leeks, potatoes, and cream.

VINAIGRETTE: A dressing of oil and vinegar often seasoned with herbs and mustard. It is used for marinating cooked leftover vegetables to turn them into an *hors d'oeuvres*. With a lot of fresh parsley added, it makes a delicious sauce for cold meat, particularly tongue and beef.

VINTAGE: A word given to the harvest of grapes relating to the year of the harvest and wine production.

VITICULTURE: The study of grape growing.

VOL-AU-VENT: A puff pastry shell filled with creamed chicken, shrimp, mushrooms, or other savory ingredients. Literally, "fly in the wind." The allusion is to the lightness of the dish.

WAFER: A thin, sweet biscuit.

WAFFLE: A light, thin batter cake baked in a special grill called a waffle iron. Basic batter is the same as for pancakes.

WATER BISCUIT: A crisp cracker that is unseasoned and goes well with cheese and butter, and *consommé*.

WATER CHESTNUT: A tuber grown for its moist crunchy texture, and mild taste. It is a staple in Oriental cooking.

WATERCRESS: A green leafy little plant that grows only in running water, and has peppery leaves prized by epicures for salads and garnishes.

WATERZOOI: A rich Belgian chicken or fish soup made with wine.

WHIP: To beat quickly. The instrument may be a fork, a whisk, or an electric beater.

WHISK: In cooking, a tool made of wire loops used for beating.

WILD RICE: A native American grain that grows wild along lake and river banks and is prepared like rice. It is scarce, expensive, and delicious, especially as stuffing for fowl or game.

WOK: A metal bowl that is broad and has handles; used in Chinese cooking, and particularly for stir-frying or flash-cooking.

WORK: In cooking, this means to knead or mix gently with the fingers.

YOGURT WITH EGGS

Yogurt gives extra lightness to an omelet and makes it particularly tender. Use 1 tablespoon of yogurt for every 2 eggs. Beat well and cook as usual. It will do as much for scrambled eggs.

Information from the Daisyfresh Yogurt Company.

YAM: A starchy root vegetable that has a wide variety of shapes and colors. It is sweet, though less so than the sweet potato, which it resembles in appearance and flavor. The flesh of the yams sold in America are generally paler than the sweet potato.

YARROW: An aromatic herb used in flavoring omeletes, stews, and salads.

YEAST: A leavening agent which comes in cakes or dried in granules. It was isolated from the desert peoples' sourdough bread by the ancient Egyptians, who used it to make risen bread.

YOGURT: Eastern curdled or cultured milk dish with custardlike consistency used in main dishes, in sauces, and in desserts.

YORKSHIRE PUDDING: A popoverlike pastry cooked in roast beef drippings, this is one of the great British inventions. When cooked successfully, it puffs as high as a giant popover, and is crusty and savory with the natural gravy of the roast.

YORKSHIRE PUDDING

Serves 4 to 6

¼ cup fatty drippings from a just-cooked roast beef, or ¼ cup
    vegetable oil, or ¼ cup butter
    1 cup cold milk
1 cup all-purpose flour
½ teaspoon salt
2 large cold eggs

1. Preheat the oven to 400 degrees.

2. Put a large heavy cast iron sauté pan in the oven to heat. During the last few minutes the pan is heating, add the drippings to the pan and let them heat.

3. While the pan is in the oven, combine the milk, flour, salt, and eggs in a mixing bowl. Beat with an electric beater for 4 or 5 minutes.

4. Remove the heated pan with the drippings from the oven, close the oven door to maintain temperature, and pour the batter into the pan all at once.

5. Return the pan to the oven and bake for 20 minutes without opening the oven door. Reduce the oven temperature to 350 degrees and bake for 20 minutes longer, or until the pastry is well browned. Serve at once—or the pudding will fall.

ZABAIONE: A rich Italian custard made by beating egg yolks until they are lemon-colored, then adding sugar and Marsala.

ZEST: The colored part of a citrus fruit rind.

ZUPPA INGLESE: Italian version of the trifle.

ZWIEBACK: A biscuit or rusk that has been twice baked.

4 GUIDE TO BUYING AND STORING FOODS

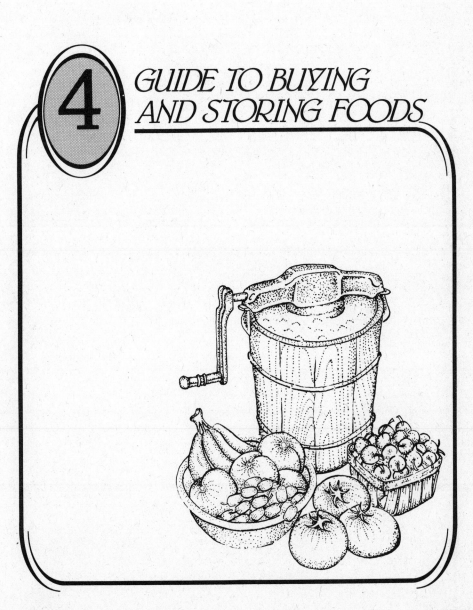

SELECTING THE BEST

The quality of the ingredients selected for a meal has as much to do with the success of the end product as does the method selected for cooking them. The best way to learn how to select superior vegetables, meats, fish, and other fresh foods, is to be born into a family of chefs or devoted food buffs. While still knee-high to a carving knife, you come to understand talk about the relationship between freshness (or ripeness), and the snapability of beans (or the tenderness of steak), and what it means when a fish's eyes aren't as shiny as yours.

The next best way to learn to select good quality from poor, and fresh from stale, is to have a vegetable garden and live near a slaughter house and a fish pier. By the simple act of getting close to where it all begins, you learn how things are when they are at their freshest. You also learn to respect the seasons of foods, and not to ask of yellowing ears of corn shipped from Texas in January what you can expect from the farmer's roadside stand in late August.

Another way to know good from poor is to look for the grading stamps the USDA places on foods that are gradable.

GUIDE TO AMOUNTS OF SOME FOODS TO BUY FOR 25 AND 100 SERVINGS

Food	Approximate size of serving	25 servings	100 servings
APPETIZERS:			
Tomato or fruit juice	½ cup	2 46-oz. cans	8 46-oz. cans
Fruit cocktail	½ cup	1 No. 10 can	4 No. 10 cans
SOUPS:			
Ready to serve soups	1 cup	1½ gal.	6 gal.
MEATS:			
Beef round, bone out, for roasting	4 oz.	9 lb.	34 lb.
Ham, bone out, cured, rolled	4 oz.	10 lb.	40 lb.
Ground beef, for meat patties	4 oz.	6 lb.	25 lb.
POULTRY:			
Turkey, ready-to-cook, for roasting	4 oz.	13 lb.	53 lb.
Chicken, ready-to-cook, small fryers	¼ bird	7 birds	25 birds
SEAFOOD:			
Fish, fillets for baking, frying, or broiling	4 oz.	10 lb.	40 lb.
VEGETABLES:			
Canned vegetables	½ cup	1¼ No. 10 cans	5 No. 10 cans
Frozen vegetables	½ cup	5-6 lb.	20-24 lb.
Carrots, for cooking	½ cup	7 lb.	25 lb.
Cabbage, for cooking	½ cup	6¼ lb.	25 lb.
Potatoes, for boiling	1 medium	9 lb.	34 lb.

GUIDE TO AMOUNTS OF SOME FOODS TO BUY FOR 25 AND 100 SERVINGS

Food	Approximate size of serving	25 servings	100 servings
SALADS:			
Cabbage for coleslaw	½ cup	4 lb.	16 lb.
Potatoes for salad	½ cup	4 lb.	16 lb.
DESSERTS:			
Pie	⅙ of pie	4 pies	17 pies
Sheet cake	3" x 3"	1¼ pans 12" x 18"	4¼ pans l2" x 18"
Ice cream, bulk	No. 12 scoop (½ c.)	1 gal.	4 gal.
FRUITS:			
Canned fruits	½ cup	1 No. 10 can	4 No. 10 cans
BEVERAGES:			
Coffee, urn grind	1 cup	⅔ lb.	2½ lb.
Coffee, instant powdered	1 cup	1 2-oz. jar	1 8-oz. jar
Coffee, instant freeze dried	1 cup	¾ cup	3 cups
Tea	1 cup	1½ oz.	6 oz.
Punch	½ cup	1 gal. (scant)	3¼ gal.
OTHER:			
Butter or margarine	1 pat (1 tsp.)	½ lb.	2 lb.
Crackers	2 crackers	½ lb.	2 lb.
Salad Dressing	1 tbsp. (scant)	1½ cups	6 cups

From *Food for Us All*, USDA, 1969.

RECOMMENDED STORAGE TIMES FOR FOODS AFTER PURCHASE[1]

CANNED GOODS (stored in a cool, dry place)
citrus fruits, citrus juices, shrimp, berries, sauerkraut, and tomatoes .... 6 months
canned soups, meats, poultry, fish, other vegetables and fruits .... 1 year
evaporated milk (should be inverted every 6 weeks to prevent
settling out of solids) .... 1 year

MAYONNAISE, PEANUT BUTTER, AND OILS (stored in cool, dark place;
after opening, in refrigerator) .... 2 months

NONFAT DRY MILK (stored in cool place, in tightly covered container) several months

PERISHABLE FOODS (stored in refrigerator at 35° to 38°F.)[2]

    DAIRY PRODUCTS
        milk, cream, cottage cheese, cream cheese 3 to 5 days
        hard cheeses (tightly covered) several weeks
        butter and margarine (tightly covered) 2 weeks

    EGGS 1 week

    FRUITS, RIPE (uncovered)
        berries, cherries, tomatoes 1 to 2 days
        apricots, grapes, pears, peaches, plums, rhubarb 3 to 5 days
        apples 1 week

    MEATS
        ground meat, variety meat, stew, poultry, fish, leftover cooked meat 1 to 2 days
        roasts, steaks, and chops 3 to 5 days

    VEGETABLES (in crisper or plastic bags)
        asparagus, broccoli, brussels sprouts, corn, leafy vegetables 1 to 2 days
        cabbage, cauliflower, snap beans, celery, carrots 3 to 5 days

FROZEN FOODS (stored at 0°F. or lower)[3]
    fruits and fruit juice concentrates 8 to 12 months
    vegetables 8 months
    ground meat 2 to 3 months
    beef and lamb roasts, whole poultry 8 to 12 months
    pork and veal roasts 6 to 8 months
    pork, cured 2 months
    ice cream 1 month
    fish, fatty (mackerel, salmon, swordfish, etc) 1 to 3 months
        lean (haddock, cod, etc.) 4 to 6 months

[1] Storage times given are the recommended times for maintenance of good quality and nutritive value.
[2] For safe handling and storage of perishable foods, do not let stand at room temperature. Refrigerate leftovers promptly.
[3] Frozen foods stored above 0°F. have a much shorter storage life.

MEAT AND FOWL STORAGE

Meat	Fresh, uncooked, refrigerated	Cooked, refrigerated	Frozen, uncooked	Defrosted, refrigerated	Frozen, cooked	Defrosted, refrigerated
BEEF						
large cuts	4 days	3 days	6 mo.	2 days	3 mo.	2 days
steaks	3 days	2 days	6 mo.	2 days	2 mo.	2 days
pieces in gravy (stews, etc.)	---	3 days	---	---	2 mo.	2 days
small pieces	2 days	2 days	4 mo.	2 days	1 mo.	1 day
ground	1 day	1 day	4 mo.	1 day	---	---
marrow bones	4 days	---	6 mo.	1 day	---	---
marrow	2 days	6 days	2 mo.	1 day	---	---
other bones	2 days	---	6 mo.	1 day	---	---
corned beef	---	5 days	1 mo.	5 days	2 mo.	5 days

MEAT AND FOWL STORAGE

Meat	Fresh, uncooked, refrigerated	Cooked, refrigerated	Frozen, uncooked	Defrosted, refrigerated	Frozen, cooked	Defrosted, refrigerated
BEEF						
chipped beef	2 weeks	2 days	---	---	---	---
fat	7 days	---	6 mo.	2 days	---	---
VEAL						
large cuts	3 days	3 days	3 mo.	1 day	3 mo.	2 days
pieces in gravy	---	3 days	---	---	2 mo.	2 days
slices, chops	2 days	2 days	1 mo.	1 day	1 mo.	1 day
ground	1 day	1 day	1 mo.	1 day	---	---
bones	2 days	---	6 mo.	1 day		
LAMB						
large cuts	3 days	3 days	6 mo.	2 days	3 mo.	2 days
shanks	2 days	3 days	4 mo.	2 days	3 mo.	2 days
chops	2 days	2 days	4 mo.	1 day	1 mo.	1 day
pieces in gravy	---	3 days	---	---	4 mo.	2 days
ground	1 day	1 day	3 mo.	1 day	---	---
PORK, FRESH						
large cuts	3 days	3 days	4 mo.	2 days	3 mo.	2 days
chops	3 days	2 days	3 mo.	2 days	1 mo.	1 day
spareribs	3 days	2 days	4 mo.	2 days	---	---
ground	1 day	1 day	3 mo.	1 day	1 mo.	1 day
fresh fatback	6 days	---	12 mo.	6 days	---	---
lard	2 mo.	---	12 mo.	1 mo.	---	---
PORK, CURED						
ham (whole or half)	7 days	7 days	3 mo.	6 days	---	---
ham steaks	4 days	3 days	1 mo.	4 days	---	---
spareribs	3 days	4 days	3 mo.	4 days	---	---
bacon, sliced, in sealed wrap	7 days	2 days	1 mo.	1 day	6 weeks	1 day
bacon, slab bacon	2 weeks	2 days	3 mo.	3 days	6 weeks	1 day
Canadian, slices	3 days	1 day	3 weeks	1 day	---	---
Canadian, whole	7 days	5 days	6 weeks	2 days	---	---
salt pork	1 mo.	---	1 year	3 weeks	3 mo.	2 days
salted fatback	1 mo.	---	1 year	2 weeks	3 mo.	2 days
SAUSAGE						
fresh	7 days	---	6 mo.	2 days	---	---
cooked	2 weeks	---	6 mo.	2 days	---	---
bologna	5 days	---	3 mo.	2 days	---	---
frankfurters	1 day	---	3 mo.	2 days	---	---
liverwurst	7 days	---	---	---	---	---
POULTRY						
chicken	2 days	2 days	6 mo.	2 days	1 mo.	2 days
chicken, cut up	2 days	2 days	3 mo.	2 days	1 mo.	2 days
chicken pieces in gravy	---	3 days	---	---	3 mo.	2 days
duck	3 days	2 days	6 mo.	2 days	1 mo.	2 days
goose	3 days	3 days	6 mo.	3 days	3 mo.	2 days
turkey, whole	3 days	3 days	6 mo.	3 days	3 mo.	2 days

turkey, cut up	3 days	3 days	3 mo.	2 days	1 mo.	1 day
guinea hen	2 days	1 day	2 mo.	1 day	1 mo.	1 day
quail	2 days	1 day	2 mo.	1 day	1 mo.	1 day
Rock Cornish game hen	2 days	1 day	2 mo.	1 day	1 mo.	1 day
squab	2 days	1 day	2 mo.	1 day	1 mo.	1 day
poultry livers, whole	2 days	1 day	2 mo.	1 day	---	---
poultry livers, ground	1 day	---	---	---	---	---
gizzards	3 days	2 days	3 mo.	2 days	2 mo.	1 day
hearts	3 days	2 days	3 mo.	2 days	2 mo.	1 day
bones	2 days	---	1 mo.	1 day	---	---
turkey, smoked	7 days	---	6 mo.	2 days	---	---
capon, smoked	4 days	---	6 mo.	2 days	---	---
chicken, smoked	3 days	---	6 mo.	2 days	---	---

GAME

rabbit	2 days	2 days	3 mo.	2 days	2 mo.	2 days
venison, after hanging	4 days	4 days	3 mo.	2 days	3 mo.	2 days

VARIETY MEATS

brains	2 days	2 days	3 mo.	1 day	---	---
heart	3 days	6 days	6 mo.	1 day	4 mo.	1 day
kidneys	2 days	4 days	6 mo.	1 day	1 mo.	1 day
liver	2 days	1 day	4 mo.	1 day	---	---
sweetbreads	2 days	1 day	4 mo.	1 day	---	---
tongue, fresh	3 days	3 days	6 mo.	3 days	4 mo.	1 day
tongue, smoked	8 days	4 days	6 mo.	5 days	4 mo.	2 days
tripe	2 days	2 days	4 mo.	1 day	1 mo.	1 day
oxtails	3 days	4 days	2 mo.	2 days	3 mo.	1 day
calf's feet	2 days	4 days	4 mo.	2 days	2 mo.	2 days
pig's feet	2 days	4 days	4 mo.	2 days	2 mo.	2 days

BEEF CHART

Wholesale Cuts of Beef and Their Bone Structure

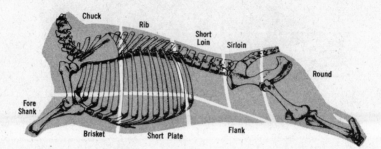

BEEF

In beef, color relates to aging. Older, or "well-hung" meat is considered best, but rumors that the finest steaks are so old they are growing green mold are denied by authorities. The head meat buyer for Gristede's, a New York Supermarket chain says, "Cut the mold off and you can eat the meat—but I don't recommend meat that old." M. Lobel & Sons in Manhattan, one of the world's most esteemed butchers, recommends you avoid meat that has a deep-red color, and choose instead meat whose color is a light cherry-red.

Another color rule applies when you are buying ground meat. Color here is affected by percentages of fat included. Ground beef that is very pink is about 70 percent lean; 30 percent fat is the maximum allowed. When the ground beef is redder than pink, content of lean is probably 80 percent. When the ground beef is very red, content is probably 90 percent lean.

Ground round has almost no fat. Pressed into a patty, it can make a good "steak". Sauté over high heat, and melt a pat of butter on the top when it is finished. Ground chuck makes the best hamburgers, meatloaf, and meatballs because the meat is tasty and has a high fat content. The inbetween, or 80 percent ground beef or ground round make the best sauces—meat sauce, chili, and so on.

The sketches and labels on the following pages will sort out much of the confusion that exist over which cut is which.

Retail Cuts of Beef and Where They Come From

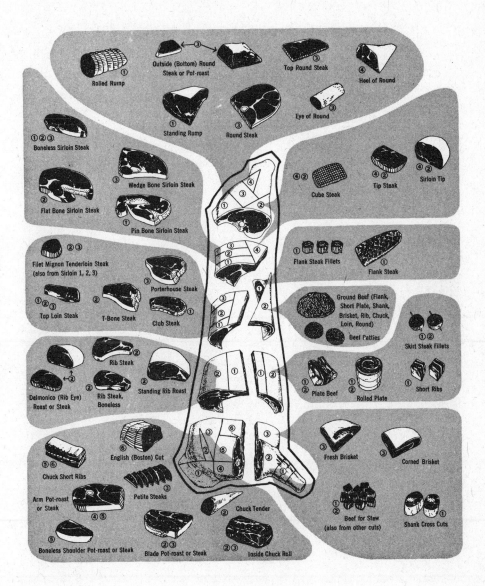

Rolled Rump ①

Outside (Bottom) Round Steak or Pot-roast ③

Top Round Steak ③

Heel of Round ④

Standing Rump ①

Round Steak ③

Eye of Round ③

Boneless Sirloin Steak ①②③

Wedge Bone Sirloin Steak ③

Cube Steak ④②

Tip Steak ④②

Sirloin Tip ④②

Flat Bone Sirloin Steak ③

Pin Bone Sirloin Steak ①

Filet Mignon Tenderloin Steak (also from Sirloin 1, 2, 3) ②③

Porterhouse Steak ③

Flank Steak Fillets ①①①

Flank Steak ①

Top Loin Steak ①②③

T-Bone Steak ②

Club Steak ①

Ground Beef (Flank, Short Plate, Shank, Brisket, Rib, Chuck, Loin, Round)

Beef Patties

Skirt Steak Fillets ①②

Rib Steak ②

Standing Rib Roast ②

Plate Beef ②

Rolled Plate ②

Short Ribs ①

Delmonico (Rib Eye) Roast or Steak ②

Rib Steak, Boneless ②

English (Boston) Cut ⑥

Fresh Brisket ③

Corned Brisket ③

Chuck Short Ribs ⑤⑥

Petite Steaks ③

Arm Pot-roast or Steak ④⑤

Chuck Tender

Beef for Stew (also from other cuts) ①②

Shank Cross Cuts ①

Boneless Shoulder Pot-roast or Steak

Blade Pot-roast or Steak ②③

Inside Chuck Roll ②③

MEATS: WHAT TO BUY, HOW TO COOK IT

BEEF

Name, Retail	Name, Wholesale	Description	Recommended Cooking Methods	Price Ranges
Arm Steak or Roast	Chuck Round	less tender; lean, dry roast with bone in or out; the steak has a small round bone	braise, stew, grind	economy
Blade Steak or Roast	Chuck Shoulder	less tender, with good flavor bone in or boneless roast, steak Also called: T-bone roast, chuck blade roast, center cut blade roast, blade cut pot roast or steak, T-bone steak, blade steak, Texas broil, cross-rib steak, fluff steak, patio steak, barbecue steak	braise, stew, pot-roast, if the steak is prime barbecue or sauté	moderate to economy
Boiling Beef	Plate, Shank, Neck	needs tenderizing, long cooking to flavor soups, beans, stocks	stew, boil	economical to moderate
Boneless Rolled Chuck Roast	Chuck	a tender roast boned, rolled and tied; usually around 3 lbs. Also called: cross-rib roast, Diamond Jim roast	braise, stew; roast if prime	moderate
Bottom Round	Round	less tender, lean, boneless, used as steak, roast, stew, and ground beef. Steaks called: Swiss steaks, minute steak, cube steak, sandwich steak, breakfast steak	stir-fry; if prime, roast, braise, stuff	moderate
Brains		considered a delicacy		
Brisket	Chuck	less tender, used for corned beef. It is flavorful and juicy. A new type has been developed that can be roasted.	sauté first, then boil, stew, braise	economy
Chateaubriand	Tenderloin Sirloin	very tender; extra thick 2-3" steak; good with sauce	sauté, broil	luxury
Chicken Fried Steak	Top or Bottom Round	thinly sliced steak cut to dip in a seasoned coating	sauté	moderate
Chipped Beef	Any	paper thin slices of salty dried beef; 1-2 oz. per person	cream, use in casseroles	moderate to expensive

Name	Origin	Description	Cooking	Price
Chuck Steaks	Chuck	flavorful; less tender 3/4 - 1" thick	braise, sauté	moderate
Chuck Tender Roast	Chuck	tender high quality lean roast usually 2-3 lb.	braise, broil, barbecue	moderate
Club Steak	Short Loin and Rib	Delicious very tender steak 3/4 - 1" thick for stuffing. Be careful not to confuse with cheaper rib steak. Also called: Jewish filet, chuck filet, Jewish tenderloin, medalion roast, Delmonico.	sauté, broil	expensive
Corned Beef	Brisket Round	see Brisket	boil with herbs 3-4 hours	moderate
Cube Steak Minute Steak	Top Butt, Round Chuck	needs tenderizing, a thin lean cut usually mechanically tenderized or pounded	sauté, grill	moderate
Delmonico Steak		see Club Steak	sauté, broil	expensive
Eye of Round	Round	a tender lean roast usually 4-6 lbs. also cut as a breakfast or sandwich steak	braise; if prime, sauté or broil	expensive
Filet Mignon	Tenderloin	a choice luxury cut, very tender small steak often sliced thin and flattened or cut in cubes for brochettes	sauté, broil, grill	expensive; luxury
Flanken	Rib Plate	German name for short ribs	see Short Ribs	moderate
Flank Steak	Flank	less tender; a lean flat boneless steak used for London broil	braise, broil, sauté	expensive
Ground	Beef	can have 33% fat; allow for shrinkage	meatloaf, patties	economy
	Chuck	15% fat, best all around, juicy	meatloaf, burgers	economy to moderate
	Round	best for sauces, to make sure of quality ask for top or bottom round roast and then grind	lasagne, meatloaf, sauces, steak tartare	moderate
	Sirloin	very lean, good for meat patties but the pan must be greased	steak tartare	expensive

MEATS: WHAT TO BUY, HOW TO COOK IT

BEEF

Name, Retail	Name, Wholesale	Description	Recommended Cooking Methods	Price Ranges
Heart		a tasty piece not as delicate as veal or pork, outstanding nutritional value	stuffed and braised, or cut and stewed	economy
Heel of Round Roast	Round	less tender; boneless roast	braise, stew	moderate to economy
Jerky	All	dried beef; salty, leatherlike strips good for snacks, backpacking	no cooking	expensive
Kansas Cube Steak	Top Loin	very tender & tasty prime steak cut from the shell. Also called New York strip	sauté, grill, broil	expensive to luxury
Kabobs	Chuck Sirloin or Top Round	tender, cut into 1 inch cubes for skewers	marinade, grill, broil	expensive
Kidney		less tender, strong flavor	soak in milk 2 hrs., then only braise	economy
Liver		once unacceptable, now with new breeding techniques it is smaller and more flavorful	braised or simmered in wine	economy
London Broil	Flank	see Flank Steak		
New York Strip	Top Loin	a shell steak from the tenderloin; excellent for saute as in steak *au poivre*	sauté, broil, grill	very expensive
Oxtails	Tail	a bony cut that is excellent for soups, stocks	braise, stew	economy
Pastrami	Brisket	a popular deli cut	rinse and braise, boil	moderate

Cut	Section	Description	Cooking Methods	Cost
Plate	Plate	less tender, stringy, used for ribs or with other meats	stew, braise	economy
Porterhouse	Short Loin	large luxury cut with T-bone separating strip and tenderloin, 1½″, usually 2 lbs.	sauté, broil	luxury
Pot Roast	Chuck Round Rump	any meat that is moist-cooked	sear, then braise or stew	moderate to economy
Prime Ribs, Rib Roast, or Standing Rib	Rib	excellent and popular thick tender roast of ribs; very moist and well marbled with fat cut into various sizes with or without short ribs	roast	luxury
Rib Eye Roast or Delmonico Steak	Rib	the center eye of the rib, a boneless tender steak	sauté, broil	very expensive
Round Steak	Round	a boneless versatile tender steak also called: breakfast steak, sandwich steak, Swiss steak, London broil, chicken fry, Salisbury steak, chili beef, barbecue steak, roulades, sukiyaki, steak tartare	sauté, broil, braise	moderate to expensive
Rump Roast	Rump	less tender, chewy, flavorful roasts, steaks, kabobs	roast, braise broil, grill	moderate to expensive
Salisbury Steak	Round	ground beef round patties	broil, grill, sauté	less expensive
Short Loin	Loin	most tender; very fine section usually devoted to steaks	sauté, broil	very expensive luxury
Short Ribs	Chuck, Rib, Plate	the small ends of rib with tender, succulent meat; use as ribs, stewed, or in soups; great stew meat	braise, barbecue, stew, boil	moderate
Sirloin	Loin	excellent flavor though not as tender as short loin, cut as steaks with or without bone	grill, roast, sauté	expensive; luxury
Sirloin Tip	Loin	roasts, kabobs; less tender and less costly than other cuts	roast, sauté, grill	expensive to moderate
Skirt Steak	Rib Plate	less tender, often tenderized commercially	braise, broil	moderate

MEATS: WHAT TO BUY, HOW TO COOK IT

BEEF

Name, Retail	Name, Wholesale	Description	Recommended Cooking Methods	Price Ranges
Standing Rib Roast		see Prime Rib	roast	luxury
Standing Rump Roast	Rump	moderately tender slightly bony roast; can be rolled and tied	braise	moderate
Stew	Chuck	boneless lean meat cut into 1½″ cubes	stew, braise	economy to moderate
Striploin Steak or Roast	Short loin	tender, succulent shell steak found as part of club, T-bone, porterhouse, New York strip	sauté, broil, grill	expensive
Sukiyaki	Round	specialty cut of very thin small slices of top round	stir-fry	moderate
Swiss Steak	Round Chuck	indicates a cooking style	dip in flour, sear, then braise in liquid; or sear, then bake at 375° for 50 minutes; slice thin against the grain	moderate
T-bone Steak	Short Loin	a thick flavorful tender and popular steak	broil, sauté	expensive
Tenderloin Steak or Filet Mignon	Beef Filet	extremely tender though it can be bland and does well with sauce	broil, sauté	luxury
Tongue		a delicate, nutritious meat	boil with herbs 2-3 hours, skin, slice thinly	moderate
Top Round Roast	Round	most tender part of the round, cut for steaks, roasts, ground beef, kabobs	broil, sauté, braise, barbecue, grill, roast	moderate

Cut	Description	Cooking method	Price
Top Sirloin	also called New York cut sirloin	sauté, broil	expensive
Sirloin			
Tournedo	a small tenderloin steak (wrapped in bacon) very tender	broil, sauté	luxury
Tenderloin			

Servings

1/3 lbs. per person boneless
1/2 lbs. per person bone-in

VEAL

Veal is the young of beef, a luxury meat since it is killed early, and not everyday fare at most supermarkets. Roasts are apt to be dry and best used stuffed. Veal hasn't had a chance to develop fat of its own so basting is in order. It is one of the most popular meats in Italian cuisine, where a little is used to go a long way, and that brings the cost down per portion. Veal shoulder cubes are relatively moderate in price and are the main ingredient in many elegant French, as well as Italian, casseroles. Shank and cross shank are delicious in stews and soups and quite inexpensive though not always available. The breast of veal, braised or roasted and basted with herbs and spices and barbecue sauce can be wonderfully savory fare.

VEAL

Name, Retail	Name, Wholesale	Description	Recommended Cooking Methods	Price Ranges
Arm Steaks	Shoulder	tender steaks also cut as a roast; premium quality	sauté or fry steak; braise or stew roast	less expensive because of bones
Birds (paupiettes)	Leg	very tender eye of cutlet, boned and pounded flat to roll and stuff	braise	expensive
Blade Steaks	Shoulder	tender steaks, also can be cut as a roast	sauté or fry steak; braise or stew roast	less expensive because of bones
Boned Shoulder	Shoulder	less tender, often stuffed, rolled, and tied	braising, stews	moderate
Breast	Breast	least tender; bone in or out often a pocket is cut for stuffing; also cut into riblets and spareribs	very long slow braising, stews	moderate
Center Leg	Rib	very tender, bone-in	long slow roasting with a coat of oil or bacon	expensive
Crown Roast	Rib	showpiece with the most tender meat; make a stuffing for the center	slow roast, basting well	luxury; allow 2 chops per person
Cutlet or Round Steak	Leg	very tender; a thin slice of leg with the tiny marrow bone left in	sauté or fry	expensive but no waste
Foreshank	Shoulder	needs tenderizing, a bony cut that has a very good taste	long slow braising, soup, stock	economy to moderate
Ground	Variety	the heel of round, flank, shank meat, or neck meat used in loaves and pâtés with pork or beef	bake, grill, poach	moderate
Hind Shank	Shoulder	a bit nicer than the foreshank; excellent for stocks	long slow braising, soups	economy

VEAL

Name, Retail	Name, Wholesale	Description	Recommended Cooking Methods	Price Ranges
Liver		pale pink when really "baby" and fresh; a great delicacy; good *pâté*	sauté, but only until pink	luxury
Loin chops	Loin	a very tender chop likened to the porterhouse or T-bone	sauté, braise, broil and baste well	expensive
Loin Roast	Loin	most tender; ask the butcher to crack the bones	slow roast, baste, braise	very expensive
Neck	Shoulder	least tender; superior for stocks and jellied veal	braise, stew	economy
Rack	Rib	a roast of rib chops; very tender as a roast, bone in or out; also used for chops	slow roast with basting; sauté chops	expensive
Shank Half of Leg	Leg	less tender than center leg, but still good quality	braise	expensive to moderate
Saddle		an extremely tender roast with bone in or out; luxurious and impressive	roast	luxury
Sweetbreads		highly valued for their delicate flavor	blanch first, then sauté, fry, roast	

Servings

⅓-½lb. per person boneless
½-¾lb. per person bone-in

LAMB CHART
Wholesale Cuts of Lamb and Their Bone Structure

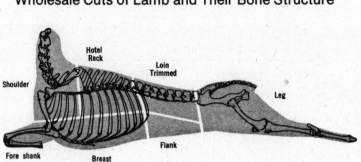

LAMB

Lamb is the young of sheep (mutton). Mutton rarely appears on the American market, though it is the staple meat in the British Isles. The smaller the lamb, the better, and usually the smaller lambs are more costly. However, the days when lamb appeared on the market only in spring (*navarin printannier* is one of the great French casseroles, a celebration of spring lamb) are gone. Today sales of lamb at off-season and sales of larger animals often make lamb one of the most advantageous roasts. If you know how to use that usually useless bit of leg (the shank) that butchers often hide under the roast in lamb packages, a leg of lamb is especially economical. The shank makes a delicious stew or soup. Neck pieces of lamb and lamb breast are among many cuts that make delicious stews and soups.

Retail Cuts of Lamb and Where They Come From

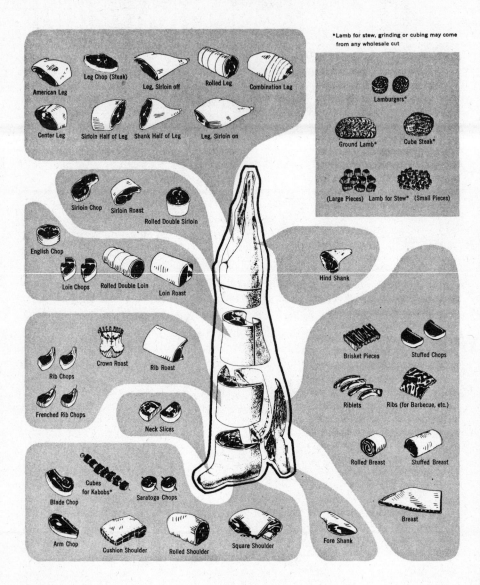

*Lamb for stew, grinding or cubing may come from any wholesale cut

American Leg
Leg Chop (Steak)
Leg, Sirloin off
Rolled Leg
Combination Leg
Center Leg
Sirloin Half of Leg
Shank Half of Leg
Leg, Sirloin on

Lamburgers*
Ground Lamb*
Cube Steak*
(Large Pieces) Lamb for Stew* (Small Pieces)

Sirloin Chop
Sirloin Roast
Rolled Double Sirloin
English Chop
Loin Chops
Rolled Double Loin
Loin Roast
Hind Shank

Rib Chops
Crown Roast
Rib Roast
Frenched Rib Chops
Neck Slices

Brisket Pieces
Stuffed Chops
Riblets
Ribs (for Barbecue, etc.)

Blade Chop
Cubes for Kabobs*
Saratoga Chops
Arm Chop
Cushion Shoulder
Rolled Shoulder
Square Shoulder
Fore Shank
Rolled Breast
Stuffed Breast
Breast

LAMB

Name, Retail	Name, Wholesale	Description	Recommended Cooking Methods	Price Ranges
Arm Chops	Shoulder	less tender	braise, broil	moderate
Baby Lamb		a whole lamb, 15-20 lbs., usually about a month old	roast in a hot quick oven (450°) 10-15 min. per lb.	very expensive
Breast Pocket Roast	Breast	a humble, less tender, popular roast when boned and rolled with a pocket for stuffing	braise	economy
Blade Chops	Shoulder	less tender with a small round bone	broil or braise	moderate
Crown Roast	Rack	a glamorous presentation of rib chops tied in a circle	roast	luxury
Cushion Shoulder	Shoulder	long boneless roll of meat	roast	expensive
English Chops	Loin	a large, thick (2") chop with the kidney attached	broil, sauté	luxury
French Rib Chop	Rack	a small rib chop used in gourmet dining	broil	expensive to luxury
Hothouse Lamb or Pascale Lamb	Whole	raised under artificial conditions for the Easter feast; slaughtered at 2-4 weeks	barbecue whole roast; stuff and roast; braise	luxury
Kabobs	Leg	leg of lamb boned and then cubed; also ground; popular for Middle Eastern dishes	marinate, then barbecue, grill	moderate to expensive
Kidney Chops	Loin	a hearty chop with kidney attached	sauté, broil	luxury
Kidney		a delicacy, must be cleaned and soaked; fresh	use in casseroles	moderate
Leg	Leg	the most popular roasting piece either whole or cut into roast, or boned and butterflied	roast, braise, broil if butterflied	expensive yet moneywise

LAMB

Name, Retail	Name, Wholesale	Description	Recommended Cooking Methods	Price Ranges
Leg Chops	Leg	a 1½" steak or chop	braise, broil	expensive
Liver		delicate and tasty as calves liver but not well known so it can be economical	sauté, broil, or roast whole	economy
Loin	Loin	the most choice lamb cut there is (a T-shaped bone with meat on both sides), sold as roasts or chops	broil, roast, sauté	expensive to luxury
Arm Chops	Shoulder	less tender	braise, broil	moderate
Loin Chop	Loin	most tender chop (the eye of the loin with a small T-bone)	broil, sauté	expensive to luxury
Neck	Shoulder	a sweet meat good for stewing or boned and ground	bake, braise, stew, use in soups	economy
Noisettes	Loin	loin chops that are boned, trimmed, and rolled usually with bacon	grill, roast, braise	very expensive
Rack or Rib Roast	Loin	a long series of rib chops makes a popular roast	roast, broil, braise	luxury
Riblets	Breast	rather sinewy, but tasty; small ribs: allow 3-5 per person	braise, stew, barbecue	economy to moderate
Rolled Double Lamb Roast	Loin	a delicate easy-to-slice roast that is boned, rolled, and tied	roast	luxury
Shank Half of Leg	Leg	the less tender half of the leg, but easiest to carve; small, attractive	roast, grill	very expensive
Shoulder Square	Shoulder	less tender, juicy, and tasty meat, usually boned and rolled	roast, braise	moderate
Sirloin Half of Leg	Leg	the most tender half of leg; it is a small roast with some bone	roast	very expensive

Sirloin Chops	a tender and flavorful chop usually cut to any thickness; also called lamb steak		moderate to expensive
Loin			
Double Loin	very elegant roast includes both loins and the bone with both kidneys	broiled, braised	luxury

Servings

$1/3$-$1/2$ lb. per person boneless
$1/2$-$3/4$ lb. per person bone-in

PORK CHART

Wholesale Cuts of Pork and Their Bone Structure

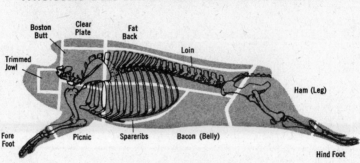

PORK

Pork is one of the sweetest and has long been one of the least expensive of meats. (The pig, by the way, is said to be the creature closest to man in physiology.) Pork should be inexpensive, since it is slaughtered young and grows rapidly on inexpensive foods. However, you have to shop carefully to get a good buy, even in pork. Pigs feet (sweet little white trotters), pigs knuckles (smoked or fresh), and other economy pieces make delicious stews and soups. Pork steak, pounded thin, makes a fine *schnitzel* at a fraction of the price of veal scallops usually used for this dish. Pork calories are surprisingly low, if you don't eat the fat around the chop.

The fresh meat of a young pig is grayish pink, and changes to a light rose color as the animal gets older. Both the fat and the lean of pork is softer than that from either beef or lamb, and it is also more oily to the touch. (This was the lard used by our grandmothers for making pies and cakes, long before vegetable shortenings became available.) The lean of pork should be fine-grained, velvety, firm, and the bones in young animals will be red, spongy, and small. Pork is the least difficult meat to buy for quality because this country produces animals of such all-round quality that there are few things for the shopper to be concerned about.

Retail Cuts of Pork and Where They Come From

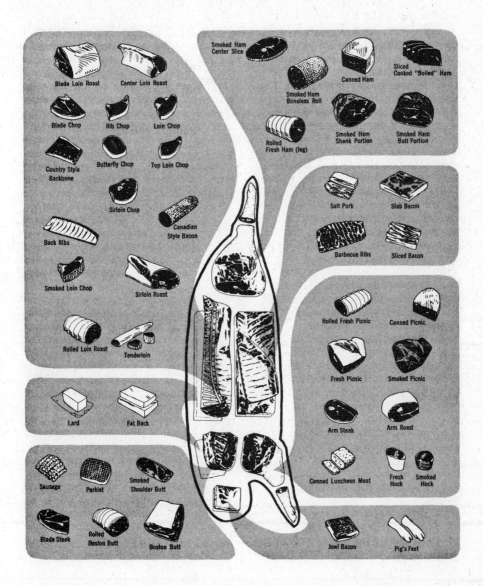

PORK

Name, Retail	Name, Wholesale	Description	Recommended Cooking Methods	Price Ranges
Arm Chops	Shoulder	less tender	braise, broil	moderate
Arm Roast of Ham	Shoulder	excellent flavor, meaty, sold fresh or cured	braise, roast	moderate
Bacon Slabs	Side Pork	tender, flavorful cured with salt or smoked	sauté, broil	economy
Blade Chops	Loin	a large meaty chop of fresh meat	braise	moderate
Blade End Roast or Rib End Roast	Loin	the meaty ribs are good for barbecue; roast the loins, or grind	roast, barbecue, grill, stir-fry	a good buy especially in summer
Blade Steak	Shoulder	a steak made from the Boston butt	braise, grill	moderate
Boneless Smoked Shoulder Butt	Shoulder	very lean rich meat cured or smoked, also fresh called a "cottage role"	braise, roast, broil	moderate
Boston Butt	Shoulder	less tender meat, very lean with a bone	braise, roast	moderate
Center Loin Roast or Rib Roast	Rib, Loin	most tender; an excellent roast for stuffing	roast, braise	moderate to expensive
Canadian Bacon	Loin	a smoked eye of loin; very tender, very little fat	sauté, broil, bake	expensive
Center Cut Roast or Steak	Leg	a roast from the heart of the leg; very little waste	roast; always braise steaks	moderate
Country-style Rib	Loin, Blade End	a blade end roast prepared by butterflying for barbecue	braise, grill, marinade	economy to moderate
Country Ham	Leg	a delightful taste, very different from processed hams; good texture, well cured or fresh	roast, if too salty soak in cold water 2 hrs.	luxury

Cut	Primal	Description	Cooking Methods	Cost
Fat Back	Loin	plain white rich fat sold for larding meat, boiling, or lining *pâtés*		hard to find; economy
Ham Butt	Leg	a desirable cut as it is boneless; sold fresh or cured	roast, braise	moderate
Ham Shank	Leg	the bony end cut of leg	roast, braise	economy
Ham Steak	Leg	lean fine-grained slices from an already cooked ham	sauté, bake, broil, boil	moderate
Hocks	Neck, Shoulder	sold fresh or cured; a tasty meat best in soups, beans, vegetables	braise, stew, soup	economy
Arm Chops	Shoulder	less tender	braise, broil	moderate
Kidneys		these tender sweet pieces of meat are hard to find	soak in milk for 1 hour, then broil, braise, sauté	economy
Liver		very good flavor with a high fat content; good for grinding	sauté or mix ground with other meats	economy
Loin Chop or Butterfly Chop	Center Loin	a small bit of tenderloin lies on one side of this T-bone chop; good for stuffing	broil, sauté, braise	moderate
Loin Roast	Loin	always sold fresh; a tender, excellent roast with a small bone	roast	expensive
Picnic Ham	Shoulder	less tender; more often smoked than fresh; smaller than a regular ham	braise, boil, roast, baste with sweet liquid	economy
Pigs Feet and Pork Hocks	Leg	pickled or fresh	simmer or pickle, great in soups, headcheese	economy
Rib Chops	Center Loin	a tender, humble chop with a long rib bone	braise, broil, roast	moderate
Rolled Loin Roast	Center Loin	any loin roast that is boned, rolled, and tied	roast, braise	moderate
Salt Pork		a fatty cut treated with a brine or salt cure; used to flavor stews (*coq au vin*, beans, chowder)	blanch before using; sauté, stew	economy

PORK

Name, Retail	Name, Wholesale	Description	Recommended Cooking Methods	Price Ranges
Sirloin Chops	Center Loin	a chop from the front part of the sirloin roast	braise, broil, barbecue	expensive
Spareribs	Loin	the breast and rib bones with the tender, moist connective meat	barbecue, broil, roast, marinate	moderate
Tongue		medium size: one person could eat 1 or 2	braise, boil with sauer-kraut	moderate
Tenderloin	Loin	the most tender section; it is very small and usually attached to the sirloin—sometimes sold separately	roasting, kabobs, broil, sauté, braise	luxury

Servings

1/3 lbs. per person boneless
1/2 lbs. per person bone-in

SAUSAGES AND DELICATESSEN PRODUCTS

Pork and some other meats are made into a number of delicatessen products, cooked, often savory, items to serve cold or use in other dishes. Since delicatessen products require manpower to produce, they are generally more expensive than untreated meats, but almost essential to sandwich-oriented lives and gourmet dining.

Sausages are a somewhat different category. Inexpensive, these descendents of farm cookery, where everything "but the squeal" was used, add savory accents to stews and work wonders for bean soups.

Packaged sausages can sit around the supermarket counter for some time, so look closely before you buy. If the casings look wizened, or the ends have a trampled look, or the skin has a greasy look (as though the fat is oozing), skip the package and look for a better one.

Here is a list describing some of the almost infinite number of sausages produced in America today, or imported from abroad, especially from Germany, which is sometimes considered the home of *charcuterie*—pork products.

SAUSAGE AND DELICATESSEN MEATS

NAME	DESCRIPTION	COMMENTS
Alesandri	Italian garlic sausage of the salami group	cured pork, seasoned
Alpino	American version of salami	
Arles	French salami	pork, beef, garlicky
Beef Bologna	beef, garlic-seasoned	regular bologna has beef, too
Beerwurst	German smoked salami	beef, pork, garlicky
Berliner	mild pork and beef sausage	

SAUSAGE AND DELICATESSEN MEATS

NAME	DESCRIPTION	COMMENTS
Biroldo	blood sausage	
Blood Sausage	cooked lamb and pork tongues and pork blood	
Bloodwurst	pork blood, pork, ham fat, jellied meats, seasonings, diced onions	also called blood sausage and blood pudding
Bockwurst	white sausage made of fresh pork, veal, chives, parsley, eggs, and milk	should be well cooked
Bologna	mild cooked, smoked, ground pork and beef sausage	almost as popular as hot dogs; favorite sandwich meat
Boterhamwurst	Dutch pork and veal sausage	should be well cooked
Bratwurst	pork and veal, or pork links with herbs and seasonings	this is fully cooked
Braunschweiger	smoked liver sausage with eggs and milk	
Calabrese	Italian pork salami with red peppers	
Cervelat	dryish salami-type sausage	sometimes called summer sausage
Chipped Beef	dehydrated beef, very thin, that has been smoked	sometimes called dried beef
Chorizo	Spanish dry link pork sausage, spicy, hot	
Chub Bologna	emulsified beef, pork, bacon	
Cold Cuts	cooked cold meats sold at delicatessen counters; usually roast beef, baked ham, tongue, corned beef	
Combination Loaf	beef and pork, with peppers and pickles	
Corned Beef	cured, spiced brisket of beef	
Cotto Salami	salami with peppercorns	
Country Sausage	fresh pork, sometimes with beef or veal added	cook or freeze soon
Deviled Ham	ground ham with seasonings	
Dutch Loaf	cold cut of pork and beef	
Easter Nola	salami from Italy, mild, dry, but well seasoned	
Farmer Cervelat	seasoned pork and beef	

Frankfurter	cured, smoked beef or pork, or both, seasoned with pepper, sugar, cloves, coriander, and nutmeg	better known as hot dog or weiner
Frizzes	chopped pork and beef, highly seasoned, dry	
Garlic Sausage	hamlike quality of the frankfurter, but more garlicky	
Genoa Salami	pork sausage made with wine and garlic	
German Salami	smoked salami	
Goettinger	spiced beef and pork, like cervelat, but hard	
Goetborg	Swedish version of cervelat touched with cardamom	
Gothaer	German cervelat, finely chopped pork	
Ham and Cheese Loaf	ground ham with cubes of cheese	
Ham Bologna	includes diced cured pork	
Headcheese	gelatinous dish including chunks of cooked pork	
Holsteiner Cervelat	ring-shaped cervelat	
Hot Dog	another name for frankfurter	
Hungarian Salami	milder than Italian	
Italian Salami	dry, chewy sausage, flavored with red wine, made of pork and strong in garlic	
Italian Sausage	fresh pork, beef seasoned with fennel and wine; may be sweet or hot	cook soon or freeze
Kielbasa	Polish sausage of ground pork and beef, seasoned with garlic	
Knockwurst	large, garlicky frankfurter	
Knoblauch	another name for knockwurst	
Kosher Salami	all-beef salami, garlicky, seasoned with mustard, coriander, and nutmeg	
Land Jaeger	smoked Swiss cervelat that is black and wrinkled	

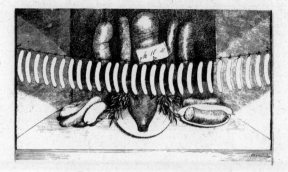

SAUSAGE AND DELICATESSEN MEATS

NAME	DESCRIPTION	COMMENTS
Lebanon Bologna	smoked beef bologna	comes from Lebanon, Pa.
Linguisa	Portuguese pork sausage, brined, garlicked, spiced with cinnamon and cumin	cook well
Liver Loaf	similar to liverwurst	
Liverwurst	cooked, ground pork and liver, flavored with onions and seasonings	
Lola	dry Italian sausage, garlicked, mild	
Lolita	small Lola link	
Longazina	dry Portuguese sausage similar to chorizo	
Luncheon Meats	combinations of beef and pork	
Lyons	dry French pork sausage	
Macoroni and Cheese Loaf	ground pork and beef, with chunks of cheese and macaroni	
Mettwurst	German beef and pork sausage, spiced with coriander, ginger, and mustard; smoked, cured, uncooked	cook well
Milano Salami	Italian salami	
Mortadella	dry sausage of pork, beef, and pork fat, licorice-flavored	
New England Sausage	cooked, chopped smoked pork	
Olive Loaf	bologna-type meat with whole stuffed olives	
Pastrami	flavored like corned beef, cured, smoked plate of beef	popular sandwich meat
Peppered Loaf	pork and beef, with cracked peppercorns	

Pepperoni	dry Italian sausage, beef and pork, peppery	
Pickle and Pimiento Loaf	pork and beef, with pimientos and sweet pickles	
Pinkel	beef, oats, and pork fat	cook well
Polish Sausage	same as kielbasa	
Polony	British version of bologna	
Pork Sausage	coarsely ground pork, seasoned with sage, nutmeg, and pepper	cook well
Salamette	link salami	
Salami	ground pork, beef, seasoned	Italian, French, German variations are flavored to the taste of the country
Salsiccia	Italian sausage, fresh pork	cook well
Scrapple	cooked ground pork with cornmeal flour	Pennsylvania Dutch
Sicilian Salami	Italian salami	
Souse	pork in vinegary jelly with pickles, peppers, and bay leaf	
Smokies	cooked links of peppered pork and beef	
Straussburg	sausage of liver and veal with pistachio nuts	
Summer Sausage	name for dry sausages, cervelat	
Swiss Sausage	bockwurst type	cook well
Thuringer	sausage of pork, with some beef or veal	
Tongue and Blood	calves' tongues, pork fat, pork skins, and beef blood	
Vienna Sausages	cocktail-type frankfurters	
Weiswurst	spicy German sausage of pork and veal	
Wiener	frankfurter, or hot dog	

FISH AND SHELLFISH

Fish and shellfish deteriorate rapidly once dead—that's why the best fish is the fish you buy at the shore. The tables below tell where some of the most popular fish in America is found. Look for these fish in their home regions and the chances are that what you will be buying will be pretty fresh. How can you tell fresh fish? Check the items on the checklist on page 163. But to generalize, shellfish must be eaten the moment it is killed—i.e., lobster must be alive when put into the cooking pot. Oysters must be alive when opened, and the same is true of other shellfish. On the other hand, certain white fish will be good enough one to three days after they have been caught—flounder, for instance, and haddock. However, though they will be good enough a couple of days after being landed, they won't be nearly as good as they are when they are cooked or flash-frozen the moment they are caught.

Buy frozen fish according to brand. Test a package, and if it is without an unpleasant fishy odor and has a good flavor, use that brand again.

You need less fish than meat per portion. A portion of less than a quarter pound, say three ounces, is enough for most appetites.

FISH: WHAT TO BUY AND WAYS TO USE IT

Name	Where Found	Ways to Cook
Amberjack	South Atlantic	Bake, broil, pan-fry
Barracuda	Atlantic, Gulf coast, California	Bake, broil, charcoal-broil
Bass (fresh water)	Most of U.S.	Bake, broil, charcoal-broil, pan-fry
Bluefish	Atlantic and Gulf coasts	Bake, broil
Butterfish (dollarfish, harvestfish)	Atlantic and Gulf coasts	Broil, pan-fry, casserole
Buffalofish (winter carp, fresh water)	East, Midwest	Bake, broil, pan-fry, poach, steam
Burbot (fresh water)	East, Midwest, Northeast	Bake, broil, pan-fry, poach, steam
Carp (fresh water)	Most of U.S.	Bake, poach
Catfish (fresh water)	All but the Pacific	Pan-fry, deep-fry, poach
Chub (mackerel)		
Cod and the many varieties, including scrod, baccalao, lufish, cush	South Atlantic, Gulf coast	Bake, broil, poach, casseroles
Croppies (fresh water)	Great Lakes, Mississippi valley	Broil, pan-fry
Croaker (hardhead)	Middle and South Atlantic coasts	Broil, pan-fry, poach
Cush (cod)		

Drum (black, red)	New York to Texas	Bake, broil, or pan-fry steaks, fillets
Eel	Maine to Texas	Bake, broil, pan-fry, deep-fry, casseroles, soup
Flounder and the many varieties, some called sole, gray sole, lemon sole, fluke or summer flounder; Pacific soles, including petrale or roundnose; California halibut, dab, rock, turbot	Atlantic, Gulf, Pacific coasts	Bake, broil, pan-fry, deep-fry, poach, casseroles
Fluke (flounder)	North Atlantic	Handle as flounder
Haddock has many varieties, including finan haddie, snapper	North Atlantic	Bake, broil, pan-fry, deep-fry, poach, casserole
Hake (whiting)		
Halibut	Atlantic and Pacific coasts	Bake, broil, pan-fry, poach, steam
Herring has many varieties, including bismark, bloater, matjes, kipper, pilchard, rollmop, sardine	Atlantic and Pacific coasts	Bake, broil, pan-fry, marinate, pickle
Kingfish (ground mullet, king, whiting, seamink)	Southern Atlantic and Gulf coasts	Bake, broil, pan-fry, casserole
Lingcod (greenling, blue, white, buffalo)	West Coast	Bake, broil, pan-fry
Mackerel has many varieties including cero, chub, jack or horse mackerel, Spanish, striped	Atlantic and Pacific	Bake, broil, pan-fry, poach
Mullet (jumping, striped or silver mullets)	Atlantic and Gulf coasts	Bake, broil, pan-fry, casserole
Ocean perch (rosefish or redfish)	North Atlantic	Bake, broil, pan-fry, deep-fry, poach

FISH: WHAT TO BUY WAYS TO USE IT

Name	Where Found	Ways to Cook
Pike (giant muskellunge)		
Pickerel	Most Eastern and Central states	Bake, broil, poach
Pollock or Boston bluefish	North Atlantic	Bake, broil, pan-fry, deep-fry, poach
Pompano	Southern Atlantic and Gulf coasts	Bake, broil, pan-fry
Porgies (scup, sheepshead)	North Atlantic; Atlantic and Gulf	Broil, pan-fry; sheepshead may be stuffed and baked
Red snapper	South Atlantic and Gulf coasts	Bake, broil, pan-fry, poach
Rockfish has many varieties including rock cod, red cod	West Coast	Bake, broil, pan-fry, poach
Sablefish	West Coast	Bake, broil, barbecue
Salmon (chinook, sockeye, Kennebec)	Pacific Northwest, North Atlantic	Whole salmon or large chunks: stuff and bake, plank, poach; steaks: broil, pan-fry
Sardines (herring)		
Scup (porgies)		
Sea bass (black, striped, white, or sea trout)	Atlantic Coast	Bake (stuffed or unstuffed), broil, casseroles
Sea squab (swellfish, puffer, blowfish)	North and mid-Atlantic coast	Broil, pan-fry, deep fry, bake, poach
Sea trout (weakfish)		
Shad	Atlantic and Pacific coasts	Bake, broil, pan-fry fillets
Shark	Atlantic and Pacific coasts	Bake, broil, sauté fillets
Skate (rajafish)	Atlantic and Pacific coasts	Poach, casseroles
Smelts (silversides, true)	Atlantic and Pacific coasts, Great Lakes	Bake, broil, pan-fry, deep-fry in batter
Spots (member of croaker family)		
Striped bass	Atlantic, Gulf, Pacific coasts	Bake, broil, charcoal-broil, poach; fry fillets

Sturgeon	North Atlantic and Pacific coasts	Bake, pan-fry, poach, casserole
Sunfish (freshwater)	Midwest and Gulf states	Broil, pan-fry, casseroles
Swordfish	South Atlantic and Pacific	Bake, plank, broil, pan-fry
Trout (freshwater) has many varieties, including brook, lake, rainbow, western	One or another species found in most of U.S. except in very warm climates	Bake, broil, pan-fry
Tuna (tunny, horse mackerel) has many varieties, including bluefin, yellowfin, skipjack, albacore	Atlantic and Pacific coasts	Bake, broil, pan-fry, poach
Whitefish	New England, Great Lakes area	Bake, broil, pan-fry, poach
Whiting (silver hake)	North Atlantic	Bake, broil, pan-fry, deep-fry, poach
Wolffish (catfish)	North Atlantic	Bake, broil, pan-fry, deep-fry, poach

CHECKLIST ON FISH

GOOD FISH

Full, clear eyes
Skin bright
Scales tight
Gills bright red
Flesh firm and elastic; does not keep a dent
 when pressed with the finger
Smells fresh, both inside and at gills
Whole fish sinks in water

Flesh sticks firmly to bones

BAD FISH

Eyes cloudy, wrinkled and sunken
Skin dull or slimy, color pale
Scales loose
Gills yellowish, gray or brown
Flesh soft and flabby and fingerprint remains

Smells stale, spoilage first noticed at gills
Whole fish floats in water
 (when badly decomposed)
Flesh separates from bones easily

Fish and shellfish as purchased	Amount to purchase (ounces)	Fish and shellfish as purchased	Amount to purchase (ounces)
FISH		King crab legs	6
Whole	11	Cooked meat	3¼
Dressed or pan-dressed	8	Canned meat	3½
Fillets, steaks, and		**LOBSTERS**	
chunks	5	In the shell	12
Portions and sticks	3½	Spiny lobster tails	6
Pickled and spiced	3	Cooked meat	3½
Salted	4¼	**OYSTERS**	
Smoked	4½	In the shell	25
Canned tuna	3	Shucked	6½
Canned salmon	3¾	Breaded, raw, or fried	3½
CLAMS		Canned whole	3
In the shell:		**SCALLOPS**	
Hard	21½	Shucked	5
Soft	10½	Breaded, raw or fried	3½
Shucked	6½	**SHRIMP**	
Breaded, raw or fried	3¾	Headless	6
Canned minced clams	3	Peeled and cleaned	5
CRABS		Cooked, peeled,	
In the shell:		and cleaned	3½
Blue	21½	Breaded, raw or fried	3½
Dungeness	12¼	Canned whole	3
Soft-shell	4½		

From *Food for Us All*, USDA 1969

VEGETABLES AND FRUITS

Vegetables and fruits are among the best buys on the market. None are cheap, but by increasing the proportion of vegetables and fruits you serve and lowering the amounts of meats and prepared desserts, you can keep your family in wholesome food with limited calories without attaching your food budget to

WHEN IS A VEGETABLE A FRUIT?

Fruit is the structure that develops from the ovary of a flower after fertilization. Vegetable is a general term for plants whose leaves, flowers, fruits, roots, or stems are edible. The term vegetable is used for those plants that are eaten in the main courses of meals. The general term fruit applies to plants used as appetizers or desserts, or eaten from the hand. Botanically, a tomato is a fruit, and so is a bean.

the rising cost of living. A slightly smaller steak can save a dollar. A slightly larger portion of salad to compensate may be just what your body needs. An apple has 80 calories; a banana 85 to 100. Regular ice cream has 255 calories; rich ice cream has 330.

There are ways to stretch your vegetable and fruit budget dollar. Buy luxury items like asparagus, for instance, in season and use the hard stems you cut off to make asparagus soup and in stews. Buy fruits in season when they are less costly and at their best. Freeze berries with a sprinkling of sugar, and use them off season. Buy good keepers (the squashes, for instance, apples and turnips) in season and store. Shop the buys—carrots year round have been the best buy for years. Try them mashed, instead of potatoes, and for salads. Iceberg lettuce may be blah, but dressing brightens it, and it goes much farther than Boston or Bibb. Use several greens in a salad—that will stretch the expensive ones.

You'll enjoy a higher vegetable content in your meals if you investigate *wok* (Chinese) cookery, and the exotic vegetables in the little greengrocers that have opened in recent years in most cities. Take up Italian cooking, too. Stretch pasta sauces with vegetables—celery and peppers—and cut down on its meat content.

ONION SAVER

When you need only a slice of an onion, take it without peeling the whole. Seal the cut end of the remaining portion with plastic and store in the refrigerator. The skin will help preserve the onion, and it will stay fresh for weeks.

GUIDE TO AMOUNTS OF VEGETABLES TO BUY TO SERVE YOUR FAMILY

	Approximate amount of cooked vegetable obtained from:				
	Frozen vegetables		Canned vegetables (drained)		1 lb. of fresh vegetable as purchased
Vegetable and style	Size of container (ounces)	Cooked, Cups	Size of container (ounces)	Heated, Cups	Cups
Asparagus, cut	10	1¼	14	1⅓	1¾
Beans, green or wax, cut	9	1⅔	15½	1¾	2¾
Beans, lima	10	1⅔	16	1¾	1⅛
Beets, sliced, diced, or whole	---	---	16	1¾	1⅞
Broccoli, cut	10	1⅓	---	---	1½

Explore vegetables you have avoided—turnips, for instance, and the free greens—dandelions and fiddleheaded ferns!

GUIDE TO AMOUNTS OF VEGETABLES TO BUY TO SERVE YOUR FAMILY

	Approximate amount of cooked vegetable obtained from:				
	Frozen vegetables		Canned vegetables (drained)		1 lb. of fresh vegetable as purchased
Vegetable and style	Size of container (ounces)	Cooked, Cups	Size of container (ounces)	Heated, Cups	Cups
Brussels sprouts	10	1 1/2	---	---	2 1/4
Cabbage, shredded	---	---	---	---	2 1/3
Carrots, diced, or sliced	10	1 2/3	16	1 3/4	2 1/8
Cauliflower	10	1 1/2	---	---	1 1/2
Corn, whole kernel	10	1 1/2	[1] 16	1 2/3	---
Kale	10	1 1/8	15	1 1/3	2 2/3
Okra	10	1 1/4	15 1/2	1 3/4	2 1/4
Peas	10	1 2/3	16	1 3/4	1
Potatoes	9	[2] 1 2/3		[3] 1 3/4	
Spinach	10	1 1/4	15	1 1/3	2
Summer squash, sliced	10	1 1/3	2		
Tomatoes			[4] 16	1 7/8	

[1] Whole kernels with liquid; a 12 oz. can of whole kernels, vacuum pack, provides 1 3/4 cups.
[2] French fries.
[3] Mashed.
[4] Undrained.

From *Food for Us All*, USDA, 1969.

STORAGE CHART FOR VEGETABLES

Vegetables can be stored in a cool cellar, attic, garage, or cold room, for as long as a year. Here is a chart prepared by the USDA indicating temperatures at which vegetables last well, and the length of time they can be expected to stay in good form at these temperatures.

Commodity	Temp. °F.	Rel. Hum.	Storage Period	Freezing Point °F.
Jerusalem Artichoke	32	95	3 mo.	27.5
Asparagus	32	90	4 wk.	29.8
Snap Beans	47	90	9 day	29.7
Limas (unshelled)	32	90	18 day	30.1
(shelled)	32	90	15 day	30.1
Beets (topped)	32	95	3 mo.	26.9
(w/tops)	32	95	13 day	26.9
Broccoli	32	95	9 day	29.2
Brussels Sprouts	32	95	4 wk.	
Cabbage	32	95	6 wk.	31.2
Carrots (no tops)	32	95	5 mo.	29.6
(w/tops)	32	95	12 day	29.6
Cauliflower	32	90	3 wk.	30.1
Celery	32	95	4 mo.	29.7
Sweet Corn	32	90	4 day	28.9
Cucumbers	50	95	3 wk.	30.5
Eggplant	50	90	10 day	30.4
Endive	32	95	3 wk.	30.9
Garlic	32	75	8 mo.	25.4
Horseradish	32	95	12 mo.	26.4
Kohlrabi	32	95	4 wk.	30.0
Leeks	32	95	3 mo.	29.2
Lettuce	32	95	3 wk.	31.2

Commodity	Temp. °F.	Rel. Hum.	Storage Period	Freezing Point °F.
Melons				
Watermelon	40	90	3 wk.	29.2
Muskmelon	50	90	2 wk.	28.4
Okra	50	95	2 wk.	30.1
Onions	32	75	8 mo.	30.1
Parsnips	32	95	4 mo.	30.0
Peas	32	90	2 wk.	30.0
Peppers (sweet)	50	90	10 day	30.1
Potatoes	40	90	8 mo.	29
Pumpkins	55	75	6 mo.	30.1
Radishes (w/tops)	32	95	14 day	29.5
(no tops)	32	95	4mo.	---
Rhubarb	32	95	3 wk.	28.4
Spinach	32	95	14 day	30.3
Squash				
Summer	40	95	14 day	29.0
Winter	55	75	6 mo.	29.3
Tomatoes				
Ripe	50	90	12 day	30.4
Mature-green	70	90	6 wk.	30.4
Turnips	32	95	5 mo.	30.5
Vegetable seed	32-50	65	1-10 yr.	---
Dried vegetables		70	1 yr.	---

From *Commercial Storage of Fruits, Vegetables, and Florist and Nursery Stocks*, USDA Handbook No. 66, September 1954.

RIPENING APPLES AND KEEPING THEM

Store slightly underripe apples for 2 weeks or less in temperatures of no more than 60 to 70 degrees to ripen them. Only perfect apples should be stored. Those with bruises will spoil.

STORAGE TIMES FOR FRESH FRUITS IN A REFRIGERATOR

Apples	1 week	Peaches	3 to 5 days
Apricots	3 to 5 days	Pears	3 to 7 days
Blackberries	1 to 2 days	Plums	3 to 6 days
Blueberries	3 to 5 days	Raspberries	1 to 2 days
Cranberries	1 to 2 weeks	Rhubarb	5 to 8 days
Figs	1 to 2 days	Strawberries	1 to 2 days
Grapes	3 to 5 days	Watermelons	5 to 8 days
Nectarines	3 to 5 days		

AMBROSIA

2 large fragrant oranges
3 small ripe bananas
¼ cup confectioners' sugar
1½ cups fresh shredded coconut or canned coconut

1. Peel the oranges, removing all the white membrane, and slice thinly. Arrange in individual cups in layers with sliced bananas. Sprinkle each layer with a little confectioners' sugar and some of the coconut.

2. Top with lots of coconut. Chill well before serving.

SERVINGS IN A CAN

There are three basic can sizes for fruits that are approximately equal to half pint, pint, and quart sizes. These are:

half pint	8 to 8¾ oz	makes 2 servings, ½ cup each
pint	15 to 17 oz	makes 4 servings, ½ cup each
quart	28 to 30 oz	makes 7 to 8 servings, about ½ cup each

From *Food For Us All*, USDA, 1969.

COOKING GUIDE FOR FRESH FRUIT

Kind of Fruit	Amount[1] of Fruit	How to prepare	Amount of water Cups	Amount of sugar Cups	Cooking time after adding fruit Minutes
Apples	8 medium-size	Pare and slice	½	¼	8 to 10, for slices 12 to 15, for sauce
Apricots	15	Halve, pit, peel if desired	½	¾	5
Cherries	1 quart	Remove pits	1	⅔	5
Cranberries	1 pound	Sort	1 or 2, as desired[2]	2	5
Peaches	6 medium-size	Peel, pit, halve, or slice	¾	¾	5
Pears	6 medium-size	Pare, core, halve, or slice	⅔	⅓	10, for soft varieties 20 to 25, for firm varieties
Plums	8 large	Halve, pit	½	⅔	5
Rhubarb	1½ pounds	Slice	¾	⅔	2 to 5

[1] Makes 6 servings, about ½ cup each.
[2] Cranberries make 6 servings with 1 cup water; 8 servings with 2 cups water.
From *Food for Us All*, USDA, 1969.

PEAR SECRET

Pears ripen from the inside out. When a pear seems ripe on the outside, it may well be mushy inside. Choose fruit that is a little firm, and has just a bit of an aroma.

PRESERVING AND FREEZING

Canning is a simple and money-saving procedure for the cook who has a garden or access to produce at wholesale prices. Freezing is faster and easier for the rest of us.

When *canning* most vegetables and fruits, the cleaned, cut-up produce must be blanched for 2 to 3 minutes before packing into scalded canning jars. The jars are then sealed and processed in a large pressure cooker for 20 minutes to an hour, depending on the ingredients (most vegetables, meats, and low-acid foods), or processed in a boiling water bath (many fruits and high-acid foods). Procedures vary according to the specific food being canned. Spoiled canned goods and those improperly handled or processed can be poisonous, so if you want to can, consult a good book on canning and follow the rules precisely.

CHEESE FREEZE

If tightly wrapped, cheese can be stored in the home freezer at 5 F., or below, without impairing its quality. The cheese should be allowed to thaw in the refrigerator for 24 hours before removing the protective wrapping. After freezing, cheese will be slightly crumbly. For the best flavor and texture, serve most cheeses at room temperature.

To *freeze* foods in small batches, use suitable containers designed for freezer storage. Blanch cut-up vegetables 2 to 3 minutes in rapidly boiling water, then plunge into a sinkful of water and ice cubes until thoroughly cool. Drain, pack into containers, and store in the freezer. Your own garden produce handled this way is usually much better in flavor and texture than commercially frozen vegetables. Berries may be lightly sugared, packed into plastic containers, and frozen. Although they may be soft when thawed, they'll be good for sauces and desserts.

RASPBERRY JAM

1 quart hulled raspberries
1¼ cups sugar (approximately)

1. Partially crush the berries in a large kettle over low heat until juices flow freely. Boil rapidly until the juice is reduced by about half.

2. Measure the fruit and return to the kettle with ⅔ cup sugar for each cup fruit. Stir over medium heat until the sugar dissolves, then boil rapidly until jelly thermometer registers 220 to 222 degrees. At this stage, syrup dripping from a spoon dipped into the kettle will sheet as it falls instead of running or falling in individual drops.

3. Remove from the heat, skim away foam, and pour into clean, dry jelly glasses or canning jars. Seal with melted paraffin to exclude all air. Store in the refrigerator.

NOT ALL FRUITS RIPEN OFF THE VINE!

Neither strawberries nor pineapples ripen beyond the state at which they were picked, so don't buy these fruits with a view to storing them until they reach perfection! Avocados that are very green and rock hard will soften, but may rot in the process, so select fruits that are already soft without being mushy.

Jams, marmalades, and relishes are fun to make in small batches. *Jellies* are made of clear juice extracted from fruits and boiled with sugar. *Jams* are chopped or crushed fruits cooked with sugar until thick. *Marmalades* are jamlike preserves made with citrus fruits. *Conserves* are made with two or more fruits. *Preserves* are whole or cut-up fruits cooked in heavy syrup. *Fruit butters* are fruit pulp cooked with sugar and spices until thick. *Relishes* are chopped vegetables or fruits cooked with vinegar. *Pickles* are vegetables and fruits in spicy, vinegary pickling liquids. For long-term storage, all these products except jellies are generally processed in a boiling water bath as are high-acid canned goods. Jellies can be stored by sealing the top with melted paraffin so no air can reach the jelly. However, paraffin may be used to temporarily seal jams and marmalades if they are stored in the refrigerator for no more than a few weeks.

The easiest preserved fruits to make are jams. You need a candy thermometer, a large kettle, and a good recipe. Here are some simple recipes for beginners that show how preserves are made.

STRAWBERRY JAM

Follow the procedure for Raspberry Jam, using 6 cups firm ripe berries, 5 cups sugar, and ⅓ cup strained lemon juice.

BLUEBERRY JAM

Follow the procedure for Raspberry Jam, using 1 quart cleaned blueberries and 1½ cups sugar.

WILD BLACKBERRY JAM

Follow the procedure for Raspberry Jam, using 2 quarts wild blackberries and 4 cups sugar. After the berries have simmered, and before you add the sugar, remove the seeds by pressing the pulp through a strainer.

ORANGE MARMALADE

4 large navel oranges
1 lemon
4 cups water
4 cups sugar

1. Peel the rind from the oranges and lemon so thinly that almost no white shows. Cut away the white pulp from the fruits, seed, and chop. With scissors, cut the rinds into the thinnest possible strips. Let fruit and peel stand overnight with 1 cup water for each cup of fruit.

2. In a large kettle over medium heat, boil the mixture rapidly for 20 minutes, stirring now and then. Measure and for each cup of fruit and juice, add 1 cup sugar. Stirring constantly with a wooden spoon, boil fruit and sugar for 30 minutes.

3. Pour into clean dry jelly glasses or canning jars. Seal with melted paraffin to exclude all air. Store in the refrigerator.

KNOWING YOUR ORANGES

There are many orange varieties, most of them grown in either Florida or California. Generally, you can tell California oranges from Florida oranges because the West Coast varieties have a thicker skin. The thick skin was bred in deliberately to enable the fruit to travel the long distance from the West to the East Coast where the greatest number of orange eaters are to be found.

The Florida oranges are excellent for eating, too, but these thinner-skinned varieties are exceptionally good for juice.

The Navel orange is California's main citrus crop, and the most important variety for eating out of hand. Florida grows more varieties and is known for the Valencia, distinguished by its first-rate juice. The West Coast Valencias are available from late April through October, while those from Florida are marketed from late March through June.

Florida produces a number of other juice oranges available most of the year. The Temple is marketed from January through March, the Hamlin from early October to December and the Pineapple from December through February.

DRYING FRUITS AT HOME

Dehydrators are sold for something between $200 and $300 or more, but the home that has an oven, or the gardener who lives in a very warm climate, can dry without special equipment.

From time immemorial in the Middle East fruits and some vegetables have been dried on flat, sun-baked roofs, a method still followed in southern Italy, New Mexico, and Latin America today.

The key feature of drying equipment is a set of trays on which small fruit, such as figs and dates, are set and then placed in the sun. Wire screens, such as old window screens, are suitable. Cover with cheesecloth. To sun-dry, place the screens where there will be daytime temperatures of 100 degrees Fahrenheit or more. Reflected heat from a tin roof can increase lower temperatures sufficiently to do the job. Bring the drying trays indoors at night if the temperature will drop 20 degrees or more.

Some fruit processors sulphur fruits before drying. Sulphuring consists in burning sulphur and fumigating the fruits on trays over the smoking container. This is said to preserve the color and the vitamin content of the fruit, but not all gardeners who dry produce sulphur fruits.

Fruit also can be dried in the home oven. Turn the heat to as low as it will go—in most stoves, somewhere between 140 and 150 degrees. Above that, you start losing color and vitamins. The difficulty with using a home oven is that it's hard to maintain the low temperatures. Some ventilation is necessary to keep moisture from accumulating, so keep the oven door open a crack.

DRIED FRUIT SOUP *Serves 4 to 6*

This is a faintly sweet, gloriously exotic curried type soup from the Near East, and much to my liking.

¾ pound meaty lamb neck, or lamb shoulder chops
½ cup yellow split peas
1 onion, peeled and chopped
8 cups water
1 teaspoon salt
¼ teaspoon freshly ground black pepper
1 teaspoon ground turmeric
¼ teaspoon saffron threads
¼ teaspoon ground coriander
½ teaspoon ground cumin
¼ cup chopped, pitted dried pruned
¼ cup chopped, pitted dried apricots
1 tablespoon strained lemon juice
Salt

Combine the lamb and all the remaining ingredients, except the fruits, the lemon juice, and salt, in a large saucepan over medium-high heat. Cover, bring to a boil, reduce the heat, and simmer for 1 hour. Add the chopped fruit, and simmer, uncovered, for 30 minutes longer. Lift out the lamb, strip the meat and return it to the soup. Discard the bones. Stir in the lemon juice, reheat for 1 minute and season with salt to taste.

From *A Feast of Soups*, by Heriteau (New York: The Dial Press, 1982).

How long does it take? The answer depends on individual conditions—humidity, primarily, and the moisture in the fruit. White figs can take 10 days to 2 weeks drying on a rooftop. In an oven, overnight drying is possible. One reason fruits to be dried are generally cut up is to expose the maximum moist

surface to the drying elements to shorten the drying time. Some dried foods will achieve an almost crisp texture—thinly sliced bananas, for instance—but most are leathery, and the thicker the fruit and the bigger, the more leathery it will remain even when well dried.

Thinly sliced vegetables dry more quickly than most fruits, since they tend to be smaller. The method is essentially the same.

BUYING AND SERVING CHEESE

The following chart describes the cheeses most commonly found in American markets, along with suggestions for the best ways to serve them. Remember to store cheese in the refrigerator, tightly wrapped in plastic or foil. Most cheeses taste best when allowed to warm to room temperature (about one hour) before serving.

ALL ABOUT CHEESES: WHAT TO BUY; HOW TO SERVE

Name, Origin, Characteristics, and Mode of Serving of Commonly Used Varieties of Cheese

Name	Origin	Consistency and Texture	Color and Shape	Flavor	Basic Ingredient	Normal Ripening Period	Mode of Serving
American pasteurized process	United States	Semisoft to soft; smooth, plastic body	Light yellow to orange; square slices	Mild	Cheddar, washed, colby, or granulated (stirred curd) or mixture of two or more	Unripened after cheese is heated to blend	In sandwiches; on crackers
Asiago, fresh, medium, old	Italy	Semisoft (fresh), medium, or hard (old); tiny gas holes or eyes	Light yellow; may be coated with paraffin, clear or colored black or brown; round and flat	Piquant, sharp in aged cheese	Cow's milk, whole or lowfat	60 days minimum for fresh (semisoft), 6 months minimum for medium, 12 months minimum for old (grating)	Table cheese (slicing cheese) when not aged; as seasoning (grated) when aged
Bel paese	Italy	Soft; smooth, waxy body	Slightly gray surface, creamy yellow interior; small wheels	Mild to moderately robust	Cow's milk, whole	6-8 weeks	As such (dessert); on crackers; in sandwiches, with fruit
Blue, Bleu	France	Semisoft; visible veins of mold on white cheese, pasty, sometimes crumbly	White, marbled with blue-green mold; cylindrical	Piquant, tangy, spicy, peppery	Cow's milk, whole or goat's milk	60 days minimum; 3-4 months usually; 9 months for more flavor	As such (dessert); in dips, cooked foods; salads and dressings
Breakfast, Fruhstuck	Germany	Soft; smooth, waxy body	Cylindrical, 2½ to 3 inches diameter	Strong, aromatic	Cow's milk, whole or lowfat	Little or none (either)	As such (dessert); on crackers; in sandwiches
Brick	United States	Semisoft; smooth open texture; numerous round and irregular-shaped eyes	Light yellow to orange; brick-shaped	Mild but pungent and sweet	Cow's milk, whole	2-3 months	As such; in sandwiches, salads. Slices well without crumbling

ALL ABOUT CHEESES: WHAT TO BUY; HOW TO SERVE

Name, Origin, Characteristics, and Mode of Serving of Commonly Used Varieties of Cheese[1]

Name	Origin	Consistency and Texture	Color and Shape	Flavor	Basic Ingredient	Normal Ripening Period	Mode of Serving
Brie	France	Soft, thin edible crust; creamy interior	White crust, creamy yellow interior; large, medium, and small wheels	Mild to pungent	Cow's milk, whole, lowfat, or skim	4-8 weeks	As such (dessert)
Caciocavallo	Italy	Hard firm body, stringy texture	Light tan surface, interior; molded into distinctive shapes, typically spindle-shaped or oblong	Sharp, similar to provolone	Sheep's, goat's, or cow's milk (whole or lowfat) or mixtures of these	3 months minimum for table use, 12 months or longer for grating	As such; as seasoning (grated) when aged
Camembert	France	Soft, almost fluid in consistency; thin edible crust, creamy interior	Gray-white crust, creamy yellow interior; small wheels	Mild to pungent	Cow's milk, whole	4-5 weeks	As such (dessert)
Cheddar	England	Hard; smooth, firm body, can be crumbly	Nearly white to orange; varied shapes and styles	Mild to sharp	Cow's milk, whole	60 days minimum; 3-6 months usually; 12 months or longer for sharp flavor	As such; in sandwiches, cooked foods
Colby	United States	Hard but softer and more open in texture than Cheddar	White to light yellow, orange; cylindrical	Mild to mellow	Cow's milk, whole	1-3 months	As such; in sandwiches, cooked foods
Cottage, Dutch, Farmers, Pot	Uncertain	Soft, moist, delicate, large or small curds	White; packaged in cuplike containers	Mild, slightly acid, flavoring may be added	Cow's milk, skim; cream dressing may be added	Unripened	As such; in salads, dips cooked foods

Name	Place of origin	Body and texture	Color and shape	Flavor	Kind of milk	Ripening time	Uses
Cream	United States	Soft; smooth, buttery	White; foil-wrapped in rectangular portions	Mild, slightly, acid, flavoring may be added	Cream and cow's milk, whole	Unripened	As such; in salads, in sandwiches, on crackers
Edam	Holland	Semisoft to hard; firm crumbly body; small eyes	Creamy yellow with natural or red paraffin coat; flattened ball or loaf shape, about 4 pounds	Mild, sometimes salty	Cow's milk, lowfat	2 months or longer	As such; on crackers; with fresh fruit
Feta	Greece	Soft, flaky, similar to very dry, high-acid cottage cheese	White	Salty	Cow's, sheep's, or goat's milk	4-5 days to 1 month	As such; in cooked foods
Gammelost	Norway	Semisoft	Brownish rind, brown-yellow interior with a blue-green tint; round and flat	Sharp, aromatic	Cow's milk, skim	4 weeks or longer	As such
Gjetost	Norway	Hard; buttery	Golden brown; cubical and rectangular	Sweet, caramel	Whey from goat's milk	Unripened	As such; on crackers
Gorgonzola	Italy	Semisoft, less moist than blue	Light tan surface, light yellow interior, marbled with blue-green mold; cylindrical and flat loaves	Piquant, spicy, similar to blue	Cow's milk, whole or goat's milk, or mixtures of these	3 months minimum, frequently 6 months to 1 year	As such (dessert)
Gouda	Holland	Hard, but softer than cheddar; more open mealy body like edam, small eyes	Creamy yellow with or without red wax coat; oval or flattened sphere of about 10 to 12 pounds	Mild, nutlike, similar to edam	Cow's milk, lowfat but more milkfat than edam	2-6 months	As such; on crackers, with fresh fruit; in cooked dishes
Gruyère	Switzerland	Hard, tiny gas holes or eyes	Light yellow; flat wheels	Mild, sweet	Cow's milk, whole	3 months minimum	As such (dessert); fondue

ALL ABOUT CHEESES: WHAT TO BUY; HOW TO SERVE

Name, Origin, Characteristics, and Mode of Serving of Commonly Used Varieties of Cheese

Name	Origin	Consistency and Texture	Color and Shape	Flavor	Basic Ingredient	Normal Ripening Period	Mode of Serving
Limburger	Belgium	Soft; smooth, waxy body	Creamy white interior; brownish exterior; rectangular	Strong, robust, highly aromatic	Cow's milk, whole or lowfat	1-2 months	In sandwiches, on crackers
Monterey, Jack	United States	Semisoft (whole milk), hard (lowfat or skim milk); smooth texture with small openings throughout	Creamy; white; round or rectangular	Mild to mellow	Cow's milk, whole, lowfat or skim	3-6 weeks for table use, 6 months minimum for grating	As such; in sandwiches, grating cheese if made from lowfat or skim milk
Mozzarella	Italy	Semisoft; plastic	Creamy white; rectangular and spherical, may be molded into various shapes	Mild, delicate	Cow's milk, whole or lowfat; may be acidified with vinegar	Unripened to 2 months	Generally used in cooking, pizza; as such
Muenster	Germany	Semisoft; smooth, waxy body, numerous small mechanical openings	Yellow, tan or white surface, creamy white interior; cylindrical and flat or loaf shapes, small wheels and blocks	Mild to mellow, between brick and limburger	Cow's milk, whole	2-8 weeks	As such; in sandwiches
Neufchâtel	France	Soft; smooth, creamy	White; foil-wrapped in rectangular retail portions	Mild	Cow's milk, whole or skim, or a mixture of milk and cream	3-4 weeks or unripened	As such; in sandwiches, dips, salads
Parmesan, Reggiano	Italy	Very hard (grating), granular, hard brittle rind	Light yellow with brown or black coating; cylindrical	Sharp, piquant	Cow's milk, lowfat	10 months minimum	As such; as grated cheese on salads and soups

Name	Origin	Texture	Appearance	Flavor	Kind of milk	Ripening	Uses
Port du salut, Oka	Trappist Monasteries	Semisoft; smooth, buttery	Russet surface, creamy white interior; small wheels, cylindrical flat	Mild to robust. Similar to gouda	Cow's milk, whole or lowfat	6-8 weeks	As such (dessert); with fresh fruit; on crackers
Primost	Norway	Semisoft	Light brown; cubical and cylindrical	Mild, sweet, caramel	Whey with added buttermilk, whole milk or cream	Unripened	As such; in cooked foods
Provolone	Italy	Hard, stringy texture, cuts without crumbling, plastic	Light golden-yellow to golden-brown, shiny surface bound with cord; yellow-white interior. Made in various shapes (pear, sausage, salami) and sizes	Bland acid flavor to sharp and piquant, usually smoked	Cow's milk, whole	6-14 months	As such (dessert) after it has ripened for 6 to 9 months; grating cheese when aged
Queso blanco, White cheese	Latin America	Soft, dry and granular if pressed; hard, open or crumbly if pressed	White; various shapes and sizes	Salty, strong, may be smoked	Cow's milk, whole, lowfat or skim or whole milk with cream or skim milk	Eaten within 2 days to 2 months or more; generally unripened if pressed	As such or later grated
Ricotta	Italy	Soft, moist and grainy, or dry	White; packaged fresh in paper, plastic, or metal containers, or dry for grating	Bland but semisweet	Whey and whole or skim milk or whole and lowfat milk	Unripened	As such; in cooked foods; as seasoning (grated) when dried
Romano	Italy	Very hard, granular interior, hard brittle rind	Round with flat sides various sizes	Sharp, piquant if aged	Cow's (usually lowfat), goat's milk, or mixtures of these	5 months minimum; usually 5-8 months for table cheese; 12 months minimum for grating cheese	As such; grated and used as a seasoning

ALL ABOUT CHEESES: WHAT TO BUY; HOW TO SERVE

Name, Origin, Characteristics, and Mode of Serving of Commonly Used Varieties of Cheese

Name	Origin	Consistency and Texture	Color and Shape	Flavor	Basic Ingredient	Normal Ripening Period	Mode of Serving
Roquefort	France	Semisoft, pasty and sometimes crumbly	White, marbled with blue-green mold; cylindrical	Sharp, spicy (pepper), piquant	Sheep's milk	2 months minimum; usually 2-5 months or longer	As such (dessert); in salads; on crackers
Sap Sago	Switzerland	Very hard (grating), granular frequently dried	Light green; small, cone-shaped	Sharp, pungent, flavored with leaves; sweet	Cow's milk, skim, slightly soured with buttermilk and whey	5 months minimum	As such; as seasoning (grated)
Schloss, Castle Cheese	Germany, Northern Austria	Soft; small, ripened	Molded in small rectangular blocks 1½" square by 4" long	Similar to, but milder than limburger	Cow's milk, whole or lowfat and / or casein	Less than 1 month; less intensively than limburger	In sandwiches; on crackers
Stirred Curd, Granular	United States	Semisoft to hard	Varied shapes and styles	Similar to mild cheddar	Cow's milk	1-3 months	Usually used to make pasteurized process cheese
Stilton	England	Semisoft-hard; open flaky texture, more crumbly than blue	White, marbled with blue-green mold; cylindrical	Piquant, spicy, but milder than roquefort	Cow's milk, whole with added cream	4-6 months or longer	As such (dessert); in cooked foods
Swiss, Emmentaler	Switzerland	Hard; smooth with large gas holes or eyes	Pale yellow, shiny; rindless rectangular blocks and large wheels with rind	Mild, sweet, nutty	Cow's milk, lowfat	2 months minimum, 2-9 months usually	As such; in sandwiches; with salads; fondue
Washed curd	United States	Semisoft to hard	Varied shapes and styles	Similar to mild cheddar	Cow's milk	1-3 months	Usually used to make pasteurized process cheese

Descriptions of additional cheeses may be found in *Cheese Varieties and Descriptions*, Agriculture Handbook No. 54, USDA, 1978, Washington, D.C.: U.S. Government Printing Office.

5 BASICS OF COOKING

ROASTING MEATS

Meats are baked in the oven, uncovered, at temperatures ranging between 325 and 425 degrees. Convection ovens do meats well, and slightly more quickly than conventional ovens. Follow the roasting timetable provided with the equipment.

The most important element for success in meat roasting is to choose a meat cut that is suitable for roasting. Tougher cuts can be delicious but should be braised, stewed, or boiled. Each type of meat—beef, veal, lamb, pork—commonly used in American cooking has its own characteristics as well and they are worth studying. An informed cook can buy wisely. The tables on the following page will be helpful in selecting cuts and choosing cooking methods for meats offered at advantageous prices.

Save drippings from the roasting pan to make gravy for the roast, or to use in soups, in braising vegetables, in cooking risotto, and as bouillon to make gravy for other roasts.

The tables for roasting meats are provided by the courtesy of the National Live Stock and Meat Board.

WHEN OVEN TEMPERATURES ARE NOT GIVEN

Very slow oven	250 to 275 degrees
Slow oven	300 to 325 degrees
Moderate oven	350 to 375 degrees
Hot oven	400 to 450 degrees
Very hot oven	475 degrees and up

TIMETABLE FOR THAWING FROZEN MEATS

Cut	40°-5°F. (Refrigerator)	70°-75°F. (Room Temperature)
Steaks, 1 inch	12 hours	2 to 3 hours
Roasts, small	3 to 4 hours per pound	1 to 2 hours per pound
large	4 to 6 hours per pound	2 to 3 hours per pound
Ground meat patties, 2½ inches		1½ to 2 hours

TIMETABLE FOR COOKING LARGE CUTS OF FROZEN MEAT

Cut	Minutes per pound		
	Rare	Medium	Well
BEEF			
Standing rib (roast at 300°F.)	47	55	63
Rolled rib (roast at 300°F.)	53	56	65
Rump (braise)			50
Porterhouse steak (broil)			
1 inch, 1¼ to 2 pounds	21	33	
1½ inches, 2 to 3 pounds	23	38	
2 inches, 2½ to 3½ pounds	33	43	
LAMB			
Leg (roast at 300°F.)			40 to 45
Boneless shoulder (roast at 300°F.)			50
PORK			
Center cut (roast at 350°F.)			50 to 55
Rib or loin end (roast at 350°F.)			70 to 75

TIMETABLE FOR COOKING SMALL CUTS OF FROZEN MEAT

Cuts	Thickness	Total cooking time
BEEF		
Club steak (broil)	¾ inch	24 to 28 minutes
	1 inch	30 minutes
Ground beef patties (panbroil)	1 inch	16 to 18 minutes
LAMB		
Loin and rib chops (panbroil)	¾ inch	15 minutes
	1½ inches	25 minutes
Shoulder chops (braise)	½ inch	20 minutes
PORK		
Chops (braise)	¾ inch	55 minutes

SERVINGS PER POUND TO EXPECT FROM A SPECIFIC CUT OF MEAT

The servings per pound are only a guide to the average amount to buy to provide 3 to 3½ ounces of cooked lean meat. The cooking method and cooking temperature, the degree of doneness, the difference in the size of bone in the bone-in cuts and amount of fat trim are some of the factors that vary and will affect the yield of cooked lean meat.

BEEF

Steaks

Chuck (Arm or Blade)	2
Club	2
"Cubed"	4
Filet Mignon	3
Flank	3
Porterhouse	2
Rib	2
Rib Eye (Delmonico)	3
Round	3
Sirloin	2½
T-bone	2
Top Loin	3

Roasts

Rib, Standing	2
Rib Eye (Delmonico)	3
Rump, Rolled	3
Sirloin Tip	3

Pot-Roasts

Arm (Chuck)	2
Blade (Chuck)	2
Chuck, Boneless	2½
English (Boston) Cut	2½

Other Cuts

Brisket	3
Cubes, Beef	4
Loaf, Beef	4
Patties, Beef	4
Short Ribs	2

Variety Meats

Brains	5
Heart	5
Kidney	5
Liver	4
Sweetbreads	5
Tongue	5

PORK

Chops and Steaks

Blade Chops or Steaks	3
Boneless Chops	4
Fresh Ham (Leg) Steaks	4
Loin Chops	4
Rib Chops	4
Smoked (Rib or Loin) Chops	4
Smoked Ham (Center Slice) Steaks	5

Roasts

Ham (Leg), Fresh, Bone-in	3½
Ham (Leg), Fresh, Boneless	5
Ham, Smoked, Bone-in	3½
Ham, Smoked, Boneless	5
Ham, Smoked, Canned	5
Boston Shoulder (Rolled) Boneless	3
Loin, Blade	2
Loin (Rolled), Boneless	3½
Loin, Center	2½
Loin, Smoked	3
Picnic Shoulder (Bone-in)	
Fresh or Smoked	2
Sirloin	2
Smoked Shoulder Roll (Butt)	3

Other Cuts

Back Ribs	1½
Bacon (Regular), Sliced	6
Canadian-Style Bacon	1½
Country-Style Back Ribs	1½
Cubes (Fresh or Smoked)	4
Hocks (Fresh or Smoked)	1½
Pork Sausage	4
Spareribs	1½
Tenderloin (Whole)	4
Tenderloin (Fillets)	4

Variety Meats

Brains	5
Heart	5
Kidney	5
Liver	4

LAMB

Chops and Steaks

Leg Chops (Steaks)	4
Loin Chops	3
Rib Chops	3
Shoulder Chops	3
Sirloin Chops	3

Roasts

Leg (Bone-in)	3
Leg (Boneless)	4
Shoulder (Bone-in)	2½
Shoulder (Boneless)	3

Other Cuts

Breast	2
Breast (Riblets)	2
Cubes, Lamb	4
Shanks	2

Variety Meats

Heart	5
Kidney	5

From *Teaching about Meat*, National Live Stock and Meat Board, 1972.

USING A MEAT THERMOMETER

A meat thermometer is helpful for the beginner who is uncertain when a roast is done. There are signs: pinkish-red juices flow from meat as they begin to cook, and stop when they are cooked. Legs in birds wobble loosely when moved when the bird is cooked. But until you get a feeling for when "done" is, use the thermometer.

Insert the thermometer into the center of the raw roast, being careful not to touch bone or to sink the point of the thermometer in fat. Place it so you'll be able to read it without opening the oven door (assuming the door is glass).

If you don't have an oven door with a glass panel, don't worry. You can open the oven door to check the temperature. The heat loss will be minimal, and the roast will take just a little longer to cook.

ROASTING BEEF

Beef tenderloin (fillet) is cooked quickly at high heat. Other cuts are cooked slowly at lower heats to preserve their juices. This method results in a roast that is pinkish to its outer edges rather than raw inside and gray outside. The British prefer beef well done, but Americans tend to prefer it medium to rare.

Before you roast the beef, sear it quickly. Heat a large cast iron pan to very hot, grease it with a bit of fat from the roast, and quickly sear (2 to 3 minutes) each side of the roast that shows meat but not fatty surfaces. To sear means to brown quickly. Then place the roast in either the searing skillet, if it is large enough to hold the roast comfortably, or in a roasting pan, uncovered. Rub it with half a teaspoon of curry powder or a teaspoon of fine prepared mustard, and with 1 tablespoon of minced onion, or 1 large clove of garlic, crushed, if you wish. Pepper, but don't salt until the roast is done. Insert the meat thermometer, and place the roast on a rack set just below the middle of the oven.

Twenty to thirty minutes before the roast is done, add ½ to 1 cup of beef stock or bouillon, or drippings, to the roasting pan. This helps to make gravy by dissolving the drippings caramelizing on the bottom of the pan.

Beef tenderloin is the most tender of all cuts, an exquisite piece of meat that should be handled a little differently. There are complicated ways of handling it—*tournedos Rossini* (with *foie gras* and truffles, for instance)—but *au jus*, or *nature*, as the French like to put it, remains the most popular.

FILLET OF BEEF, AU JUS   *Serves 4 to 6*

About 1 ¾ pounds fillet of beef, ends trimmed
Freshly ground black pepper
2 tablespoons butter
Salt

1. Preheat the oven to 425 degrees.

2. Sprinkle the meat with pepper and put the meat in a small roasting pan. Roast for 20 minutes, turning it once during the cooking. Remove any excess fat from the pan and add the butter, rubbing it all over the meat. Cook for another 3 to 6 minutes, according to whether you want it rare or medium rare.

3. Remove the pan from the oven, cover loosely with foil, and allow to rest for 10 minutes before serving. Season with salt and pepper to taste.

TIMETABLE FOR ROASTING BEEF

CUT	OVEN TEMPERATURE	AVERAGE WEIGHT	MINUTES PER POUND	INTERNAL TEMPERATURE OF MEAT
Standing Rib	300° to 325°F.	6 to 8 lbs.	23 to 25	140°F. for rare
			27 to 30	160°F. for medium
			32 to 35	170°F. for well-done
		4 to 6 lbs.	26 to 32	140°F. for rare
			34 to 38	160°F. for medium
			40 to 42	170°F. for well-done
Rolled Rib	300° to 325°F.	5 to 7 lbs.	32	140°F. for rare
			38	160°F. for medium
			48	170°F. for well-done
Rib Eye (Delmonico)	350°F.	4 to 6 lbs.	18 to 20	140°F. for rare
			20 to 22	160°F. for medium
			22 to 24	170°F. for well-done
Tenderloin, whole	425°F.	4 to 6 lbs.	45 to 60 total cooking time	140°F. for rare
Tenderloin, half	425°F.	2 to 3 lbs.	45 to 50 total cooking time	140°F. for rare
Rolled Rump	300° to 325°F.	4 to 6 lbs.	25 to 30	150° to 170°F.
Sirloin Tip	300° to 325°F.	4 to 6 lbs.	30 to 35	140° to 170°F.
		3½ to 4 lbs.	35 to 40	140° to 170°F.

ROASTING VEAL

Veal is the young of beef; it is drier meat, however, that benefits from
rubbing well with lots of butter before roasting. Because the animal has developed little fat, drippings are lean. Augment them by adding chicken or veal
bouillon to the pan 20 to 30 minutes before the roast is done. Sear the roast on
top of the stove, as described for roasting beef, then rub with a little curry, and
pepper well before placing in the roasting pan, uncovered, and setting just below
the middle rack in a preheated oven. Veal is preferred pink—medium to rare—
and is most tender when cooked to this stage.

TIMETABLE FOR ROASTING VEAL

CUT	AVERAGE WEIGHT	OVEN TEMPERATURE	INTERNAL TEMPERATURE OF MEAT	MINUTES PER POUND
Leg	5 to 8	300° to 325°F.	170°F.	25 to 35
Loin	4 to 6	300° to 325°F.	170°F.	30 to 35
Rib (rack)	3 to 5	300° to 325°F.	170°F.	35 to 40
Rolled Shoulder	4 to 6	300° to 325°F.	170°F.	40 to 45

ROASTING LAMB

Lamb leg is fatty and is handled somewhat differently from the other
lamb roasts. Make incisions—10 or so—1 inch deep in the leg and press into
each a sliver of fresh garlic. Rub the meat with ½ teaspoon of curry powder and
sprinkle with salt. Place uncovered in a roasting pan, and set into a preheated
oven just below the middle rack. When the roast is done, remove the meat and
keep warm at the back of the stove. Remove the fat from the pan drippings, and
add a little veal, chicken, or beef bouillon to the pan drippings. Cook on top of
the stove until the gravy reduces. Salt and pepper the roast before serving.

In France it is the custom to cook small white navy beans and serve these in
the pan drippings from a leg of lamb. The fatty lamb gravy is very good with

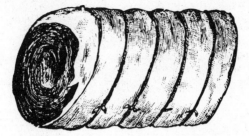

beans of various sorts. Frozen baby lima beans, cooked and mixed with the pan drippings, make a very good accompaniment for a leg of lamb. In Britain and in America, it is the custom to serve mint jelly or fresh mint in a vinaigrette sauce with lamb.

In Europe, lamb is served medium-rare, or medium-to-well-done, and that is becoming a preferred way in America as well. Other roasts of lamb may be cooked as a leg of lamb, or simply rubbed with a littly curry before roasting.

SAVE THE SOUP BONE

The bone from a leg of lamb is a great addition to almost any barley, bean, or vegetable soup. The shin portion of a leg of lamb roast is usually too dry to serve with the roast, so remove it before you roast the leg (unless the roast is meant for a formal presentation), and freeze it to use in a lamb or mutton soup.

TIMETABLE FOR ROASTING LAMB

CUT	AVERAGE WEIGHT	OVEN TEMPERATURE	INTERNAL TEMPERATURE OF MEAT	MINUTES PER POUND
Leg	5 to 8	300° to 325°F.	175° to 180°F.	30 to 35
Shoulder	4 to 6	300° to 325°F.	175° to 180°F.	30 to 35
rolled	3 to 5	300° to 325°F.	175° to 180°F.	40 to 45
cushion	3 to 5	300° to 325°F.	175° to 180°F.	30 to 35
Rib	1½ to 3	375°F.	170° to 180°F.	35 to 45

ROASTING PORK

Pork is particularly good when roasted with a hint of garlic or sprigs of fresh thyme. Prepare the roast with garlic and curry as described for roasting lamb. Salt and pepper well before serving. To make gravy, add chicken, veal, or beef bouillon to the pan drippings 20 to 30 minutes before the roast is done.

DRIPPINGS

One of the secrets of good cooking is to use the leftover gravies and pan drippings, those strongly flavored juices that are browned-on or caramelized in the bottom of a cooking dish or pan. One reason for cooking with heavy cast iron pans and pots is that the juices caramelize in this type of utensil, whereas they tend to burn in thinner, lighter vessels. A cup of warm water poured into the pan about 20 minutes before a roast is done makes a delicious gravy and, usually, lots of it. If fat settles on the top, as it will with a fatty roast, like lamb or pork, chill the gravy, and when the fat rises to the top, skim it off. Almost any dish, from plain boiled rice to a Chinese mix of the chop suey variety will taste better with a few spoonfuls of real gravy added to the sauce. One old chef's tale that may be true is that a great Chinese chef had in his family drippings that had been added-on to from generation to generation for 200 years!

Pork generally has a better flavor when it is very well done, and many Americans like to serve with an accompaniment of cold applesauce, or small baked cinnamon-flavored apples.

Pork loin is the best roast. Ribs generally are better barbecued in a sauce than roasted.

TIMETABLE FOR ROASTING PORK

CUT	AVERAGE WEIGHT	OVEN TEMPERATURE	INTERNAL TEMPERATURE OF MEAT	MINUTES PER POUND
Loin, center	3 to 5	325° to 350°F.	170°F.	30 to 35
half	5 to 7	325° to 350°F.	170°F.	35 to 40
blade or sirloin	3 to 4	325° to 350°F.	170°F.	40 to 45
rolled	3 to 5	325° to 350°F.	170°F.	35 to 45
Picnic shoulder	5 to 8	325° to 350°F.	170°F.	30 to 35
rolled	3 to 5	325° to 350°F.	170°F.	35 to 40
cushion style	3 to 5	325° to 350°F.	170°F.	30 to 35
Boston shoulder	4 to 6	325° to 350°F.	170°F.	40 to 45
Leg (fresh ham)				
whole, bone in	12 to 16	325° to 350°F.	170°F.	22 to 26
rolled	10 to 14	325° to 350°F.	170°F.	24 to 28
half, bone in	5 to 8	325° to 350°F.	170°F.	35 to 40
Spareribs		325° to 350°F.	well done	1½ to 2½ hours

BAKING HAM

Ham is, of course, pork, which has been cured, usually by smoking. Fully cooked roasts bear a set of instructions on heating times required. Almost any ham can be dressed with pineapple rings, and should be basted often with citrus (preferably orange) or pineapple juice during cooking, even the small, can-shaped hams. But a whole or half ham really should be garnished this way.

Remove a portion of the brown skin to show a portion of the creamy white fat. Score ¼ inch deep all over the top of the roast with a sharp knife, and press a whole clove into the meeting points of the score marks. Mix a paste of brown sugar with just enough prepared mustard to moisten it, and spread all over the fat, including the scored portion. An hour before the ham is done, use wooden toothpicks to fix rounds of canned pineapple across the top of the roast, and arrange a maraschino cherry in the center of each round, then return the roast to the oven and complete the cooking. Bring to the table with all the garnishes in place.

HOW MUCH TO BUY PER SERVING
INGREDIENT PER SERVING

Meat, boneless	¼ to ⅕ pound
Meat, with small section of bone	⅓ to ¼ pound
Meat, with medium section of bone	⅓ to ½ pound
Meat, mostly bone	½ to 1 pound
Broiler-fryer	¼ to ½ bird
Capon, roaster, fowl	½ pound
Game hens, squab	1 bird
Turkey, to 12 pound	¾ to 1 pound
12 to 24 pounds	½ to ¾ pound
Boneless	¼ to ⅓ pound
Duck	1 pound
Goose	1 pound

Ham drippings can be very useful. Jellied ham drippings may be added to split pea and lentil soups, bean soups and bean dishes. Ham skin, cooked and still soft and warm, may be pureed with pea soup in a blender. A ham bone is the classic addition to split pea soup. So, throw nothing away. Often, the sugar in the coating for the ham roast will burn during the cooking. It is hard to get off the roasting pan, so line the pan with foil that can be discarded.

What to serve with ham? Baked sweet potatoes and yams, or plain white potatoes are first rate with ham. So are corn dishes and corn biscuits.

TIMETABLE FOR BAKING HAM

CUT	AVERAGE WEIGHT	OVEN TEMPERATURE	INTERNAL TEMPERATURE OF MEAT	MINUTES PER POUND
Ham (cook before eating)				
whole	10 to 14	300° to 325°F.	160°F.	18 to 20
half	5 to 7	300° to 325°F.	160°F.	22 to 25
shank or butt	3 to 4	300° to 325°F.	160°F.	35 to 40
Ham (fully cooked)*				
half	5 to 7	325°F.	130°F.	18 to 24
Picnic Shoulder	5 to 8	300° to 325°F.	170°F.	35
Shoulder Roll	2 to 3	300° to 325°F.	170°F.	35 to 40
Canadian-style Bacon	2 to 4	325°F.	160°F.	35 to 40

*Allow approximately 15 minutes per pound for heating whole ham.

TIMETABLE FOR COOKING VARIETY MEATS

Kind	Broiling	Braising'	Cooking in Liquid
LIVER			
Beef, 3- to 4-pound piece		2 to 2½ hrs.	
sliced		20 to 25 min.	
Veal (calf), sliced	8 to 10 min.		
Pork, 3 to 3½ pounds		1½ to 2 hrs.	
sliced		20 to 25 min.	
Lamb, sliced	8 to 10 min.		
KIDNEY			
Beef		1½ to 2 hrs.	1 to 1½ hrs.
Veal (calf)	10 to 12 min.	1 to 1½ hrs.	¾ to 1 hr.
Pork	10 to 12 min.	1 to 1½ hrs.	¾ to 1 hr.
Lamb	10 to 12 min.	¾ to 1 hr.	¾ to 1 hr.
HEART			
Beef, whole		3 to 4 hrs.	3 to 4 hrs.
sliced			1½ to 2 hrs.

HEART			
Veal (calf), whole		2½ to 3 hrs.	2½ to 3 hrs.
Pork		2½ to 3 hrs.	2½ to 3 hrs.
Lamb		2½ to 3 hrs.	2½ to 3 hrs.
TONGUE			
Beef			3 to 4 hrs.
Veal (calf)			2 to 3 hrs.
Pork ⎫ usually sold			
Lamb ⎭ ready-to-serve			
TRIPE			
Beef	10 to 15 min.**		1 to 1½ hrs.
SWEETBREADS	10 to 15 min.**	20 to 25 min.	15 to 20 min.
BRAINS	10 to 15 min.**	20 to 25 min.	15 to 20 min.

*On top of range, or in a 300°F. to 325° oven.
**Time required after precooking in water.
Courtesy National Live Stock and Meat Board

MICROWAVE AND CONVECTION OVENS

New to the cooking scene in the last decade, microwave and convection ovens are now popular as second ovens. They require special cooking and timing tables, and these are supplied by the oven manufacturers. Generally, both cook more rapidly than conventional ovens, but similarities between microwave and convection cooking end there.

The microwave oven uses electromagnetic radiation to break down food fibers from the inside out. It cooks food in one-half to one-quarter of the time required by conventional ovens, according to manufacturers' claims. The microwave oven cooks vegetables as beautifully as a Chinese cook, but doesn't crisp or brown anything. Many cooks say these ovens are excellent for thawing frozen foods rapidly. The prospective microwave oven owner should be aware of two precautions: Special wiring may be required before installation; and metal utensils, or those with even a small quantity of metal on them, can damage the oven. Some ceramicware has metal in it, so it is safest to use only glass vessels and utensils. You can also cook on paper plates!

The convection oven cooks with electric heat, but circulates the heat rapidly. The result is superbly crisp, brown meats, potatoes, and other foods in as little as 75 percent of the time required in a conventional oven. I use mine for everything except very large roasts (which are too big for it) and for baking (the moving air builds slopes on my cakes and muffins). Custards and other delicate foods should be baked at 25 to 50 degrees lower than the recipe specifies. The convection oven bakes fish beautifully in a matter of minutes.

ROASTING BIRDS

Birds are baked in the oven, uncovered, at temperatures ranging around 400 degrees. In a convection oven, reduce cooking times by 5 to 10 minutes for each hour. Convection ovens make the crispest roast birds.

Stuffing a chicken provides a starch and saves the labor and cost of preparing a vegetable. Turkey without a stuffing would disappoint most guests.

The roasting timetable for chicken allows for a preliminary searing at 425 degrees, then baking at a lower temperature. This makes a tastier bird with richer gravy. Bigger birds that must cook longer don't need the searing period.

If you don't use the drippings from the cooked bird, store them in a covered container in the refrigerator, remove the fat that will solidify on the surface, and use the jelled consommé beneath to make gravy for other roasts, or in soups.

ROASTING CHICKEN

This information applies to stuffed fresh or thawed birds which have been exposed to room temperatures for an hour or so. If the bird is just out of the refrigerator or has just been thawed, it will need another 5 to 10 minutes of cooking. These roasting periods must be reduced by 15 to 20 minutes (for larger birds) if the birds are unstuffed. Turn the oven to the required setting, while you rub the breast of the bird with a little soft butter, and sprinkle with salt, pepper, and a pinch of curry powder. Roast, uncovered, preferably in a heavy cast iron or enameled cast iron pan, or a roasting pan. (The heavier utensils caramelize the drippings and tend to produce a richer gravy.)

BIRD STUFFING

The table on page 195 is a general guide to stuffing quantities needed. The rule of thumb is that 1 cup of uncooked stuffing will yield 2 servings of cooked stuffing. Spoon the stuffing loosely into the bird. Bake extra stuffing in a heavy casserole covered with foil or a lid. Put it into the oven ¾ hour before the bird should be done. Serve when the stuffing cooked inside the birds runs out.

About 2 quarts of dry or moist bread cubes are required to make 2 quarts of stuffing.

Baste the bird every 20 minutes during roasting with stock (see instructions under Roasting Turkey). The inner juices, which are clear and pinkish, will seep

from the bird as it cooks. To test for doneness, wiggle the legs. If they are loose, the bird is cooked. This is true for chicken, but not quite accurate for birds with shorter forelegs, like duck.

Capon, which is a fattened unsexed male, 7 to 10 months old and especially heavy and tender, and big chickens, may be handled as turkeys; that is, remove a little early from the oven, and rest on the back of the stove while you are making giblet gravy from the drippings (see instructions under Roasting Turkey). If you don't choose to make gravy, remove the bird at the end of the correct cooking time, skim the fat from drippings, and serve the drippings as gravy.

TIMETABLE FOR ROASTING CHICKEN AND CAPON

WEIGHT	OVEN TEMP.	ROASTING TIME	THERMOMETER READING WHEN DONE
Up to 2 pounds	425°F. 375°F.	for 20 minutes, 45 minutes more	190°F.
2 to 4 pounds	425°F. 375°F.	for 20 minutes, 1 hour	190°F.
4 to 6 pounds	425°F. 350°F.	for 20 minutes, 1½ to 2 hours	190°F.
6 to 7 pounds (capon)	325°F.	2½ to 3 hours	180° to 190°F.
Halves, quarters	400°F.	¾ to 1 hour	

QUANTITY OF STUFFING	SIZE OF BIRD	SERVINGS
2 cups	3 to 4 pounds	4 to 5
3 cups	5 to 6 pounds	6 to 8
4 cups	6 to 8 pounds	8 to 10
8 cups	12 to 14 pounds	12 to 16
12 cups	15 to 20 pounds	18 to 24

CORNISH HENS AND SQUAB

(baste every 10 to 15 minutes)		
3/4 to 1 1/2 pounds	400°F.	3/4 to 1 hour

GUINEA HEN AND DOMESTIC GAME BIRDS

2 to 4 pounds	350°F.	1 1/2 to 2 1/2 hours

BEEF-UP SUPERMARKET CHICKEN

Improve the flavor of supermarket chicken and meats by rubbing them all over with half a teaspoon of curry powder before cooking. Add salt and pepper, too.

BREAD STUFFING, BASIC RECIPE
Makes 8 cups

2 medium-sized onions, peeled and minced
2 stalks celery, and leaves, minced
1/2 cup butter or bacon drippings
8 cups bread cubes or coarse bread crumbs
2 teaspoons poultry seasoning, or 3/4 teaspoon each of
    thyme, sage, and marjoram
1 1/2 teaspoons salt
1/2 teaspoon pepper
1/2 cup minced parsley
1/3 cup chicken bouillon or water, optional
Salt and freshly ground black pepper to taste

1. In a large skillet over medium-high heat, sauté the onion and celery in the butter until the onion is translucent. Mix in the bread and seasonings, tossing to keep fluffy. Add the parsley and cook for 1 minute longer. If you like a very moist stuffing, add up to 1/3 cup of broth or water, tossing as you mix, and enough additional salt and pepper to make a well-seasoned stuffing.

2. Up-end the bird and spoon in the stuffing, but do not pack it down.

GIBLET STUFFING

Cook giblets and liver in stock before making the stuffing. Chop them and add them to the Basic Recipe for Bread Stuffing with the bread crumbs.

ROASTING TURKEY

Thaw the bird, if frozen. Use the giblets and neck for stock to make the gravy. Prepare the stuffing, cool it, and refrigerate it until just before you are ready to roast the bird. It is a good idea to do all this the night before. Let the bird stand at room temperature for 2 to 3 hours before roasting. Preheat the oven to 425 degrees while you stuff and truss the bird, rub the breast generously with soft butter, and sprinkle with salt, pepper, and a pinch of curry powder. Roast, uncovered, in a large pan, following the chart below.

Baste the bird every ½ to ¾ hour with hot stock, and with drippings from the pan. Just scoop up the drippings with a big spoon and pour over the breast. Do it quickly so as not to lose too much heat from the oven. Thirty minutes before the bird is done, pour 1 cup of stock into the pan. This will mix with the drippings caramelizing on the bottom of the pan and make the base for the gravy. If the bird is browning too quickly, cover loosely half way through cooking with a big sheet of foil.

TRUSSING THE BIRD

Use wooden or metal skewers or big sturdy toothpicks for fixing togeth-er the vents and neck skin on big birds and small turkeys. This is easier than sewing, both to prepare and to remove once the bird is cooked.

To make stock: In a small covered pot over high heat, simmer the gizzard, heart, and neck, with enough water to cover—3 to 4 cups plus 1 small onion stuck with 2 whole cloves, ¼ teaspoon dried thyme, 1 small bay leaf, 1 large sprig fresh parsley, 2 teaspoons salt, and ¼ teaspoon pepper. Total cooking time will be 1 to 1½ hours, depending on how large the giblets are. In the last 20 minutes of cooking time, add the liver. Add more water if the level gets so low that the meat is uncovered. Strain, reserving the meat and broth only.

To make giblet gravy: About 15 minutes before the bird is to be done, coarsely chop the heart, gizzard, and liver, in a processor or by hand. Combine with 2 cups of the stock. Remove the bird and keep warm on its serving plate at the back of the stove. Place the roasting pan on 1 or 2 medium-hot burners, and stir the stock mixture into the pan drippings. If the bird was very fat, skim the excess fat from the surface of the drippings before adding the stock. Simmer the gravy, stirring, until it boils and begins to thicken. Season with salt and pepper to taste.

To freeze leftover turkey: Slice cooled breast and leg meat thinly, and seal tightly into freezer paper or foil after dribbling a small amount of gravy over the slices.

To warm leftover turkey (try this with thawed turkey slices as well): Lay slices of turkey over mounds of stuffing, cover with a moist paper towel, and heat for 20 minutes in a 325-degree oven. Or, just before serving, warm leftover gravy in a heavy casserole over medium heat on top of the stove, and place slices of turkey in the gravy just long enough to warm them, about 2 minutes. Serve with gravy, warm leftover stuffing and cranberry sauce.

POULTRY THAWING TIME AT ROOM TEMPERATURE

4 to 10 pounds	6 to 10 hours
10 to 16 pounds	10 to 14 hours
16 to 24 pounds	14 to 18 hours

TIMETABLE FOR ROASTING TURKEY

WEIGHT	OVEN TEMP.	ROASTING TIME	THERMOMETER READING WHEN DONE
8 to 12 pounds	375°F.	2 to 2½ hours	180° to 185°F.
12 to 16 pounds	375°F.	2½ to 3 hours	180° to 185°F.
16 to 20 pounds	375°F.	3 to 3½ hours	180° to 185°F.
20 to 24 pounds	375°F.	3½ to 4 hours	180° to 185°F.

Half turkeys take a little less time proportionately.

5 to 8	325°F.	2½ to 3 hours	180° to 185°F.
8 to 10 pounds	325°F.	3 to 3½ hours	180° to 185°F.
10 to 12 pounds	325°F.	3½ to 4 hours	180° to 185°F.

Rolled, boneless turkey is more dense and takes a little more time.

3 to 5 pounds	325°F.	2½ to 3 hours	170° to 175°F.
5 to 7 pounds	325°F.	3 to 3½ hours	170° to 175°F.
7 to 9 pounds	325°F.	3½ to 4 hours	170° to 175°F.

ROASTING DUCK AND GOOSE

Duck is usually not stuffed, although seasoned wild rice makes a nice stuffing. Duck is often served in a sweet sauce, sour cherry sauce, for instance, or an orange sauce. It also is good dredged with a liqueur, such as Amaretto, the last 10 minutes of cooking. Skim the fat from the drippings before making gravy. Goose is usually stuffed. Stuffings made of bread and giblets or wild rice are nice. See accompanying recipes for holiday treatments.

Both duck and goose are fatty birds, so the first step in roasting properly is to rid the bird of some of the fat. Prick the bird all over with a fork, then sear either in an oven, preheated to 450 degrees, or 4 inches below a broiler on high, for 20 minutes. Turn once. Salt and pepper the bird and set, breast up, in a roasting pan and roast, uncovered, following the charts below.

Follow the instructions for basting and making gravy and stock under Roasting Turkey. Let the bird rest, covered, on top of the stove 15-20 minutes after roasting before serving.

TIMETABLE FOR ROASTING DUCK

WEIGHT	OVEN TEMP.	ROASTING TIME	THERMOMETER READING WHEN DONE
3 to 5 pounds	350°F.	2 to 2½ hours	190°F.
Halves, quarters	350°F.	1 hour	

TIMETABLE FOR ROASTING GOOSE

WEIGHT	OVEN TEMP.	ROASTING TIME	THERMOMETER READING WHEN DONE
4 to 6 pounds	325°F.	2 ¼ to 2¾ hours	190°F.
6 to 8 pounds	325°F.	2¾ to 3 hours	190°F.
8 to 12 pounds	325°F.	3 to 4 hours	190°F.
12 to 14 pounds	325°F.	4 to 4½ hours	190°F.

ROASTING GAME BIRDS

Wild birds should hang in a cool place for at least 24 hours and preferably 48 hours, before cooking. Bleed the bird soon after killing and allow it to hang by the head. To pluck birds, remove the large feathers, then dip the bird in a mixture of ⅜ pound paraffin dissolved in 7 quarts boiling water. Repeat 4 or 5 times until the feathers are coated with paraffin, let paraffin harden, then strip off the paraffin and feathers. Singe and remove any remaining small feathers. Remove the head, feet, entrails, and wipe with a damp cloth, and dry.

TIMETABLE FOR ROASTING GAME BIRDS

BIRD	OVEN TEMP.	ROASTING TIME	THERMOMETER READING WHEN DONE
Grouse	425°F.	20 to 25 minutes	
Guinea Hen	350°F.	1½ to 2 hours	190°F.
Partridge	350°F.	40 to 50 minutes	190°F.
Pheasant	325°F.	1½ to 2 hours	190°F.
Squab	400°F.	40 to 50 minutes	
Wild Duck (or follow instructions for domestic duck)	450°F.	(halved) 25 minutes	
Wild Goose	325°F.	25 minutes per pound	190°F.

MARINADE FOR GAME BIRDS

½ cup dry red or dry white wine
¼ cup vegetable oil
¼ cup boiling water
1 teaspoon juniper berries
1 small onion, peeled and minced
⅛ teaspoon dried thyme
1 small bay leaf
1 teaspoon salt
⅛ teaspoon freshly ground black pepper
1 teaspoon minced garlic, optional

Combine all the ingredients together in a glass dish and coat all parts of the game bird liberally. Let marinate for at least 4 hours or overnight. If the bird seems tough, choose the longer marinating period. Use the marinade to make a sauce for the bird, and to baste it if roasting or barbecueing.

MARINADE FOR DOMESTIC BIRDS

Follow the recipe above and the instructions for game bird marinade, but omit the juniper berries.

SPIT-ROASTING POULTRY

The roasting times given below are for birds at refrigerator temperature cooked in a kitchen. Done outdoors on a spit, on a cool or windy day, spit-roasting will take longer. Test for doneness by inserting a sharp-pointed roasting fork, and by wiggling the legs. If the fork goes in very easily, and if the legs wiggle easily, the bird is done. Allow the birds to rest for 15 to 20 minutes after cooking before serving.

BIRD AND WEIGHT	ROASTING TIME
Cornish Hens and Squab, ¾ to 1½ pounds	40 to 45 minutes
Guinea Hen and domestic game birds, 2 to 4 pounds	1 to 2 hours
Chicken, 2 to 3 pounds	1 to 1¼ hours
Chicken, 4 to 5 pounds	1½ to 2 hours
Duck, 4 to 5 pounds	1½ to 2½ hours
Goose, 4 to 6 pounds	2 to 3 hours
Turkey, 4 to 6 pounds	2 to 3 hours
Turkey, 6 to 8 pounds	3 to 3½ hours
Turkey, 8 to 10 pounds	3½ to 4 hours
Turkey, over 10 pounds	4 to 5 hours

CLAMBAKE FOR 25

Before the party: You will need 6 to 7 bushels of seaweed, a large sheet of canvas, and enough kindling and split logs (⅛ cord) to make a roaring fire. The traditional drink is beer; the traditional dessert, icy watermelon chunks. The clambake can be held in the backyard if you make a "pit" by building a space using cinder blocks, and cook the food on a sheet of metal (an old paintless car hood, for instance?) large enough to cover the pit. Don't forget to get paper cups to serve the melted butter and offer a generous supply of napkins.

2 packages cheesecloth
1 bushel soft shell clams
25 white baking potatoes
4½ dozen ears corn
25 live 1-pound lobsters and/or broiler chickens, halved
3 pounds butter, melted and hot

1. Cut the cheesecloth into 10-inch squares. Scrub the clams to remove all sand and tie them into the cheesecloth squares, about 8 to a bundle.

2. Scrub the potatoes and tie each one into a cheesecloth square.

3. Shuck the corn, removing the coarse outer leaves and the silk. Let the thin inner husk remain.

4. About 4 hours before dinnertime, prepare the fire. Dig a 5-foot-square pit about 2 feet deep and line it with brick or large flat stones. Lay kindling covered with logs on the rock bed. Light the fire and let it burn down completely. By the time the fire dies down completely, the rocks should be very hot and ready to cook on.

5. Rake away the embers and logs that haven't burned, then spread a 3-inch layer of wet seaweed on the hot rocks. Place a layer of clams on the seaweed, then a layer of corn, then a layer of potatoes. Arrange the live lobsters on top of the pile. If you are using the chickens, season them, then seal each half in foil before you lay it in the pit. Cover these layers with a 2-inch layer of seaweed, and seal the pit with a large canvas cover, anchored securely on all sides so no steam can escape. Set the butter in a covered kettle in the center of the canvas where it will melt while the food cooks.

6. Allow the food to cook for about 1 hour. Then roll back the cover, rake off the seaweed and, using tongs, help the guests to help themselves. Serve melted butter in a paper cup to each guest.

ROASTING (BAKING) VEGETABLES

Most vegetables can be roasted (or baked) successfully in the drippings of roasts, or in their own skins.

BEANS, PEAS, GREENS: Snap beans, peas, kale, and spinach, may be baked in a little butter in a covered casserole. Preheat the oven to 425 degrees, and cover well. The vegetables will be done in 10 to 30 minutes, depending on how thick they are. Spinach cooks very rapidly; thick green beans and big peas take longer.

CARROTS, TURNIPS, AND OTHER ROOT VEGETABLES: Root vegetables (such as carrots, salsify, and peeled, cut-up turnips) may be baked at 375 to 400 degrees until tender—between 45 minutes and 1 hour. Place them in a covered Dutch oven or seal into heavy duty foil, with a little butter. Or, halve or quarter them and roast with meats in the bottom of the roasting pan.

POTATOES, SWEET (ALSO YAMS): Bake in oven preheated to 400 degrees (450 degrees if you are in a hurry) for 45 minutes (or until pierced easily with a fork).

POTATOES, WHITE: Bake in an oven preheated to 425 degrees (500 degrees if you are in a hurry) for 1 hour (or until pierced easily with a fork). Wash well first, and pierce with a fork in one or two places so steam can escape. (Smaller potatoes occasionally explode when baked unpierced.)

SQUASH, ACORN (ALSO BUTTERNUT): Bake halved, seeded squash at 375 degrees for 45 minutes or until fork-tender. Salt, pepper, and butter each half, and brace in foil. Then set on an oven rack or in a baking pan. Corn syrup, brown sugar, and lemon juice, are some popular seasonings for squashes.

SQUASH, HUBBARD: Bake slices wrapped in foil, and seasoned, at 400 degrees for 1 hour, or until easily pierced with a fork. Salt and pepper and add lots of butter before serving.

TOMATOES: Place tomatoes, halved, cut side up, in a buttered roasting pan, dot with butter, and season with salt and pepper. Bake for 15 to 20 minutes, or until tender. Crushed garlic, slivered onions, and minced basil, are among seasonings for baked tomatoes. Or, smother in a mixture of bread crumbs and crushed garlic, then bake.

COUNTRY CORN ROAST

Start the fire about half an hour before cooking time, and set the rack 4 to 6 inches above the coals.

For each guest:
2 ears fresh sweet corn
2 teaspoons butter
Salt
½ broiler chicken
Freshly ground black pepper
Pinch of dried rosemary

1. Shuck the corn. Put each ear on a piece of foil, spread with half the butter, and sprinkle with salt and pepper. Wrap foil securely around each ear. Don't seal the seam, but do twist the foil at the ends to hold in the butter. That way, steam will escape and the corn will roast instead of steaming. Sprinkle the chicken with the pepper and a bit of rosemary.

2. Place the chicken pieces on the grill over coals hot enough to be covered with ash. Cook for 15 to 20 minutes. Add the corn and roast until tender, turning the ears often. Turn the chicken once or twice. Total cooking time should be about 30 to 40 minutes.

PAN-ROASTING POTATOES, TURNIPS, ETC.

Pan-roasting is a popular method for cooking an accompaniment for a roast. Potatoes are most often chosen for this method, but baby turnips (small, white and purple type), cut-up rutabaga, parsnips, carrots, pineapple chunks, and other popular accompaniments for roasts may be pan-roasted.

Vegetables intended for pan-roasting should be peeled and cut into chunks the size of a medium-small potato. Add the vegetable to the roaster in which the meat is cooking about 1 hour before the roast will be done, if it is cooking at between 375 and 400 degrees. If it is cooking at a lower temperature, allow 1½ hours for the vegetables to cook. Turn two or three times during the cooking so all sides have the opportunity to brown.

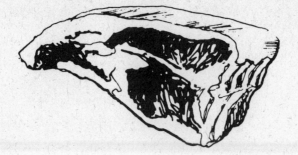

BROILING MEATS, VEGETABLES AND FISH

The "broil" setting in a home oven is about 550 degrees F. Commercial ranges go to 700 to 1000 degrees. You won't, therefore, get the same results from a home broiler as you see in meat or fish that has been broiled in a restaurant—the luscious charring. A good outdoor broiler may get to higher temperatures, and a really glowing coal fire in an outdoor grill often does.

The heat in a broiler setting (if there is a setting; many just offer low or high broiler settings) is not very pertinent. What counts is how close, or how far from the fire, the food to be cooked has been placed. You control what happens by raising or lowering the racks of the broiler. Most broilers have a 3-inch space between the top rack and the heat source. The first or second rack is the right place for not-too-thick steaks (about 1 inch), fish, and chops. The second or third rack is the place to put very thick meats, and also sauces and cheese toppings that are to be browned.

Meat to be broiled will cook more quickly if it has been out of the refrigerator for an hour. Only the best cuts of meat should be selected for broiling—steaks, fillets, first quality chops. Season with salt and pepper before placing under the broiler. If the meat is very lean, brush it with oil to give it a little more sizzle. It's the fat and marbling that burns fastest and gives broiled meat its characteristic charred glamor.

Cooking times on outdoor broilers are variable, easily affected by wind and temperature of the air. If cool outdoors, lower the grill to keep food closer to the source of heat. Grilling times can only be an indication. If in doubt, taste for doneness before serving.

THE OUTDOOR FIRE FOR BROILING

Here are some pointers from experts:

Line the bottom of the broiler with heavy aluminum foil to reflect heat and increase intensity of fire.

If the bottom of the bowl is not perforated, add a layer of pea gravel (¼ to ¾ inch stones). This will make a base for the fire that will allow it to breathe.

It is critical to success in broiling that the fire be well heated before the meat or fish is put on to cook. One method, which takes about 45 minutes, is to stack briquets in a pyramid and soak them with a lighting fluid, following instructions on the container. Pour on the fluid, let stand 1 minute, then light, and wait.

The fire is ready when the briquets are covered evenly with a layer of gray ash. Do not try to cook before this happens.

Spread the briquets to make an even bed a little wider than the space occupied by the food to be cooked.

Water-soaked wood chips (hickory, apple, pear) give a smoky, flavorful touch to the food, but don't use pine for this purpose. Dried sage, thyme, or rosemary scattered lightly over the coals for chicken or lamb add a hint of flavor you'll enjoy.

TIMETABLE FOR BROILING MEATS

CUT		TEMPERATURE	DISTANCE FROM HEAT	MINUTES PER SIDE RARE	MEDIUM	WELL DONE
CHARCOAL BROILING						
All tender steaks	1"	hot	4"	4 to 5	7 to 8	9 to 10
	1½"	hot	4"	5 to 6	9 to 10	12 to 15
	2"	moderate	5"	9 to 10	13 to 15	17 to 20
	2½"	moderate	5"	12 to 14	19 to 22	22 to 25
INDOOR BROILING						
Boneless tender steaks, including	1"	high broil	2 to 3"	4	6	7
rump, skirt, eye of	1½"	high broil	3"	7	8	9 to 12
the round, etc.	2"	high broil	4"	8 to 10	15 to 17	18 to 19
London broil	3 to 4"	high broil	4"	3	4	5
Note: broil to color sides, then bake at 375 degrees in oven for 10 minutes more.						
Bone-in steaks	1"	high broil	3"	7	9	10 to 12
	1½"	high broil	4"	9 to 10	10 to 12	13 to 15
	2"	high broil	5"	14 to 16	17 to 19	19 to 21

TIMETABLE FOR BROILING LAMB

CUT		TEMPERATURE	DISTANCE FROM HEAT	MINUTES PER SIDE MEDIUM	WELL DONE
INDOOR BROILING					
Loin lamb chops	¾"	high broil	3"	5 to 6	6 to 7
	1"	high broil	3"	6 to 7	8 to 9
	1½"	high broil	3"	7 to 8	10 to 11

BROILING HAM

The best meats for broiling are marbled, fatty meats. Ham doesn't qualify, though it is surrounded in a coat of fat because ham slices for broiling do not have interior veining of fat. Yet, broiled ham is good if handled well. Select uncooked ham slices barely ½ inch thick for broiling. Wash in warm water, trim off excess fat, and score the fat. Place on a broiler rack positioned as suggested in chart below. As soon as the surface of the ham appears dry (about 1 minute) brush it with melted butter, and brush every minute or so of cooking. Or, brush with melted bacon fat, or fat drippings from a ham roast. When the top side is well browned, turn and brush the other side with butter.

Ham slices may be touched lightly with a good mustard here and there before broiling, and benefit from basting with a little orange juice during the cooking.

For gala occasions, broil 1½ inch-thick slice of fresh pineapple, 1 thick orange sections, and 2 thick grapefruit sections for each slice of ham, and drizzle with a little brown sugar melted in orange juice.

TIMETABLE FOR BROILING HAM

CUT		TEMPERATURE	DISTANCE FROM HEAT	MINUTES PER SIDE
CHARCOAL BROILING				
Precooked ham steaks	½"	moderate	4"	3 to 4
	¾"	moderate	4"	4 to 5
	1"	moderate	4"	5 to 6
Uncooked ham steaks	½"	moderate	4"	5
	¾	moderate	4"	6 to 8
	1"	moderate	5"	10
INDOOR BROILING*				
Precooked ham steaks	½"	high broil	3"	3
	¾"	high broil	3"	4
	1"	high broil	4"	5
Uncooked ham steaks	½"	high broil	3"	4
	¾"	high broil	3"	7
	1"	high broil	4"	9

* Brush with oil on each side, baste with a little orange juice.

BROILING POULTRY

Birds, halved or quartered, make excellent broiling meats. Domestic birds are more tender, and better for broiling than game birds, unless the game has been tenderized by hanging for as long as you dare. In some parts of Europe a winter delicacy is a *brochette* (skewer) of small birds, well ripened, plucked, brushed with a strong garlic sauce, and spit-broiled until deep brown.

Birds to be barbecued may be marinated for 3 to 4 hours before cooking. Brush the birds often during broiling with the marinade.

Birds may be broiled over a charcoal fire at moderately high heat, or under the oven broiler. Turn the pieces every 15 or 20 minutes. Prick ducklings and fatty birds during the broiling to release fats.

BIRD AND WEIGHT	HEAT	DISTANCE FROM BROILER	BROILING TIME
Chicken, 1 to 3 pounds	High	5 to 6 inches	35 to 45 minutes (turn once)
Duck, 3 pounds	High	7 to 8 inches	1 hour (turn twice)
Turkey, 4 to 6 pounds	High	8 to 9 inches	1½ hours (turn twice)

CHICKEN SIZES

Supermarkets usually classify chickens this way:

Broilers	2½ pounds
Fryers	2½ to 3 pounds
Roasters	3½ to 5 pounds
Fowl	6 to 8 pounds
Capons	6 to 8 pounds

The difference between a fryer and a broiler is primarily size and age. Broilers are usually slaughtered at 6 weeks; fryers at 11 weeks; roasters at 12 weeks or more. Capons are usually kept until they are 18 weeks or older.

FISH BROILING

Broil fish 4 to 6 inches below the flame at medium high. Do not attempt to turn the fillets. Fish comes apart easily when cooking. Whole fish such as mackerel, and meaty fish, such as salmon and swordfish steaks, may be turned without breaking, and should be turned halfway through cooking time so each side can color nicely. Baste fillets and whole fish and steaks before or during the broiling with butter combined with a little dry white wine, or strained lemon juice, or a teaspoon or two of vinegar. If you wish, add chopped chives, mushrooms, or your favorite herb—tarragon is good. Strongly flavored fish, such as bluefish, may be topped with a mixture of mayonnaise and Parmesan cheese and broiled.

SMOKE YOUR CATCH

Smoking, which is primarily viewed as a method of preserving fish, shellfish, and some meats, coats it with a creosote deposit that slows the development of bacteria and allows the product to be stored for months. The initial investment is small. You need a smoker, about $45, which can be ordered from a mail order house such as L. L. Bean, Inc., Freeport, Maine 04033. Or you can improvise one from a grill by devising a hood made of several layers of aluminum foil shaped around a wire (a coat hanger will do), bent into the shape of a bonnet. Leave a small opening at the top.

Besides the smoker, you will need a thermometer and chunks of fragrant wood (such as hickory, apple, cherry, or walnut) or sawdust, and water.

The method is this: Heat the charcoal in the grill, wet several chunks of the fruity wood and place them among the coals, so the wood will smoke, without burning. Put the fish or meat to be smoked on the barbecue rack over the charcoal. Cover with the hood and smoke 2½ to 3 hours, or until the fish fillets flake easily. Fillets should be about 1 inch thick. Thicker chunks will take much longer. The temperature inside the smoker should be between 160 and 180 degrees during the cooking.

Never smoke food with resinous or piny woods: The flavor will be awful!

From *Food For Us All*, USDA, 1969

TIMETABLE FOR BROILING FISH

TYPE OF FISH CUT	DISTANCE FROM BROILER	TIME TO BROIL
Steaks, ½ inch thick	2 inches	6 to 8 minutes
Steaks, 1 inch thick	2 inches	7 to 10 minutes
Fillets, ½ inch thick	2 inches	4 to 5 minutes
Fillets, 1 inch thick	2 inches	8 to 10 minutes
Flat fish or half fish, 1 plus pounds	3 inches	8 to 10 minutes
Whole fish, 1 to 2 pounds	3 inches	8 to 12 minutes
Whole fish, 3 to 5 pounds	5 to 6 inches	12 to 18 minutes

Garnish cooked fish with lemon wedges and sprigs of fresh parsley.

If you like to broil fish in metal dishes meant to go to the table, withdraw the fish a little before it is done. The heated metal will continue to cook the fish after it is withdrawn from the broiler.

BROILING VEGETABLES

Vegetables are not generally broiled in American cuisine. The exception is the skewer broiling of various kebab combinations, described below.

Another exception is the broiled sweet pepper, which is very good as an accompaniment to lamb, chicken, or beef. To broil a sweet pepper (or similar vegetable), spear it at one end with a two-pronged fork. Hold the pepper over a gas flame or red hot coals, turning it often until it is charred all over and on either end. Hold the pepper under cold running water and peel away the thin outer skin. Trim off the stem end and clean out the seeds and inner veins. Serve warm.

BROILING ON SKEWERS

Kebab cooking is another name for broiling on skewers. You will need skewers at least 10 inches long, but the 12 to 16 inch sizes are easier to work with. The first step in this method of cookery is to choose items that will cook at the same rate of speed. If you choose to broil shrimp on a skewer loaded with onions, mushrooms, and green peppers, for instance, blanch the onions for 2 or 3 minutes in rapidly boiling water before placing them on the skewer so they will complete cooking at the same time that the shrimp are ready.

Cut the vegetables to sizes that will cook at the same rate. Select cherry tomatoes, if tomatoes are called for. Protect dry and delicate meats, such as livers and sweetbreads, by wrapping in fatty portions of thinly cut bacon.

Cook skewered foods under moderate heat. Set the skewers 6 to 12 inches from the heat—6 inches for rapidly cooking foods, thin slices of meat, fish—12 inches for thicker cuts of meat. Turn the skewers often.

BRAISING MEATS AND VEGETABLES

Braising is a slow-cook method in which meat is browned in a preheated heavy skillet or pot in a little fat over high heat, then a small amount of liquid is added, the pot is covered, and the meat simmers very slowly until tender. It is a method adapted to turning tough cuts into tender meats. It is recommended for pork and thick veal chops, and also for thick, tough steaks and roasts.

Vegetables may be braised, too, but they usually are not browned. Simmer for 4 or 5 minutes in a little butter, then simmer, covered, in a very small amount of beef broth, water, or leftover clear soup of some sort until tender—15 to 20 minutes for most.

The key to success in braising either meat or vegetables, is to avoid burning them. Since very little liquid is employed (to avoid "boiled" flavors), the utensil used must have a very tight lid or all the liquid will be lost in the course of the cooking. It is wise when braising to check liquid levels often, and to expect to replenish the supply once or twice during cooking.

A Dutch oven (a heavy, cast iron casserole with a very tight lid) is recommended for long-time braising. Another method is to brown the meat in a heavy skillet, then transfer the meat and fat from the cooking to an electric crockery pot of the slow-cooking type, along with the drippings from the skillet dissolved in the braising liquid, and to cook on low for 6 to 10 hours, depending on the cut, and on the recommendations of the slow-cook pot manual.

The timetable for braising on the chart below is for cooking meats in a Dutch oven, or other tight-lidded casserole, over very low heat.

TIMETABLE FOR BRAISING MEATS

MEAT	WEIGHT	COOKING TIME (brown then simmer)
Beef pot roast; chuck roast; rump; heel of round, etc.	3 to 5 pounds	3½ to 4 hours
Swiss steak (round) 1" thick	2 pounds	1½ to 2 hours
Flank steak	1½ to 2 pounds	1½ hours
Beef short ribs	2 to 2½ pounds	2 to 2½ hours
Oxtails	1½ pounds	3 to 4 hours
Rolled lamb shoulder pot roast	3 to 5 pounds	2 to 2½ hours
Lamb shoulder chops	4 to 5 ounces each	35 to 40 minutes
Lamb neck slices	½ pound each	1½ hours
Lamb shanks	1 pound each	1½ hours
Pork chops	4 to 5 ounces each	35 to 40 minutes
Pork shoulder steaks	5 to 6 ounces each	35 to 40 minutes
Veal rolled shoulder pot roast	4 to 5½ pounds	2 to 2½ hours
Veal cutlets or round	2 pounds	45 to 50 minutes
Veal loin or rib chops	3 to 5 ounces each	45 to 50 minutes

WHAT'S A ROOT VEGETABLE?

Root vegetables are those whose crop matures underground, such as carrots, turnips, and potatoes. The rule of thumb in cooking vegetables is that root vegetables are started in cold water while vegetables matured above ground are generally started in boiling water.

PAN-FRYING

Pan-frying is a fast and very good way to do some foods—tender steaks, for instance, hamburgers, sausages, liver, pancakes, bacon. Preheat the pan, and grease it before adding the food. Fat from a meat chop, oil, or butter are suitable for greasing the pan.

PENNY PINCHER

Use yogurt as a substitute for sour cream.
Substitute beans or bean curd (*tofu*) for beef in chili.
Fresh haddock isn't quite a substitute for lobster, but when poached and served with drawn butter, it tastes almost as good.
Turkey breast can be successfully substituted for veal in dishes such as *schnitzel*.
Sliced chicken breast can also be used instead of veal.

TIMETABLE FOR PAN-FRYING

FOOD	UTENSIL	HEAT	TIME	REMARKS
Steaks 1" thick; lamb chops	heavy pan	Very hot, 375°F.	2 to 3 minutes per side	Reduce heat when you turn
Liver 1" thick	heavy pan	Very hot, 375°F.	2 minutes first side, 1 minute second side	Use butter
Veal chops 1"	heavy pan	Hot, 350°F.	2 to 3 minutes per side	Sprinkle with lemon juice
Pork chops 1"	heavy pan	Hot, 350°F.	5 to 7 minutes per side	Off heat, and let rest in hot pan 10 minutes
Bacon; burgers, ground meats	any pan	Hot, 350°F.	2 minutes per side	Cook bacon until crisp; drain
Sausages	any pan	Low, 300°F.	5 to 6 minutes per side	untill brown all over; prick before cooking

FOOD	UTENSIL	HEAT	TIME	REMARKS
Fish fillets	any pan	Hot, 350°F.	2 to 3 minutes per side	Dredge in flour before cooking
French toast; pancakes	any pan	Very hot, 375°F.	until golden brown on each side	Keep hot until ready to serve

SEASONING CAST IRON

To season a new cast iron frying pan, heat it to very hot, pour in a little vegetable oil, and rinse off before the oil begins to smoke. Coat the pan again with oil and put it in a 450-degree oven for about 30 minutes. Rinse again, wipe dry, then dry on top of the pilot light of the stove or on a burner on the stove. When you use the pan, if you put it under hot water the minute you have emptied out the cooked contents, the baked-on juices will usually lift off very easily with a brush, and the pan can be returned to the hot burner and heat-dried. This avoids the scouring pad, which will remove the seasoning.

FATS FOR FRYING

Butter burns easily. Clarified butter or *ghee* won't burn, and fries meats to a golden brown. It has the best flavor. To fry fish in butter, add to the pan an equal amount of vegetable oil first, then the butter. You get the butter flavor, without burning.

Peanut, corn, and *sesame seed oils* can become very hot before burning, and are preferred for stir-frying and deep-frying.

Olive oil has a special flavor and is suitable for frying only when called for in a recipe. Also, it is very costly, and usually saved for use only in salads.

Pork and *vegetable shortenings*—creamy white fats—are used for deep-frying and to make cakes and piecrusts.

DEEP-FRYING

Deep-frying produces crispy foods that are favorites in most families. Anything can be deep-fried, but most popular are batter-coated fish, fruits, onion rings, string-cut potatoes, and batter-coated vegetables. Many of the best *dim sum* of Chinese cuisine are batter-coated and fried. Here is a table that gives some idea of the uses of deep-frying. Always preheat fats to temperatures called

for. Pour oil or fat 3 inches deep into pan. A deep skillet or an electric deep-frying pan are suitable.

BATTER FOR FRITTERS

2 eggs
1 cup all-purpose flour
½ teaspoon salt
1 tablespoon granulated sugar (for sweet fritters, such as
    fruit fritters, only)
1 tablespoon melted butter
2 tablespoons strained lemon juice
Milk
2 cups vegetables or fruits

1. Beat the eggs until thick. Add the flour, salt, and sugar, if it is to be used. Mix well. Add the butter, lemon, and enough cold milk to make a paste as thick as heavy cream. Beat smooth and let stand for 20 minutes.

2. Dip the fruit chunks or vegetable chunks into the batter, and deep-fry in 3 to 6 cups of fat or vegetable oil heated to 365 degrees. Cook until the fritters are golden brown all over, and drain on paper towels. Keep hot until ready to serve.

TIMETABLE FOR DEEP FRYING

FOOD	HEAT	TIME	REMARKS
Onion rings ¼" thick, in rounds	375°F.	1 minute per side	Keep warm in oven at 250°F. while you complete cooking
Potatoes in strips ⅜" wide	375°F.	10 to 15 minutes (until golden brown)	Soak cut potatoes in cold water first (10 minutes), then pat dry
Vegetable pieces Zucchini rounds, Carrot rounds, Cauliflower ½" to 1" thick	380°F.	2 to 5 minutes (until golden brown)	Drain and keep warm until ready to serve; dip in batter first

TIMETABLE FOR DEEP FRYING

FOOD	HEAT	TIME	REMARKS
Fruit pieces ½" to 1" thick	365°F.	2 to 6 minutes (until golden brown)	Drain and keep warm until ready to serve; dip in batter first
Fish 1" thick, shrimp	375°F.	1 to 4 minutes	Dip in batter first
Chicken pieces	350 to 375°F.	10 to 20 minutes	Use lower temperature and longer period for bigger pieces
Doughnuts	375 to 400°F.	2 to 4 minutes	These will turn over when ready to cook on second side

SAUCES AND STOCKS

There are something like twelve basic recipes in the world; the rest are variations. Many of those variations are created by the addition of sauces. This is particularly true of French *haute cuisine*. Paris intellectual Christiane Gremillon tells the story of the fabulous fish recipe she brought back from Provence to make for friends. She spent five hours on the sauce, but was disappointed with the dish. Some hours later, she discovered that in her preoccupation with the sauce, she had forgotten to cook the fish she poured it over!

To make wonderful sauces, you must begin with good stock (broth). Here are some basic stocks and sauces to prepare and store in measured cupfuls in your freezer. Use them frequently to make wonderful casseroles, flavorful soups, elegant creamed vegetables, rich gravies, and other delectable creations.

WHITE STOCK (*FOND BLANC*)   *Yield: 3 to 4 quarts*

This is delicate, elegant, and perfect for making cream soups or chicken, veal, and vegetable casseroles. Use it whenever a light stock is called for.

    3 pounds veal bones, cracked
    2 pounds veal shanks or shoulder
    2 pounds chicken trimmings, including giblets, neck, back, and wings, but not liver
    1½ tablespoons salt
    6 quarts water
    2 medium carrots, in chunks
    2 medium leeks, cleaned and halved
    2 large stalks celery and leaves
    4 sprigs parsley
    1 medium bay leaf
    1 teaspoon dried thyme
    4 whole cloves stuck in a medium onion
    8 peppercorns

1. In a large pot over high heat, combine bones, meats, salt, and water. Bring to a boil. Remove scum. When it stops foaming, add remaining ingredients. Cover partially, reduce heat, and simmer 4 hours. As water falls below level of ingredients, replenish.

2. Strain through a colander lined with two thicknesses of cheesecloth. Allow broth to cool, then refrigerate or freeze for future use in 1- or 2-cup containers.

Note: The vegetables and meats reserved from preparing the stock make an excellent meal when served in a soup plate with a little of the broth. Offer coarse salt on the side, crisp bread and butter, and a green salad.

SALT SCAM

To remove excess salt from soup or stew, peel and cut a raw potato in half. Add the potato halves to the liquid. About 15 minutes later, the food should taste properly unsalty. You can save the potato halves for frying. This trick will not work with a spaghetti sauce.

BEEF STOCK (*FOND BRUN*)   *Yield: 3 to 4 quarts*

For the first three ingredients of the White Stock recipe, substitute 1 meaty veal knuckle, 2 pounds beef shin or other soup bones, and 2 pounds beef neck, brisket, flanken, or chuck. Add 2 parsnips cut into chunks. Roast the bones until brown in a 450 degree oven (30 to 40 minutes). Follow instructions for White Stock.

COURT BOUILLON (FOR FISH)   *Yield: Approximately 7 cups*

2 quarts cold water
2 pounds trimmings (heads,
    bones, tails) from white fish
    (sole, flounder, whiting)
1 sliced onion
1 sliced carrot
1 small bay leaf
¼ teaspoon dried thyme
3 sprigs parsley, chopped
1 cup white wine
1 tablespoon lemon juice

Combine all ingredients in a large pot. Bring to a rapid boil, skimming off the accumulated foam, then simmer uncovered 20 minutes. Strain and store.

CHICKEN STOCK OR BROTH   *Yield: 2 to 3 quarts*

For the meats and bones of the White Stock recipe, substitute

3 pounds chicken backs, necks, wings, gizzards, and hearts. Reduce water to 4 quarts and add salt to taste when cooking is done. Follow instructions for White Stock, reducing cooking time to 2½ hours. For a "kosher-style" chicken broth, add a clove of garlic and 3 large branches of fresh dill with the other vegetables.

VEGETABLE STOCK
Yield: 1 to 2 quarts

3 tablespoons butter
4 medium carrots
2 onions
2 large celery stalks and leaves
4 leeks
3 quarts cold water
1 medium bay leaf
4 large sprigs parsley
½ teaspoon dried thyme
2 teaspoons salt
¼ teaspoon pepper

1. In butter in a large pot, sauté diced or chopped carrots, scallions, onion, celery, and leeks until golden, about 15 minutes.

2. Cover vegetables with cold water, bring to a boil, and skim off foam. Reduce heat. Add bay leaf, parsley, thyme, salt, and pepper, and simmer covered 2 hours. Strain and store.

WHITE SAUCE (*SAUCE BÉCHAMEL*)
Yield: 2 cups

2 tablespoons butter
3 tablespoons all-purpose flour
2 cups hot White Stock
Salt and pepper to taste

Melt the butter in an enamel saucepan over low heat. With a wire whisk, stir in the flour until smooth, making a *roux*. Add the hot liquid all at once, stirring constantly. Keep stirring until the sauce thickens, about 5 to 10 minutes.

BROWN SAUCE (*SAUCE BRUNE*)

Yield: 2 cups

Follow the procedure for White Sauce, but use Beef Stock instead of White Stock. Cook the *roux* very slowly until it turns a rich brown. While browning the *roux*, keep it from drying out with small additions of stock. This is the basis of some famous Creole recipes. The flavor key is the cooking of the *roux*, which can take literally 8 to 12 hours.

LEMON BUTTER SAUCE

Yield: 2 to 4 portions

This is a classic sauce to use on green vegetables such as asparagus, and artichokes.

2 tablespoons lemon juice
⅛ teaspoon salt
½ cup butter (1 quarter-pound stick)

In a small saucepan, simmer the lemon juice and salt until the liquid is reduced by half. Remove from the heat and stir in the butter in pats until all the butter has melted. Return the pan to the heat now and then if necessary to keep the butter melting. Don't let it brown or boil.

BOILING OVER

Rub the top two inches of the pot all around with fat or oil before making pea soup and other types of starchy foods that tend to boil over.

STEWS AND CASSEROLES

Stews and casseroles combine pan-frying, or sautéing, with braising. Casserole is the French word for pot, and when applied to a stew, it generally means one that has several ingredients other than meat. A stew is apt to be meat with some flavorings, such as onions.

Once you have made one stew, you should be able to make any stew. The first step is to brown the meat in a little fat, although you may slice and sauté an onion first, and even add a clove or two of garlic to flavor the dish. The secret to tasty stews is to really brown the meat. All that takes is the patience to stand over a moderately hot burner turning the meat pieces until they are well colored. Flour may be added at this point to thicken the stew. Liquid, preferably stock or broth, is added next. Scraping up the pan juices after this liquid has been added is another secret to tasty stews. Get up all that browned-on gravy so it will make a rich sauce for the stew.

The next step is to cook the stew slowly, covered, until tender, usually an hour or two. Chicken dishes are ready within an hour, but most meats benefit from slow cooking at 325 degrees or so in the oven, or at "simmer" on the top of the stove. A tightly fitted lid is essential to keep the liquid from escaping and the dish from drying. Check a stew often to make sure it hasn't dried and is on its way to incineration, especially if there are starches in it that absorb liquid, such as beans or rice. A crockpot is the ideal way to handle the cooking of a stew or casserole from step 2 on as it lets no liquid escape.

ELECTRIC CROCKERY POTS

A great help to the working homemaker is a slow-cooking electric crockery pot for making stews, soups, and pot roasts. These come with their own recipe booklets, but you can use them with your favorite recipes, too. Most pots have two settings. "Low" is used if you are going to be away all day or if you want to cook overnight to take advantage of low electricity rates. "High" is used if you want the food to be ready in three to four hours. Add an automatic timer to the equipment if you want the pot to turn itself off at a specific time.

For maximum flavor in slow-cooked stews, you must brown the meat before putting it into the pot, just as if you were going to cook in a Dutch oven or casserole. If you throw all the ingredients into the slow cooker, add water, and make no further effort, the food will taste like soup. On the "low" setting, no steam escapes, so sauces tend to be thin. When cooking is completed, thicken these sauces with a *roux*. When preparing regular casserole recipes (not especially formulated for electric crockery pots), reduce the water specified in the recipe by one-half or one-third. Vegetables cooked for hours turn golden brown. If you want pure white potatoes or pure orange carrots, cook them separately and add to the slow-pot stew just before serving.

MAKING SOUPS

There are two basic approaches to soup making. The first is to put all the ingredients into a large pot, including, of course, plenty of water, bring this to a boil, covered, then reduce the heat and simmer until the soup tastes good (you will surely need to season it a little at the end) and all the ingredients are tender. If there are beans, rice, barley, or other liquid-absorbing grains in the soup, you will probably need to add more water toward the end of the cooking.

Another approach to soup-making calls for sautéing a sliced onion in butter or a little fat until the onion is translucent, then either browning meat pieces a little, or cooking vegetable pieces a little—say 5 minutes for vegetables, 10 for

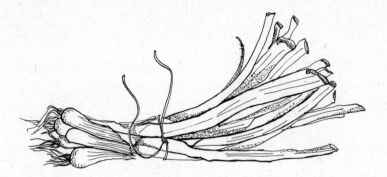

meats—then adding liquid and cooking as described above. Your own taste in seasonings dictates the final flavor of the dish.

TOMATO SOUP SAVER

To keep cream of tomato soup from curdling as you add the cream or milk, beat a pinch of baking soda into the tomato mixture before adding the cream or milk.

FROM-SCRATCH BAKING RECIPES

The grand art of baking has succumbed in most households to the depredations of the ready-boxed mix. Many are excellent as well as easy. Possibly, the only incentive to a return to from-scratch baking is the high cost of these labor-saving packages. To make boxed mixes more personal, add your own flavorings: chopped nuts, grated citrus rind, liqueurs, raisins, chocolate chips, whatever seems desirable. And underbeat the cakes. Below are a handful of from-scratch recipes for classic baked goods, handy when you run out of mix and face an emergency.

CAKE COOLER

To get a hot cake layer out of the pan before it cools, turn the cake upside down on a plate and rub ice cubes on the bottom of the pan. The cake will fall out.

BASIC LAYER CAKE

Serves 10 to 12

A good recipe for birthday cakes. Freezes well, too.

3 cups sifted cake flour
3 teaspoons baking powder
⅛ teaspoon salt
1 cup shortening,
   preferably butter
2 cups granulated sugar
4 eggs
1 cup milk
1 teaspoon vanilla, almond,
   lemon, or orange extract
Icing

1. Preheat the oven to 375 degrees.

2. Measure the flour, baking powder, and salt into a sifter and sift into a large bowl.

3. In another large bowl, using an electric beater, beat the shortening and sugar until creamy, adding the eggs one at a time. Add ⅓ of the flour mixture at a time, alternately with the milk. Add the extract.

4. Turn into two 8 inch square or round cake pans. Bake for 25 minutes, or until a straw comes out clean. Cool on a rack for 10 minutes, then turn out of the pans and cool thoroughly.

5. Lay one layer on a cake plate and cover with icing. Place the other layer on top, and cover the whole cake with the remaining icing.

BASIC CREAM FROSTING

Fills and frosts 1 layer cake

½ cup butter
½ cup flavoring, such as maple syrup, or frozen orange
   concentrate, or melted semisweet chocolate
½ teaspoon salt
1 egg
2 teaspoons vanilla extract
2¾ or more cups confectioners' sugar
½ cup chopped walnuts or pecans, or chocolate chips
12 whole nuts, optional

Cream the butter with an electric beater. Then beat in the flavoring, salt, egg, and vanilla. Beat in the confectioners' sugar until the icing reaches a consistency that will spread easily, but hold its shape. Mix in the nuts or chocolate chips, or other flavor accents, if you wish, and use to fill and ice a layer cake. Garnish with the whole nuts.

CAKE DISASTERS AND THEIR CAUSES

Heavy soggy cakes: too slow an oven.

Coarse-grained cakes: too much leavening, too slow an oven, insufficient creaming, or insufficient beating before addition of egg whites.

Large holes in angelfood cakes: egg whites weren't blended in well enough. Too hot an oven will produce the same effect.

Cake falling: not enough flour, too hot an oven, or opening the oven door before the cell walls have become firmed by the heat.

Bready cake: too much flour.

Uneven surface: too much heat.

BAKING PIE SHELLS

When baking a pastry shell for a pie, prick the bottom of the dough all over and turn a bit of the pastry under the rim on each side of the pie plate to hold it in place.

BASIC PIE CRUST RECIPE   *Makes 2 crusts*

---

2 cups all-purpose flour
½ teaspoon salt
2 teaspoons granulated sugar
   (omit if for a meat pie)
½ teaspoon baking powder
⅔ cup shortening
1 tablespoon butter
4 tablespoons ice water
Milk

---

1. Sift together the flour, salt, sugar, and baking powder. Using two knives, or the chopping blade of the food processor, cut the shortening and butter into the dry ingredients. Dribble in the water. Press the crumbs together with a fork, or beat with the chopper, until a ball forms. Shape the ball into two flattish rounds, one for a top, and one for a bottom crust.

2. Roll the dough out on a floured board. Flip it a quarter turn at each rolling until it is the size of your pie plate. Fold the pastry in four, gently lift onto the plate and unfold. Let rest for 5 minutes, then pat to fit the pie plate. (Note: If the pastry bottom is to be used as a shell and precooked, bake at 425 degrees for 15 to 20 minutes, after pricking all over with a fork to keep it from bubbling.)

3. Add the filling, top with the second ball of dough rolled out, prick with a fork to let steam escape. Flute the edges with a fork. Brush the pastry with milk to help it color while cooking. Bake at 425 degrees for 15 to 20 minutes, then at 325 degrees for 20 to 30 minutes longer.

LEVITATING NUTS

To prevent nuts and fruits from sinking to the bottom of a batter during cooking, warm them a little in the oven and toss them with flour (shaking off any excess flour) before you mix them into the batter.

CARROT CAKE   *Serves 10 to 12*

2 cups all-purpose flour
2 cups granulated sugar
2 teaspoons baking powder
1 teaspoon salt
2 teaspoons ground cinnamon
4 eggs
1 cup vegetable oil
4 cups raw grated carrot
   (about 8 carrots)
½ cup chopped pecans
Cream Cheese Frosting

1. Preheat the oven to 350 degrees.

2. Measure the flour, sugar, baking powder, salt, and cinnamon into a sifter and sift three times.

3. Break the eggs into a large bowl and beat until thick. Dribble in the oil, still beating, then the flour. Fold in the carrots and nuts. Pour into 2 well-greased and floured 8-inch cake pans.

4. Bake for 25 to 30 minutes. Cool in the pan for 10 minutes, then turn the cakes out onto racks and cool completely. Spread the frosting between the layers, and over the top of the cake.

THE MAGIC OF BAKING POWDER

Most recipes today call for "double acting" baking powder, which reacts very slowly, releasing about one-fifth to one-third of its carbon dioxide when liquid is added at room temperature, the balance when it becomes heated. Phosphate baking powder also reacts slowly, releasing one-third of its gases when heated. Tartrate powder reacts rapidly and begins its action as soon as liquid is added. Nationally sold brands indicate the type of baking powder they contain right on the label and give instructions for use of their product with heavy flours, such as whole wheat, and with fruits. Check these rather than blindly following recipe instructions concerning baking powder.

CREAM CHEESE FROSTING

6 tablespoons sweet butter
10 ounces cream cheese
1½ cups confectioners' sugar
1 teaspoon vanilla extract
1 teaspoon maple flavoring
Cream

1. Cream the butter and cheese. Then beat in the sugar and flavorings and enough cream to make the frosting of spreading consistency—probably a tablespoon or two.

BASIC RECIPE FOR BISCUITS FROM SCRATCH   *Makes 8 to 10 small biscuits*

2 cups all-purpose flour
2 teaspoon baking powder
2 teaspoon granulated sugar
½ teaspoon salt
6 tablespoons butter
½ to 1 cup milk

1. Preheat the oven to 450 degrees.

2. Sift the flour, baking powder, sugar, and salt into a mixing bowl. Cut in the butter as for pie dough. Add the milk, omitting a portion if the dough is reaching the point where it won't hold its shape.

3. Grease and dust a cookie sheet with flour. Drop the dough by table-spoonfuls onto the sheet and brush with a little of the remaining milk to help color while cooking. Bake for 12 to 15 minutes, or until golden brown on top.

BASIC RECIPE FOR DROP COOKIES   *Makes 4 to 5 dozen*

1½ cups cake flour
½ teaspoon salt
3 eggs
1 cup packed light brown sugar

¾ cup broken walnut meats
⅓ cup melted butter
½ teaspoon vanilla extract
½ cup raisins, chocolate chips, or other flavor accents

1. Preheat the oven to 350 degrees.

2. Sift the flour and salt together.

3. In a large bowl, beat the eggs until thick and lemon-colored. Gradually beat in the sugar. Add the nuts, butter, vanilla, and flour mixture. Drop far apart on a greased cookie sheet, and bake for 12 to 15 minutes.

BASIC RECIPES FOR PANCAKES FROM SCRATCH   *Makes 12*

Pancakes are large; hot cakes are small pancakes. The same batter is used for waffles. You may add blueberries, thin apple slices, and other fruits to the batter before frying. Serve with butter, preferably sweet, and maple or other syrup.

1 cup sifted all-purpose flour
½ teaspoon salt
1 tablespoon granulated sugar, optional
2 teaspoons baking powder
1 egg
¾ cup milk, or more
2 tablespoons melted bacon fat, or butter

1. Preheat the griddle or a heavy frying pan to very hot— 375 degrees on your electric griddle, or until a drop of water sizzles, rolls rapidly across the surface, and vanishes.

2. Sift the dry ingredients, or not; it's not critical. Beat in the egg and milk. If you like thin pancakes, add ¼ to ⅓ cup more milk. Beat in the melted fat. Turn into a large pitcher to make it easier to control the amount to be poured on griddle or frying pan.

3. Grease the griddle generously.

4. Pour enough batter to make a 4-inch round, and as many more of these as the griddle or pan will hold, separately. When the surface begins to look dry and bubbles have formed all over, flip with a spatula. If the cakes are getting too dark, remove the pan from the heat for a minute or two to cool it down. Keep finished cakes warm in a 250 degree oven while you cook the rest.

6 CALORIE COUNTER

COUNTING CALORIES

CALORIE CHART

MILK, CHEESE, AND ICE CREAM

Milk, Fluid:

Whole	1 cup or glass	160
Skim	1 cup or glass	90
Partly skimmed, 2% nonfat milk solids added	1 cup or glass	145
Buttermilk	1 cup or glass	90
Evaporated, undiluted	½ cup	175
Condensed, sweetened, undiluted	½ cup	490

Cream:

Half-and-half (milk and cream)	1 cup	325
	1 tablespoon	20
Light, coffee or table	1 tablespoon	30
Sour	1 tablespoon	25
Whipped topping (pressurized)	1 tablespoon	10
Whipping, unwhipped (volume about double when whipped):		
Light	1 tablespoon	45
Heavy	1 tablespoon	55

Imitation cream products

Creamers: (made with vegetable fat):		
Powdered	1 teaspoon	10
Liquid (frozen)	1 tablespoon	20
Sour dressing (imitation sour cream) made with nonfat dry milk	1 tablespoon	20
Whipped topping:		
Pressurized	1 tablespoon	10
Frozen	1 tablespoon	10
Powdered, made with whole milk	1 tablespoon	10

Cheese:

Natural:		
Blue or Roquefort type	1 ounce	105
	1 cubic inch	65
Camembert, packed in 4-ounce package with 3 wedges per package	1 wedge	115
Cheddar	1 ounce	115
	1 cubic inch	70
	½ cup grated (2 ounces)	225

CALORIE CHART

MILK, CHEESE, AND ICE CREAM

Cheese:

Cottage, large or small curd:		
Creamed	1 cup curd (pressed down)	260
	2 tablespoons (1 ounce)	30
Uncreamed	1 cup curd (pressed down)	170
	2 tablespoons (1 ounce)	20
Cream	1 ounce	105
	1 cubic inch	60
Parmesan, grated	1 tablespoon	25
	1 ounce	130
Swiss	1 ounce	105
	1 cubic inch	55
Pasteurized processed:		
American	1 ounce	105
	1 cubic inch	65
Swiss	1 ounce	100
	1 cubic inch	65
Pasteurized process cheese food:		
American	1 tablespoon	45
	1 cubic inch	55
Pasteurized process cheese spread:		
American	1 tablespoon	40
	1 ounce	80

Milk beverages:

Chocolate, homemade	1 cup	240
Cocoa, homemade	1 cup	245
Chocolate-flavored drink made with skim milk and 2% added butterfat	1 cup	190
Chocolate-flavored drink made with whole milk	1 cup	215
Malted milk	1 cup	245
Chocolate milkshake	One 12-ounce container	430

Milk desserts:

Custard, baked	1 cup	305
Ice cream:		
Regular (about 10% fat)	1 cup	255
Rich (about 16% fat)	1 cup	330
Ice milk:		
Hardened	1 cup	200
Soft-serve	1 cup	265
Yogurt:		
Made from partially skimmed milk	1 cup	125
Made from whole milk	1 cup	150

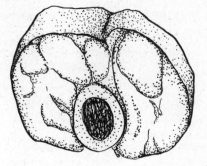

MEAT, POULTRY, FISH, EGGS, DRY BEANS AND PEAS, NUTS

MEAT, COOKED, WITHOUT BONE:

Beef:

Pot roast, braised, or simmered:

Lean and fat	3 ounces (1 thick or 2 thin slices, 4 by 2⅛ inches).	245
Lean only	3 ounces (1 thick or 2 thin slices, 4 by 2⅛ inches).	165

Oven roast:

Cut relatively fat, such as rib:

Lean and fat	3 ounces (1 thick or 2 thin slices, 4 by 2¼ inches)	375
Lean only	3 ounces (1 thick or 2 thin slices, 4 by 2¼ inches)	205

Cut relatively lean, such as round:

Lean and fat	3 ounces (1 thick or 2 thin slices, 4 by 2¼ inches)	220
Lean only	3 ounces (1 thick or 2 thin slices, 4 by 2¼ inches)	160

Steak, broiled:

Cut relatively fat, such as sirloin:

Lean and fat	3 ounces (1 piece, 3½ by 2 inches by ¾ inch)	330
Lean only	3 ounces (1 piece, 3½ by 2 inches by ¾ inch)	175

Cut relatively lean, such as round:

Lean and fat	3 ounces (1 piece, 4 by 2 inches by ½ inch)	220
Lean only	3 ounces (1 piece, 4 by 2¼ inches by ½ inch	160

Hamburger patty:

Regular ground beef	3-ounce patty, 2⅝ inches in diameter, ¾ inch thick (about 4 patties per pound of raw meat)	245
Lean ground beef	3-ounce patty, 2⅝ inches in diameter, ¾ inch thick (about 4 patties per pound of raw meat)	185
Corned beef, canned	3 ounces (1 piece, 4 by 2½ inches by ½ inch)	185

MEAT, POULTRY, FISH, EGGS, DRY BEANS AND PEAS, NUTS

MEAT, COOKED, WITHOUT BONE:

Beef:

Corned beef hash, canned	3 ounces (about 2/5 cup)	155
Dried beef, chipped	2 ounces (about 1/3 cup)	115
Dried beef, creamed	1/2 cup	190
Beef and vegetable stew, canned	1/2 cup	95
Beef potpie, home-prepared, baked	1/4 pie, 9 inches in diameter	385
Chili con carne, canned:		
Without beans	1/2 cup	240
With beans	1/2 cup	170

Veal:

Cutlet, broiled, meat only	3 ounces (1 piece, 3 3/4 by 2 1/2 inches by 3/8 inch)	185
Roast	3 ounces (1 thick or 2 thin slices, 4 by 2 1/4 inches)	230

Lamb:

Loin chop (about 3 chops to a pound, as purchased):		
Lean and fat	3 1/2 ounces	355
Lean only	About 2 1/3 ounces	120
Leg, roasted:		
Lean and fat	3 ounces (1 thick or 2 thin slices, 4 by 2 1/4 inches)	235
Lean only	3 ounces (1 thick or 2 thin slices, 4 by 2 1/4 inches)	160
Shoulder, roasted:		
Lean and fat	3 ounces (1 thick or 2 thin slices, 4 by 2 1/4 inches)	285
Lean only	3 ounces (1 thick or 2 thin slices, 4 by 2 1/4 inches)	175

Pork:

Fresh:		
Chop (about 3 chops to a pound, as purchased):		
Lean and fat	About 2 2/3 ounces	305
Lean only	2 ounces	150
Roast, loin:		
Lean and fat	3 ounces (1 thick or 2 thin slices, 3 1/2 by 2 1/2 inches)	310
Lean only	3 ounces (1 thick or 2 thin slices, 3 1/2 by 2 1/2 inches)	215

Cured:
Ham:

Lean and fat	3 ounces (1 thick or 2 thin slices, 3½ by 2½ inches)	245
Lean only	3 ounces (1 thick or 2 thin slices, 3½ by 2½ inches)	160
Bacon, broiled or fried crisp	2 thin slices (28 slices per pound)	60
	2 medium slices (20 slices per pound)	85
Bacon, Canadian, cooked	1 slice, 3⅜ inches in diameter, 3/16 inch thick	60

Sausage and variety and luncheon meats:

Bologna sausage	2 ounces (2 very thin slices, 4½ inches in diameter)	170
Braunschweiger	2 ounces (2 slices, 3⅛ inches in diameter)	180
Vienna sausage, canned	2 ounces (3½ sausages)	135
Pork sausage:		
Link	4 links, 4 inches long (4 ounces, uncooked)	250
Bulk	2 patties, 3⅞ inches by ¼ inch (4 ounces, uncooked)	260
Liver, beef, fried (includes fat for frying)	3 ounces (1 piece, 6½ by 2⅜ inches by ⅜ inch)	195
Heart, beef, braised, trimmed of fat	3 ounces (1 thick piece, 4 by 2½ inches)	160
Salami	2 ounces (2 slices, 4½ inches in diameter)	175
Tongue, beef, braised	3 ounces (1 slice, 3 by 2 inches by ⅜ inch)	210
Frankfurter	1 frankfurter, 2 ounces (8 per pound)	170
Boiled ham (luncheon meat)	2 ounces (2 very thin slices, 6¼ by 4 inches)	135
Spiced ham, canned	2 ounces (2 thin slices, 3 by 2 inches)	165

Poultry, cooked, without bone:

Chicken:		
Broiled (no skin)	3 ounces (about ¼ of a broiler)	115
Fried	½ breast, 2⅘ ounces, meat only.	160
	1 thigh, 1⅘ ounces, meat only	120
	1 drumstick, 1⅓ ounces, meat only	90
Canned	3½ ounces (½ cup)	200
Poultry pie, home-prepared, baked	¼ pie, 9 inches in diameter	410
Turkey, roasted:		
Light meat (no skin)	3 ounces (1 thick or 2 thin slices, 4¼ by 2 inches)	150
Dark meat (no skin)	3 ounces (1 thick or 2 thin slices, 4¼ by 2 inches)	175

Fish and shellfish:

Bluefish, baked with fat	3 ounces (1 piece, 3½ by 2 inches by ½ inch)	135
Clams, shelled:		
Raw, meat only	3 ounces (about 4 medium clams)	65
Canned, clams and juice	3 ounces (1 scant half cup, 3 medium clams and juice)	45

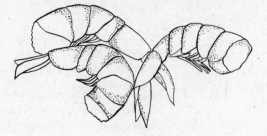

MEAT, POULTRY, FISH, EGGS, DRY BEANS AND PEAS, NUTS

MEAT, COOKED, WITHOUT BONE:

Fish and shellfish:

Crabmeat, canned or cooked	3 ounces (½ cup)	80
Fish sticks, breaded, cooked, frozen (including breading and fat for frying)	3 ounces (3 fish sticks, 4 by 1 inch by ½ inch)	150
Haddock, breaded, fried (including fat for frying)	3 ounces (1 fillet, 4 by 2½ inches by ½ inch)	140
Mackerel:		
Broiled with fat	3 ounces (1 piece, 4 by 3 inches by ½ inch)	200
Canned	3 ounces, solids and liquids (about ⅖ cup)	155
Ocean perch, breaded, fried (including fat for frying)	3 ounces (1 piece, 4 by 2½ inches by ½ inch)	195
Oysters, raw, meat only	½ cup (6 to 10 medium size oysters, selects)	80
Salmon:		
Broiled or baked	4 ounces (1 steak, 4½ by 2½ inches by ½ inch)	205
Canned (pink)	3 ounces, solids and liquids (about ⅗ cup)	120
Sardines, canned in oil	3 ounces, drained solids (7 medium sardines)	170
Shrimp, canned, meat only	3 ounces (27 medium shrimp)	100
Tunafish, canned in oil	3 ounces, drained solids (½ cup)	170

Eggs:

Fried (including fat for frying)	1 large egg	100
Hard or soft cooked, "boiled"	1 large egg	80
Scrambled or omelet (including milk and fat for cooking)	1 large egg	110
Poached	1 large egg	80

Dry beans and peas:

Red kidney beans, canned or cooked	½ cup, solids and liquid	110
Lima, cooked	½ cup	130
Baked beans, canned:		
With pork and tomato sauce	½ cup	155
With pork and sweet sauce	½ cup	190

Nuts:

Almonds, shelled	2 tablespoons (15 almonds)	105
Brazil nuts, shelled	2 tablespoons (4 to 5 large kernels)	115
Cashew nuts, roasted	2 tablespoons (11 to 12 medium nuts)	100
Coconut, fresh, shredded meat	2 tablespoons	55
Peanuts, roasted, shelled	2 tablespoons	105
Peanut butter	1 tablespoon	95
Pecans, shelled halves	2 tablespoons (10 jumbo or 15 large)	95
Walnuts, shelled:		
Black or native, chopped	2 tablespoons	100
English or Persian, halves	2 tablespoons (about 6 to 7 halves)	80
Chopped	2 tablespoons	105

VEGETABLES AND FRUITS

Vegetables:

Asparagus, cooked or canned	6 medium spears or ½ cup cut spears	20
Beans:		
Lima, green, cooked, or canned	½ cup	90
Snap, green, wax or yellow, cooked or canned	½ cup	15
Beets, cooked or canned	½ cup, diced, slices, or small whole	30
Beet greens, cooked	½ cup	15
Broccoli, cooked	½ cup chopped or 3 stalks, 4½ to 5 inches long	25
Brussels sprouts, cooked	½ cup, 4 sprouts, 1¼ to 1½ inches in diameter	25
Cabbage:		
Raw	½ cup, shredded, chopped, or sliced	10
Coleslaw, with mayonnaise	½ cup	85
Coleslaw, with mayonnaise-type salad dressing	½ cup	60
Cooked	½ cup	15
Carrots:		
Raw	1 carrot, 7½ inches long, 1⅛ inches in diameter	30
	½ cup, grated	25
Cooked or canned	½ cup	25
Cauliflower, cooked	½ cup flower buds	15
Celery:		
Raw	3 inner stalks, 5 inches long	10
Cooked	½ cup, diced	10
Chard, cooked	½ cup	15
Chicory, raw	½ cup, ½-inch pieces	5
Chives, raw	1 tablespoon	trace

Vegetables:

Collards, cooked	½ cup	25
Corn:		
On cob, cooked	1 ear, 5 inches long, 1¾ inches in diameter	70
Kernels, cooked or canned	½ cup	70
Cream style	½ cup	105
Cress, garden, cooked	½ cup	15
Cucumbers, raw, pared	6 center slices, ⅛ inch thick	5
Dandelion greens, cooked	½ cup	15
Eggplant, cooked	½ cup, diced	20
Endive, raw	½ cup, small pieces	5
Kale, cooked	½ cup	20
Kohlrabi, cooked	½ cup	20
Lettuce, raw	2 large leaves	5
	½ cup, shredded or chopped	5
	1 wedge, ⅙ of head	10
Mushrooms, canned	½ cup	20
Mustard greens, cooked	½ cup	15
Okra, cooked	½ cup, cuts and pods	35
	½ cup, sliced	25
Onions:		
Young, green, raw	2 medium or 6 small, without tops	15
	1 tablespoon, chopped	5
Mature:		
Raw	1 tablespoon, chopped	5
Cooked	½ cup	30
Parsley, raw	1 tablespoon, chopped	trace
Parsnips, cooked,	½ cup, diced	50
	½ cup, mashed	70
Peas, cooked or canned	½ cup	65
Peppers, green:		
Raw	1 ring, ¼ inch thick	trace
	1 tablespoon, chopped	trace
Cooked	1 medium, 2¾ inches long, 2½ inches in diameter	15
Potatoes:		
Baked	1 potato, 4¾ inches long, 2⅓ inches in diameter	145
Boiled	1 potato, 2½ inches in diameter	90
	½ cup, diced	55
Chips	10 chips, 1¾ by 2½ inches	115
French-fried:		
Cooked in deep fat	10 pieces, 3½ to 4 inches long	215
Frozen, heated, ready-to-serve	10 pieces, 3½ to 4 inches long	170

Pan fried from raw	½ cup	230
Hash browned	½ cup	175
Mashed:		
Milk added	½ cup	70
Milk and tablefat added	½ cup	100
Made from granules		
with milk and tablefat added	½ cup	100
Au gratin	½ cup	180
Scalloped without cheese	½ cup	125
Salad:		
Made with cooked salad dressing	½ cup	125
Made with mayonnaise or		
french dressing and eggs	½ cup	180
Sticks	½ cup, pieces ¾ inch to 2¾ inches long	95
Pumpkin, canned	½ cup	40
Radishes, raw	5 medium	5
Rutabagas, cooked,	½ cup, diced or sliced	30
Sauerkraut, canned	½ cup	20
Spinach, cooked or canned	½ cup	25
Squash:		
Summer, cooked	½ cup	15
Winter:		
Baked	½ cup, mashed	65
Boiled	½ cup, mashed	45
Sweetpotatoes:		
Baked in skin	1 potato, 5 inches long, 2 inches in diameter	160
Candied	½ potato, 2½ inches long	160
Canned	½ cup, mashed	140
Tomatoes:		
Raw	1 tomato, 2⅖ inches in diameter	20
Cooked or canned	½ cup	30
Tomato juice, canned	½ cup	25
Tomato juice cocktail, canned	½ cup	25
Turnips:		
Raw	½ cup, cubed or sliced	20

Vegetables:

Cooked	½ cup, diced	20
Turnip greens, cooked	½ cup	15
Vegetable juice cocktail	½ cup	20
Watercress, raw	10 sprigs	5

Fruits:

Apples, raw	1 medium, 2¾ inches in diameter (about ⅓ pound)	80
Applejuice, canned	½ cup	60
Applesauce:		
Sweetened	½ cup	115
Unsweetened	½ cup	50
Apricots:		
Raw	3 (about 12 per pound as purchased)	55
Canned:		
Water pack	½ cup, halves and liquid	45
Heavy syrup pack	½ cup, halves and syrup	110
Dried, cooked, unsweetened	½ cup, fruit and juice	105
Avocados:		
California varieties	½ of a 10-ounce avocado, 3⅛ inches in diameter	190
Florida varieties	½ of a 16-ounce avocado, 3⅝ inches in diameter	205
Bananas, raw	1 banana, 6 to 7 inches long (about ⅓ pound)	85
	1 banana, 8 to 9 inches long (about ⅖ pound)	100
Berries:		
Blackberries, raw	½ cup	40
Blueberries:		
Fresh, raw	½ cup	45
Frozen, sweetened	½ cup	120
Frozen, unsweetened	½ cup	45
Raspberries:		
Fresh, red, raw	½ cup	35
Frozen, red, sweetened	½ cup	120
Fresh, black, raw	½ cup	50
Strawberries:		
Fresh, raw	½ cup	30
Frozen, sweetened	½ cup, sliced	140
Cantaloup, raw	½ melon, 5 inches in diameter	80
Cherries:		
Sour:		
Raw, with pits	½ cup	30

Canned, water pack, pitted	½ cup	50
Sweet:		
Raw, with pits	½ cup	40
Canned:		
Water pack, with pits	½ cup	65
Syrup pack, with pits	½ cup	105
Dates, "fresh" and dried, pitted, cut	½ cup	245
Figs:		
Raw	3 small, 1½ inches in diameter (about ¼ pound)	95
Canned, heavy syrup	½ cup	110
Dried	1 large, 2 inches by 1 inch	60
Fruit cocktail, canned in heavy syrup	½ cup	95
Grapefruit:		
Raw:		
White	½ medium, 3¾ inches in diameter	45
	½ cup sections	40
Pink or red	½ medium, 3¾ inches in diameter	50
Canned:		
Water pack	½ cup	35
Syrup pack	½ cup	90
Grapefruit juice:		
Raw	½ cup	50
Canned:		
Unsweetened	½ cup	50
Sweetened	½ cup	65
Frozen concentrate, diluted, ready-to-serve:		
Unsweetened	½ cup	50
Sweetened	½ cup	60
Grapes, raw:		
American type (including Concord, Delaware, Niagara, and Scuppernong), slip skin	1 bunch, 3½ by 3 inches (about 3½ ounces)	45
	½ cup with skins and seeds	35
European type (including Malaga, Muscat, Thompson seedless, and Flame Tokay), adherent skin	½ cup	55
Grapejuice:		
Bottled	½ cup	85
Frozen, diluted with 3 parts water by volume	½ cup	65
Honeydew melon, raw	1 wedge, 2 by 7 inches (1/10 of melon)	50
Lemon juice, raw or canned	½ cup	30
	1 tablespoon	5
Oranges, raw	1 orange, 2⅝ inches in diameter	65

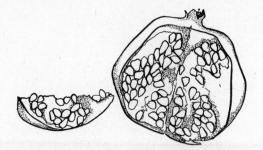

VEGETABLES AND FRUITS

Fruits:

Orange juice:

Raw	½ cup	55
Canned, unsweetened	½ cup	60
Frozen concentrate, diluted, ready-to-serve	½ cup	55

Peaches:

Raw	1 medium, 2½ inches in diameter (about ¼ pound)	40
	½ cup, sliced	30
Canned:		
Water pack	½ cup	40
Heavy syrup pack	½ cup	100
Dried, cooked, unsweetened	½ cup (5 to 6 halves and liquid)	100
Frozen, sweetened	½ cup	110

Pears:

Raw	1 pear, 3½ inches long, 2½ inches in diameter	100
Canned:		
Water pack	½ cup	40
Heavy syrup pack	½ cup	95

Pineapple:

Raw	½ cup, diced	40
Canned in heavy syrup:		
Crushed, tidbits, or chunks	½ cup	95
Sliced	2 small or 1 large slice and 2 tablespoons juice	80
Pineapple juice, canned, unsweetened	½ cup	70

Plums:

Raw:		
Damson	5 plums, 1 inch in diameter (about 2 ounces)	35
Japanese	1 plum, 2⅛ inches in diameter (about 2½ ounces)	30
Canned, syrup pack, with pits	½ cup	105

Prunes, dried, cooked:

Unsweetened	½ cup, fruit and liquid	125
Sweetened	½ cup, fruit and liquid	205
Prune juice, canned	½ cup	100
Raisins, dried	½ cup, packed	240
Rhubarb, cooked, sweetened	½ cup	190
Tangerine, raw	1 medium 2⅜ inches in diameter (about ¼ pound)	40

Tangerine juice, canned:

Unsweetened	½ cup	55
Sweetened	½ cup	60
Watermelon, raw	1 wedge, 4 by 8 inches (about 2 pounds, including rind)	110

BREAD AND CEREALS

Bread:

Cracked wheat	1 slice, 9/16 inch thick	65
Raisin	1 slice, ½ inch thick	65
Rye	1 slice, 7/16 inch thick	60
White:		
Soft crumb:		
Regular slice	1 slice, 9/16 inch thick	70
Thin slice	1 slice, 7/16 inch thick	55
Firm crumb	1 slice, 7/16 inch thick	65
Whole wheat:		
Soft crumb	1 slice, 9/16 inch thick	65
Firm crumb	1 slice, 7/16 inch thick	60

Other baked goods:

Baking powder biscuit:		
Home recipe	1 biscuit, 2 inches in diameter	105
Mix	1 biscuit, 2 inches in diameter	90

Cakes, cookies, pies (see Desserts)
Crackers:

Butter	1 cracker, 2 inches in diameter	15
Cheese	1 cracker, 2 inches in diameter	15
Graham	4 small or 2 medium	55
Saltines	4 crackers, 1⅞ inches square	50
Oyster	10 crackers	35
Rye	2 wafers, 1⅞ by 3½ inches	45

Doughnuts:

Cake-type, plain	1 doughnut, 3¼ inches in diameter	165
Yeast-leavened, raised	1 doughnut, 3¾ inches in diameter	175

Muffins:

Plain	1 muffin, 3 inches in diameter	120
Blueberry	1 muffin, 2³/₈ inches in diameter	110
Bran	1 muffin, 2⁵/₈ in diameter	105
Corn	1 muffin, 2³/₈ inches in diameter	125

Pancakes (griddle cakes):

Wheat (home recipe or mix)	1 cake, 4 inches in diameter	60
Buckwheat (with buckwheat pancake mix)	1 cake, 4 inches in diameter	55

Pizza (cheese) — 5¹/₃-inch sector, ¹/₈ of a 13³/₄-inch pie — 155

Pretzels:

Dutch, twisted	1 pretzel	60
Stick	5 regular (3¹/₈ inches long) or 10 small (2¹/₄ inches long)	10

Rolls:

Danish pastry, plain	1 pastry, 4¹/₂ inches in diameter	275
Hamburger or frankfurter	1 roll (16 per pound)	120
Hard, round or rectangular	1 roll (9 per pound)	155
Plain, pan	1 roll (16 per pound)	85
Waffles	1 waffle, 7 inches in diameter	210

Cereals and other grain products:

Bran flakes (40 percent bran)	1 ounce (about ⁴/₅ cup)	85
Bran flakes with raisins	1 ounce (about ³/₅ cup)	80
Corn, puffed, presweetened	1 ounce (about 1 cup)	115
Corn, shredded	1 ounce (about 1¹/₆ cups)	110
Corn flakes	1 ounce (about 1¹/₆ cups)	110
Corn flakes, sugar coated	1 ounce (about ²/₃ cup)	110
Corn grits, degermed, cooked	³/₄ cup	95
Farina, cooked, quick-cooking	³/₄ cup	80
Macaroni, cooked	³/₄ cup	115
Macaroni and cheese:		
Home recipe	¹/₂ cup	215
Canned	¹/₂ cup	115
Noodles, cooked	³/₄ cup	150
Oats, puffed	1 ounce (about 1¹/₆ cups)	115
Oats, puffed, sugar coated	1 ounce (about ⁴/₅ cup)	115
Oatmeal or rolled oats, cooked	³/₄ cup	100
Rice, cooked, instant	³/₄ cup	135
Rice flakes	1 ounce (about 1 cup)	110
Rice, puffed	1 ounce (about 2 cups)	115
Rice, puffed, presweetened	1 ounce (about ²/₃ cup)	110
Rice, shredded	1 ounce (about 1¹/₈ cups)	115

Spaghetti, cooked	3/4 cup	115
Spaghetti with meat balls:		
Home recipe	3/4 cup	250
Canned	3/4 cup	195
Spaghetti in tomato sauce with cheese:		
Home recipe	3/4 cup	195
Canned	3/4 cup	140
Wheat, puffed	1 ounce (about 1⅞ cups)	105
Wheat, puffed, presweetened	1 ounce (about ⅘ cup)	105
Wheat, rolled, cooked	3/4 cup	135
Wheat, shredded, plain (long, round, or bite-size)	1 ounce (1 large biscuit or ½ cup bite-size)	100
Wheat flakes	1 ounce (about 1 cup)	100
Wheat flours:		
Whole wheat	3/4 cup, stirred	300
All-purpose	3/4 cup, sifted	315
Wheat germ	1 tablespoon	25

FATS, OILS, AND RELATED PRODUCTS

Butter or margarine	1 tablespoon	100
	1 pat, 1 inch square, ⅓ inch thick	35
Margarine, whipped	1 tablespoon	70
	1 pat, 1¼ inches square, ⅓ inch thick	25
Cooking fats:		
Vegetable	1 tablespoon	110
Lard	1 tablespoon	115
Salad or cooking oils	1 tablespoon	120
Salad dressings:		
Regular:		
French	1 tablespoon	65

FATS, OILS, AND RELATED PRODUCTS

Salad dressings:

Blue cheese	1 tablespoon	75
Home-cooked, boiled	1 tablespoon	25
Italian	1 tablespoon	85
Mayonnaise	1 tablespoon	100
Salad dressing, commercial, plain (mayonnaise-type)	1 tablespoon	65
Russian	1 tablespoon	75
Thousand Island	1 tablespoon	80
Low calorie:		
French	1 tablespoon	15
Italian	1 tablespoon	10
Thousand Island	1 tablespoon	25

SUGARS, SWEETS, AND RELATED PRODUCTS

Candy:

Caramels	1 ounce (3 medium caramels)	115
Chocolate creams	1 ounce (2 to 3 pieces, 35 to a pound)	125
Chocolate, milk, sweetened	1-ounce bar	145
Chocolate, milk, sweetened, with almonds	1-ounce bar	150
Chocolate mints	1 ounce (1 to 2 mints, 20 to a pound)	115
Fondant:		
Candy corn	1 ounce (20 pieces)	105
Mints	1 ounce (3 mints, 1½ inches in diameter)	105
Fudge, vanilla or chocolate:		
Plain	1 ounce	115
	1-inch cube	85
With nuts	1 ounce	120
	1-inch cube	90
Gumdrops	1 ounce (about 2½ large or 20 small)	100
Hard candy	1 ounce (3 to 4 candy balls, ¾ inch in diameter)	110
Jellybeans	1 ounce (10 beans)	105
Marshmallows	1 ounce (4 marshmallows, 63 to a pound)	90
Peanut brittle	1 ounce (1½ pieces, 2½ by 1¼ inches by ⅜ inch)	120

Syrup, honey, molasses:

Chocolate syrup:		
Thin type	1 tablespoon	45
Fudge type	1 tablespoon	60
Honey, strained or extracted	1 tablespoon	65
Molasses, cane, light	1 tablespoon	50

Syrup, table blends	1 tablespoon	55
Cranberry sauce, canned, sweetened	1 tablespoon	25
Jam, preserves	1 tablespoon	55
Jelly, marmalade	1 tablespoon	50
Sugar: White, granulated, or brown (packed)	1 teaspoon	15

SOUPS

Bean with pork	1 cup	170
Beef noodle	1 cup	65
Bouillon, broth, and consommé	1 cup	30
Chicken gumbo	1 cup	55
Chicken noodle	1 cup	60
Chicken with rice	1 cup	50
Clam chowder, Manhattan	1 cup	80
Cream of asparagus:		
With water	1 cup	65
With milk	1 cup	145
Cream of Chicken:		
With water	1 cup	95
With milk	1 cup	180
Cream of mushroom:		
With water	1 cup	135
With milk	1 cup	215
Minestrone	1 cup	105
Oyster stew (frozen):		
With water	1 cup	120
With milk	1 cup	200
Tomato:		
With water	1 cup	90
With milk	1 cup	170
Vegetable with beef broth	1 cup	80

DESSERTS

Apple betty	½ cup	160
Brownie, with nuts	1 piece, 1¾ inches square, ⅞ inch thick	90
Cakes:		
Angelcake	2½-inch sector (¹⁄₁₂ of 9¾-inch round cake)	135
Butter cakes:		
Plain, without icing	1 piece, 3 by 3 by 2 inches	315
	1 cupcake, 2¾ inches in diameter	115

DESSERTS

Cakes:

Plain, with chocolate icing	1¾-inch sector (¹⁄₁₆ of 9-inch round layer cake)	240
	1 cupcake, 2¾ inches in diameter	170
Chocolate, with chocolate icing	1¾-inch sector (¹⁄₁₆ of 9-inch round layer cake)	235
Fruit cake, dark	1 piece, 2 by 1½ inches by ¼ inch	55
Gingerbread	1 piece, 2¾ by 2¾ by 1⅜ inches	175
Pound cake, old fashioned	1 slice, 3½ by 3 inches by ½ inch	140
Sponge cake	1⅞-inch sector (¹⁄₁₆ of 9¾-inch round cake)	145

Cookies:

Chocolate chip	1 cookie, 2⅓ inches in diameter, ½ inch thick	50
Figbars, small	1 figbar	50
Sandwich, chocolate or vanilla	1 cookie, 1¾ inches in diameter, ⅜ inch thick	50
Sugar	1 cookie, 2¼ inches in diameter	35
Vanilla wafer	1 cookie, 1¾ inches in diameter	20
Custard, baked	½ cup	150
Fruit Ice	½ cup	125

Gelatin desserts, ready-to-serve:

Plain	½ cup	70
Fruit added	½ cup	80

Ice cream, plain:

Regular	½ cup	70
Rich	½ cup	165

Ice milk:

Hardened	½ cup	100
Soft serve	½ cup	135

Pies:

Apple	3½-inch sector (⅛ of 9-inch pie)	300
Blueberry	3½-inch sector (⅛ of 9-inch pie)	285
Cherry	3½-inch sector (⅛ of 9-inch pie)	310

Chocolate meringue	3½-inch sector (⅛ of 9-inch pie)	285
Coconut custard	3½-inch sector (⅛ of 9-inch pie)	270
Custard	3½ inch sector (⅛ of 9-inch pie)	250
Lemon meringue	3½-inch sector (⅛ of 9-inch pie)	270
Mince	3½-inch sector (⅛ of 9-inch pie)	320
Peach	3½-inch sector (⅛ of 9-inch pie)	300
Pecan	3½-inch sector (⅛ of 9-inch pie)	430
Pumpkin	3½-inch sector (⅛ of 9-inch pie)	240
Raisin	3½-inch sector (⅛ of 9-inch pie)	320
Rhubarb	3½-inch sector (⅛ of 9-inch pie)	300
Strawberry	3½-inch sector (⅛ of 9-inch pie)	185
Prune whip	½ cup	70
Puddings:		
Cornstarch, vanilla	½ cup	140
Chocolate, from a mix	½ cup	160
Rennet desserts, ready-to-serve	½ cup	115
Tapioca cream	½ cup	110
Sherbert	½ cup	130

BEVERAGES (not including milk beverages and fruit juices)

Carbonated beverages:		
Ginger ale	8 ounce glass	75
	12 ounce can or bottle	115
Cola-type	8 ounce glass	95
	12 ounce can or bottle	145
Fruit flavored soda	8 ounce glass	115
	12 ounce can or bottle	170
Root beer	8 ounce glass	100
	12 ounce can or bottle	150
Alcoholic beverages:		
Beer, 3.6 percent alcohol by weight	8 ounce glass	100
Whisky, gin, rum, vodka:		
100-proof	1 jigger (1½ ounces)	125
90-proof	1 jigger (1½ ounces)	110
86-proof	1 jigger (1½ ounces)	105
80-proof	1 jigger (1½ ounces)	95
Wines:		
Table wines (such as Chablis, claret, Rhine wine, and sauterne)	1 wine glass (about 3½ ounces)	85
Dessert wines (such as muscatel, port, sherry, and Tokay)	1 wine glass (about 3½ ounces)	140
Fruit drinks, canned:		
Apricot nectar	½ cup	70
Cranberry juice cocktail, canned	½ cup	80
Grape drink	½ cup	70
Lemonade, frozen concentrate, sweetened, diluted, ready-to-serve	½ cup	55

BEVERAGES (not including milk beverages and fruit juices)

Fruit drinks, canned:

Orange juice-apricot juice drink	½ cup	60
Peach nectar	½ cup	60
Pear nectar	½ cup	65
Pineapple juice-grapefruit juice drink	½ cup	70
Pineapple juice-orange juice drink	½ cup	70

MISCELLANEOUS

Bouillon cube	1 cube, ½ inch	5
Olives:		
Green	5 small, 3 large, 2 giant	15
Ripe	3 small or 2 large	15
Pickles, cucumber:		
Dill	1 pickle, 4 inches long, 1¾ inches in diameter	15
Sweet	1 pickle, 2½ inches long, ¾ inch in diameter	20
Popcorn, popped (with oil and salt added)	1 cup large kernels	40
Sauces:		
Cheese sauce (medium white sauce with 2 tablespoons grated cheese per cup)	½ cup	205
Chili sauce, tomato	1 tablespoon	15
Gravy	2 tablespoons	35
Tomato catsup	1 tablespoon	15
White sauce, medium (1 cup milk, 2 tablespoons fat, and 2 tablespoons flour)	½ cup	200

MORE INFORMATION

Additional help in weight control is given in *Calories and Weight: The USDA Pocket Guide,* AIB 364. Single copies are available from the Office of Communication, U.S. Department of Agriculture, Washington, D.C. 20250. Send your request on a post card, and be sure to include your ZIP Code in your return address.

Calorie Chart from *Food and Your Weight*, U.S. Department of Agriculture, Home and Garden Bulletin No. 74.

7 MEASUREMENTS SUBSTITUTES AND EQUIVALENTS

METRIC MEASUREMENTS

American recipes are the only directions in the world not yet converted to the metric system of measurements. They are based on a system called *avoirdupois*, a set of French words run together: *voir*, to have; *du*, some; *pois*, weight. It is expected that the United States will go metric within the next decade, and already, food researchers use metric measurements because they are more precise.

When metric measurements become standard in this country we will weigh dry ingredients on a good scale rather than measure them. Smaller quantities of ingredients such as vanilla will still be measured in standard measuring spoons. Liquids will be measured in containers with the calibrations marked in liters and milliters.

Already major food shops are selling measuring cups marked with metric and *avoirdupois* equivalencies.

Below is a small table showing some of these equivalencies. Abbreviations used in recipes based on metric measurements are: G, gram; kg, kilogram; cm, centimeter; dl, deciliter.

METRIC WEIGHTS AND MEASURES

DRY

1 teaspoon = about 5 grams
1 ounce = 28.35 grams
1¾ ounces = 50 grams
3½ ounces = 100 grams
8 ounces = 227 grams
2 pounds 3¼ ounces = 1000 grams = 1 kilogram

VOLUME

1 teaspoon (¹⁄₁₆ oz.) = 5 milliliters
1 tablespoon (3 tsp.) = 15 milliliters

METRIC WEIGHTS AND MEASURES

VOLUME

1 cup (8 oz.) = ¼ liter
2 cups (1 pt.) = ½ liter
4 cups (1 quart) = 0.946 liter
6 tablespoons plus 2 teaspoons = 1 deciliter
1 cup plus 2¼ teaspoons = ¼ liter
1 pint plus 4½ teaspoons = ½ liter
1 quart plus 4 scant tablespoons = 1 liter
1 gallon plus 1 scant cup = 4 liters
2½ gallons plus 2½ cups = 10 liters

LINEAR

1 inch = 2½ centimeters
39⅓ inches = 100 centimeters = 1 meter

DULL BOTTOMS SAVE MONEY

Don't worry if the bottom of your aluminum pan is dull. It will absorb heat more easily and cut down on your fuel bills for the stove.

CONVERSION TABLE

Inches to centimeters = multiply inches by 2.54
Centimeters to inches = multiply centimeters by .39
Ounces to grams = multiply ounces by 28.35
Grams to ounces = multiply grams by .035

STANDARD METRIC MEASUREMENTS

This is the standard conversion table of equivalents used by cooks.

WEIGHTS

10 milligrams = 1 centigram
10 centigrams = 1 decigram
10 decigrams = 1 gram
10 grams = 1 decagram
10 decagrams = 1 hectogram
10 hectograms = 1 kilogram

FLUID MEASURES

10 milliliters = 1 centiliter
10 centiliters = 1 deciliter
10 deciliters = 1 liter
10 liters = 1 decaliter
10 decaliters = 1 hectoliter
10 hectoliters = 1 kiloliter

CUBIC MEASURES

1000 cubic millimeters = 1 cubic centimeter
1000 cubic centimeters = 1 cubic decimeter
1000 cubic decimeters = 1 cubic meter

METRIC FLUID EQUIVALENTS

1 kiloliter = 1000 liters
1 liter = 1000 milliliters
1 milliliter = 1 cubic centimeter
1 teaspoon = 4.93 milliliters
1 tablespoon = 14.79 milliliters
1 fluid ounce = 29.57 milliliters
1 cup = 237 milliliters
1 pint = 473 milliliters
1 quart = 946 milliliters
1 gallon = 3.78 liters
1 milliliter = .03 fluid ounce
100 milliliters = 3.38 fluid ounces
250 milliliters = 8.45 fluid ounces = 1.06 cups
500 milliliters = 16.91 fluid ounces = 1.06 pints
1 liter = 33.81 fluid ounces = 1.06 quarts
10 liters = 2.64 gallons

CONVERTING CELSIUS TO FAHRENHEIT

Multiply Celsius reading by nine, divide by five, add 32
(100 C. x 9 = 900 ÷ 9 = 100 C.)

CONVERTING FAHRENHEIT TO CELSIUS

Subtract 32 from Fahrenheit reading, multiply by five, divide by nine
(212 F. -32 = 180 x 5 = 900 ÷ 9 = 100 C.)

FAHRENHEIT CELSIUS TEMPERATURE CONVERSION

Fahrenheit		Celsius	Fahrenheit		Celsius
600		316	110		43.3
500		260	100		37.8
400		204	90		32.2
300	(boiling point of water)	149	80		26.7
212		100	70		21.1
200		93.3	60		15.6
190		87.8	50		10
180		82.2	40		4.4
170		76.7	32	(freezing point of water)	0
160		71.1	0		-17
150		65.5	-10		-23
140		60.0	-40		-40
130		54.4	-459		-273
120		48.9			

EQUIVALENTS FOR MEASUREMENTS

1 drop = about 1/50 fluid ounce

1 dash = about 5 drops or 1/10 ounce

1 teaspoon = 50 drops

3 teaspoons = 1 tablespoon = 1/2 fluid ounce

2 tablespoons = 1 fluid ounce = 1/8 cup

1 jigger = 1 1/2 fluid ounces

4 tablespoons = 1/4 cup

5 tablespoons plus 1 teaspoon = 1/3 cup

8 tablespoons = 1/2 cup = 4 fluid ounces

10 tablespoons plus 2 teaspoons = 2/3 cup

12 tablespoons = 3/4 cup = 6 fluid ounces

16 tablespoons = 1 cup

1 cup = 8 fluid ounces

2 cups = 1 pint

2 pints = 1 quart

4/5 quart = 25.6 fluid ounces

1 quart = 32 fluid ounces

2 quarts = 1/2 gallon

4 quarts = 1 gallon

2 gallons (dry) = 1 peck

4 pecks = 1 bushel

4 ounces = 1/4 pound

8 ounces = 1/2 pound

16 ounces = 1 pound (dry)

PENNY SAVER

Con Edison of New York estimates that it costs 8 cents an hour to operate a self-cleaning oven, 10 cents an hour for a conventional oven, and 11 cents an hour for a small portable broiler. However, a chicken will cook faster in the smaller oven, and, therefore, it is more economical to operate.

LIQUID INGREDIENTS

1 teaspoon = 1/6 ounce = 5 grams = 5 milliliters
3 teaspoons = 1 tablespoon = 1/2 fluid ounce = 15 grams = 15 milliliters
2 tablespoons = 1/8 cup = 1 fluid ounce
8 tablespoons = 1/2 cup = 1/4 pint = 4 fluid ounces
1 cup = 1/2 pint
2 cups = 1 pint
4 cups = 1 quart

SOLID INGREDIENTS

Ingredient	Ounces	Grams
Rice, 1 teaspoon	1/6 ounce	5 grams
Salt, 1 tablespoon	1/2 ounce	15 grams
Butter, 1 cup	8 ounces	240 grams
Dried beans, 2 cups	16 ounces (1 pound)	500 grams
Spices, 1 teaspoon	1/2 ounce	2 1/2 grams
Grated cheese, 1 cup	4 ounces	100 grams
Flour, 1 tablespoon	1/2 ounce	15 grams

FRACTIONAL MEASURES

AMOUNT	EQUALS
1/8 cup	2 tablespoons
1/6 cup	2 tablespoons plus 2 teaspoons
1/4 cup	4 tablespoons
1/2 of 3/4 cup	1/4 cup plus 2 tablespoons
1/3 of 1/4 cup	1 tablespoon plus 1 teaspoon
1/3 of 1/3 cup	1 tablespoon plus 2 1/3 teaspoons
1/3 of 1/2 cup	2 tablespoons plus 2 teaspoons
1/3 of 2/3 cup	3 tablespoons plus 1 2/3 teaspoons
1/3 of 3/4 cup	1/4 cup or 4 tablespoons

SEASONING THE SALAD BOWL

Wooden salad bowls are the most popular. They have a particular virtue, which is that the rough interior surfaces allow you to mash garlic with salt to begin the base of a good dressing. Do wash the salad bowl after using, even if it is wooden. The oily dressing residue will quickly make the bowl rancid if you don't. However, just wash it quickly in warm-to-hot sudsy water, rinse it well, and wipe dry at once.

EQUIVALENT MEASURES OF FOOD

Ingredient	Weight	Measure
Dried beans	1 pound	2 cups +
Cheese, grated	½ pound	2 cups
Sour cream	16 ounces	2 cups
Garlic	1 large clove	1 tablespoon
Meat	1 pound	2 cup, chopped
Mushrooms	1 pound	4 cups, sliced
Potatoes	1 pound	2 cups, grated
Tomatoes	1 large ripe tomato	1 cup, chopped

CHEAP ENAMEL IS NO BARGAIN

Buy only good enameled equipment. Less expensive enamel utensils will chip very quickly and become useless.

CAN SIZES IN CUPS AND OUNCES

Can	Weight	Cups
6-ounce	6 ounces	¾ cup
8-ounce	8 ounces	1 cup
#1	9 ounces	1 cup
#1	10½ to 12 ounces	1¼ cup
#300	14 to 16 ounces	1¾ cups
#303	16 to 17 ounces	2 cups
#2	20 ounces	2½ cups
#2½	1 pound, 13 ounces	3½ cups
#3 (46 ounces)	3 pounds, 4 ounces	5¾ cups
#10	7 pounds +	12-13 cups

HIGH-ALTITUDE TEMPERATURES

High above sea level, the boiling temperature of water is lower. In the mountains you must cook foods longer since the boiling water will not be as hot. Altitude affects other culinary methods, including baking, candy-making, leavening, and whipping egg whites.

ALTITUDE	BOILING POINT OF WATER
0'	212 F.
1000'	210 F.
2000'	208 F.
3000'	207 F.
4000'	205 F.
5000'	203 F.
7500'	198 F.
10,000'	194 F.

VEGETABLES, FROZEN AND CANNED PACKAGES SIZES AND YIELD

VEGETABLE	FROZEN		CANNED	
	Package size	Cups, approximate	Can size	Cups, approximate
Asparagus, cut	10 ounce	1 1/4	14 ounce	1 1/3
Beans, cut green or wax	10 ounce	1 1/2	15 1/2 ounce	1 3/4
Beans, lima	10 ounce	1 2/3	16 ounce	1 3/4
Beets, sliced or diced	16 ounce	1 3/4		
Broccoli and cauliflower	10 ounce	1 1/2		
Carrots, sliced	10 ounce	1 2/3	16 ounce	1 3/4
Corn, while kernel	10 ounce	1 1/2	16 ounce	1 2/3
Kale	10 ounce	1 1/8	15 ounce	1 1/3
Okra	10 ounce	1 1/4	15 ounce	1 1/3
Peas	10 ounce	1 1/2	16 ounce	1 3/4
Spinach	10 ounce	1 1/4	15 ounce	1 1/3
Squash, zucchini or summer, sliced	10 ounce	1 1/3		
Squash, mashed	10 ounce	1 1/2		
Tomatoes, in juice	16 ounce	1 7/8		
Tomato sauce	15 ounce	2 (scant)		

COMMON CAN SIZES

Recipe designation	Weight	Servings, approximate	Cups	Type of Food
6 ounce	6 ounce	4 to 6	3/4	Juice concentrates, frozen
8 ounce	8 ounce	1 to 2	1	Vegetables, fruits
Picnic	10 1/2 to 12 ounce	2 to 3	1 1/4	Soups, condensed, prepared foods
12 ounce vacumn	12 ounce	3	1 1/2	Corn
No. 300	14 to 16 ounce	3 to 4	1 3/4	Cranberry sauce, meat dishes, pork and beans

COMMON CAN SIZES

Recipe designation	Weight	Servings, approximate	Cups	Type of Food
No. 303	16 to 17 ounce	4	2	Fruits, vegetables
No. 2½	1 pound, 13 ounces	5	2½	Juices, pineapple slices
No. 2½	1 pound, 13 ounces	7	3½	Fruits, vegetables
No. 3 or 46 fluid ounces	3 pounds, 3 ounces or 1 quart, 14 fluid ounces	10-12	5¾	Fruits, vegetables, pork and beans ("family size") and juices
No. 10	6½ to 7¼ pounds	25	12-13	Fruits, vegetables

EQUIVALENTS

1 teaspoon fresh herb	=	½ teaspoon dried
1 teaspoon	=	one sixth ounce
1 tablespoon	=	3 teaspoons or ½ fluid ounce
1 cup	=	16 tablespoons
16 fluid ounces	=	1 pint
4 cups	=	32 fluid ounces
1 pound sliced carrots	=	about 4 cups
2 large celery stalks cut	=	about 1 cup
½ pound mushrooms sliced	=	about 2 ½ cups
1 medium onion	=	about ⅓ cup
1 pound chopped onions	=	about 4 cups
1 cup raw rice	=	about 3 cups cooked rice

THE RICE TRICK

To keep rice from yellowing as it cooks, add a teaspoon of strained lemon juice to the water before you add the rice.

DON'T PANIC -- SUBSTITUTE

When you are preparing a dish and discover that a necessary ingredient is missing, don't panic—substitute. The following table lists some of the things I run out of occasionally and the substitutes I use.

TABLE OF SUBSTITUTES

Bouillon or stock	1 bouillon cube dissolved in 8 ounces hot water
Bread crumbs	Rolled-out saltines
Butter	Margarine, rendered chicken fat, vegetable oil, shortening, or rendered pork fat
Carrots	Parsnips or baby white turnips
Cream, light	Whole milk or heavy cream thinned with milk
Croutons	Cubes of crustless white bread, sauteed in butter
Curry powder	Turmeric plus cardamom, ginger powder, and cumin
Flour, all-purpose as a thickener	Cornstarch
Garlic	Garlic salt or garlic powder
Ginger, fresh	Powdered ginger. One slice ginger equals about ¼ teaspoon powdered
Lemon juice	White vinegar, lime juice, or white wine
Lettuce	Spinach or any leafy green
Mayonnaise, fresh	For ½ cup mayonnaise; commercial mayonnaise plus ½ teaspoon lemon juice and ½ teaspoon prepared mustard
Milk	Powdered milk and water, blended
Mustard, prepared	Powdered mustard
Olive oil	Vegetable oil
Parsley	Chervil
Pepper, black	White pepper or paprika
Scallions	Green, plain, or frozen onions, or onion powder to taste
Shallots	⅔ onion plus a garlic clove
Vinegar, tarragon	Pinch of dried tarragon heated in wine vinegar for 3 minutes, then strained
Vinegar, wine	Cider, or red or white vinegar with a little wine

SOURING A SWEET

If a dish is too sweet, add a dash of vinegar or lemon juice to it.

SUBSTITUTING SYRUPS & HONEY IN PLACE OF GRANULATED SUGAR*

Honey: To substitute honey for sugar in baking use ¾ cup of honey for every cup of sugar, but reduce the other liquid required by ¼ cup. Cakes or cookies made with honey are improved in keeping qualities as honey tends to retard drying out. It is well to lower baking temperature about 25 degrees which prevents overbrowning of honey baked goods. Honey should be warmed in simmering water and then mixed with other liquids in recipe.

Maple syrup or Maple sugar: One cup of either syrup or maple sugar can be used in place of 1 cup of granulated sugar. For each cup of syrup used, reduce the amount of liquid required by several tablespoons.

Molasses: In cooking or flavoring, use ½ cup to 1 cup of sugar. In baking, use 1 cup of molasses to 1 cup of sugar plus ½ teaspoon of baking soda.

Sorghum: Sorghum is a tall cereal plant resembling corn. Its stalk produces a sweet juice from which syrup is made. Sorghum syrup can be used in place of sugar in the same way as molasses.

*Honey & syrups will tend to make the final baked produce less crispy and more chewy. If a crispy product is desired, add several tablespoons of additional flour.

MAPLE SUGARING

"The early settlers learned maple sugaring from the Indians. The Indians reduced the syrup to granulated sugar which was much easier to transport than syrup. Maple sugar can be used the same as white sugar. To make, boil maple syrup until it reaches 227 F. Cool to 160 F. Beat until grainy and cool. After it begins to crystallize, beat for a few minutes more. When it reaches the consistency of medium-thick cream pour it into a glass or tin storage container. It can be kept in a cool, dry place for several months."

Information from the Vermont General Store and Grist Mill.

HEALTHFOOD SUBSTITUTES FOR...

BREAD CRUMBS: Soy grits (absorbs liquid in the same way as bread), wheat germ.

BUTTER: Corn germ oil (for use in baking and cooking), nut butters, tahini paste (finely ground sesame seeds)

CHOCOLATE: Carob confections for snacking; carob powder or flour for drinks and cooking (it has a flavor closer to chocolate when toasted before using). 3 tablespoons of carob powder combined with 2 tablespoons of water equals 1 square of chocolate.

COFFEE: Pero and Yano (made from grains), herbal teas.

MILK: Nut milk (made from raw nuts and water), soy flour and water (made from ground soy beans and water). Both should be combined with a natural sweetener if the taste is not palatable to you.

PEPPER: Paprika

PROTEIN: Miso (made from soybeans and often used in soups), raw nuts, nut milk, vegetable protein (concentrated), soy grits, brewers yeast (Torumel brand has a milder flavor than some others), wheat germ, and white rice substitutes.

RICE (white): Organically grown, short grain brown rice, rice grits (coarsely ground brown rice), wild rice, buckwheat, bulgur wheat; for use in soups, stews, etc: soybeans (almost complete protein), millet, barlet grits, and gruenken (unripened green wheat kernels that have been dried).

SALT (refined): Earth or sea salt, both unrefined and rich in minerals; vegetable salt (made from dried vegetables that have been finely ground).

SOY SAUCE (most brands contain MSG): Tamari sesame paste with the addition of water.

SWEETENERS: Date sugar or syrup, maple syrup, sorghum, carob syrup, unrefined honey or molasses, malt syrup (less sweet than most other sweeteners), fruit concentrates (particularly apple), and blackstrap molasses (combine with other syrups; it has a bitter flavor, but it is high in nutrients).

TEA: Herb combinations with mint or peppermint.

THICKENERS (in place of cornstarch and white refined flour): Unrefined flour, arrowroot (in equal amounts as for cornstarch), agar-agar (use 2 tablespoons to each 2 ½ cups of liquid), Irish moss also called carragreen (used in thickening desserts), rice cream, wheat cereal, tapioca starch, potato flour, and plain gelatin.

VINEGAR: Naturally processed apple cider vinegar, wine vinegar, or lemon juice.

WHAT IS MARGARINE?

Oleomargarine or margarine may contain pasteurized cream, cow's milk, skim milk, a combination of nonfat dry milk and water, vegetable oils, or finely ground soybeans and water. The finished product must contain at least 80 percent fat according to USDA regulations, and the label must indicate what fats are used.

SUBSTITUTIONS IN BAKING

In a pinch, any of the following ingredient substitutions can be made successfully except in temperamental cakes, breads, cookies, or pastries.

Leavening

—1 ½ teaspoons phosphate or tartrate baking powder = 1 teaspoon double-acting baking powder.

—¼ teaspoon baking soda + ½ teaspoon cream of tartar = 1 teaspoon double-acting baking powder.

—¼ teaspoon baking soda + ½ cup sour milk = 1 teaspoon double-acting baking powder in liquid mixtures; reduce recipe content by ½ cup.

Thickening

—1 tablespoon cornstarch = 2 tablespoons all-purpose flour.

—1 tablespoon potato flour = 2 tablespoons all-purpose flour.

—1 tablespoon arrowroot = 2 ½ tablespoons all-purpose flour.

—2 teaspoons quick-cooking tapioca = 1 tablespoon all-purpose flour (use in soups only).

Sweetening, Flavoring

—1 ¼ cups sugar + ⅓ cup liquid = 1 cup light corn syrup or honey.

—3 tablespoons cocoa + 1 tablespoon butter = 1 (1-ounce) square unsweetened chocolate.

—¼ teaspoon cayenne pepper = 3 to 4 drops liquid hot red pepper seasoning.

Flour

—1 cup sifted all-purpose flour

—2 tablespoons = 1 cup sifted cake flour.

—1 cup + 2 tablespoons sifted cake flour = 1 cup sifted all-purpose flour.

—1 cup sifted self-rising flour = 1 cup sifted all-purpose flour + 1 ¼ teaspoons baking powder and a pinch of salt; when using, substitute measure for measure for all-purpose flour, then omit baking powder and salt in recipe.

SOFTENING HARD SUGAR

When brown sugar cakes into a lump and won't crumble, put it and a piece of fresh white bread in a sealed container and let sit for twenty-four hours. The bread will humidify the sugar, and it will be good as new again. Or, you can put the brown sugar (box and all) in a slow oven for a while, and it will soften up nicely.

INDEX

Kellogg, Dr. John Harvey, 65
Ketchup, 63
Kettle, 101
Kipper, 101
Kirsch, 101
Kisses, 101
Kitchiner, Dr. William, *The Cook's Oracle*, 29
Knead, 101
Knuckle, 101
Kofta, 101
Korma, 101
Kosher, 101
Kulich, 102
Kummel, 102

Lactic acid, 102
Ladyfingers, 102
Lager, 102
Lamb
  broiling, 205
  calories in, 230
  how to cook, 147-149
  roasting, 188-189
  servings per pound, 185
  storing, 132
  what to buy, 145-149
Lamb *Korma*, 43
Lamb's fry, 102
Lamb's lettuce, 102
Lamb's wool, 102
Langouste, 102
Lard, 102
Larding needle, 101, 102
Lasagne, 102
Laurel, 102
Layer cake, 102
Layer Cake, Basic, 220
Lazy Susan, 102
Leaven, 102
Lebanon, 21, 46
Lees, 102
Le fond brun, 84
Legume, 102-103
Lemon Butter Sauce, 217
Lemon sole, 103
Lemon Soup, 44
Liaison, 103
Lights, 103
Lillet, 73

Linzer torte, 103
Liqueur, 103
Liquor
  calories in, 245
  see also Wine
Littleneck clams, 103
Lobster, 160, 164
Loquat, 103
Lotus root, 103
Lotus seeds, 103
Louis XIV, 15, 25, 84
Louis XVI, 20
Love Potion, 13
Luau, 103
Lychee, 103
Lyonnaise, à la, 103

Macadamia nut, 103
Macaroni, 103
Mace, 32
Madeleine, 104
Madrilène, 104
Magnum, 104
Maintenon, Madame de, 84
Maître d'hôtel, 104
Maître d'hôtel butter, 104
Maize, 84
Maize bread, 104
Malaysian Chicken Curry, 41
Malt, 104
Malted milk, 104
Mango, 104
Manioc, 104
Maraschino, 104
Marbled, 104
Marc, 104
Marchpane, 105
Maréchale, à la, 104
Marennes, 104
Margarine, 104, 259
Marie Antoinette, 20, 25
Marinade, 104
  for Domestic Birds, 200
  for Game Birds, 200
  with Tarragon for Vegetables, 36
Marinière, 105
Marmalade, 105
Marmite, 105
Marmite, petite, 105

WORLD ALMANAC PUBLICATIONS
200 Park Avenue
Department B
New York, New York 10166

Please send me, postpaid, the books checked below:

☐ THE WORLD ALMANAC® AND BOOK OF FACTS 1984 . . . . $4.95
☐ THE WORLD ALMANAC BOOK OF WORLD WAR II $10.95
☐ 101 LISTS: HOW TO DO PRACTICALLY EVERYTHING FASTER,
   EASIER, & CHEAPER $4.95
☐ THE WORLD ALMANAC DICTIONARY OF DATES. $8.95
☐ THE SNOOPY COLLECTION $9.95
☐ THE LAST TIME WHEN $8.95
☐ WORLD DATA $9.95
☐ THE CIVIL WAR ALMANAC $10.95
☐ THE OMNI FUTURE ALMANAC $8.95
☐ THE LANGUAGE OF SPORT $7.95
☐ THE COOK'S ALMANAC. $8.95
☐ THE GREAT JOHN L $3.95
   WORLD OF INFORMATION:
☐ MIDDLE EAST REVIEW 1983. . . . . $24.95
☐ ASIA & PACIFIC 1983 . . . . $24.95
☐ LATIN AMERICA & CARIBBEAN $24.95
☐ AFRICA GUIDE 1983. . . . . $24.95

(Add $1 postage and handling for the first book, plus 50 cents for each additional
book ordered.)
Enclosed is my check or money order for $_____

NAME_____

ADDRESS_____

CITY_____ STATE_____ ZIP_____